Preface

In 1940 my uncle made a decision as a very young man, a decision that took him on a remarkable adventure. He joined the Royal Air Force and served in Bomber Command. An experience shared with more than 125,000 men, most under 25, from all over the world and a multitude of backgrounds. Their motivations to volunteer were wide ranging, they had differing abilities and varying capacities to handle the stresses and strains of operational life. For many, bombing operations were unsettling, exhausting and sometimes terrifying ordeals to be endured. For others, although difficult for us to understand, they were relished, challenging, stimulating and satisfying. For the pilots particularly, the overriding emotion was excitement as many just wanted to fly.

Brian's decision to volunteer resulted in him being one of the youngest, if not the youngest, RAF bomber pilot in the Second World War, when he and his crews climbed into huge, hurriedly made but often highly sophisticated cutting-edge aircraft where night after night the survival odds became shorter and shorter.

I discovered him in my parents' attic. I was about 10, just tall enough to open the hatch unaided, and found an old pigskin suitcase in which I met a world, a time and people who were never mentioned. An unspoken mystery that captivated me in that dark and dusty space where, by torchlight, I read his logbook, handled his medals, wore his cap and imagined. He was my mother's only sibling and to me with wide eyes, he was a war hero, but we had no photographs of him in our house, no small brass model bombers, no RAF ashtrays, no squadron plaques or prints. Nothing about him or his time. He was never spoken of and at times I assumed they knew nothing about him. Why had they kept all these items shut away. Were they ashamed of him? It's taken many compelling hours over several years to research the story, which uncovered some wonderful characters and their part in some of the key events of the war's strategic bombing campaign. My regret is not having started much earlier when more of the people he knew and who he served with were alive.

I am not a military historian, and I can add nothing to the existing extensive writing about the Second World War. That war though, is the essential background to him joining Bomber Command and participating in one of its longest and more controversial campaigns. Nor am I a researcher engrossed in the detailed statistics of that campaign and once again I can add nothing to the phenomenal weight of data that provides daunting proof about the death and destruction of the time. Those authors and researchers have my boot marks on their shoulders. This is just an amateur's biography but for the story to have relevance it needs to be seen alongside the broad historical context of the time and should not be distanced from the sometimes staggering statistics those researchers revealed.

In researching and writing this tale I was also curious whether my own experiences of service life would help to understand what these young men went through. My knowledge of the RAF of the Second World War was of schoolboy standard until my fellow cadets and I whistled through the difference between the British night bombing strategy and US daylight operations while doing war studies at Sandhurst.

During my military service the only part of the RAF I saw at close quarters was the helicopter squadrons, the fixed-wing boys being all rather distant and even at close range, aloof, grey and serious. During peacetime my aerial taxi drivers and heavy lifters were constantly restricted by lack of fuel, hours, daylight and a morbid belief that bad weather was round the corner. Too many times I cursed them as their helicopters disappeared into in a bright blue sky leaving half my gun battery on the other side of Salisbury Plain. But, in anything approaching an operational situation they were wonderful. Highly professional, skilful risk takers happy to break the rules and put themselves in harm's way if it helped us out. I suspect it was much the same in my uncle's time.

My military experience, albeit as a 'brown job' as I would have been described by aircrew, gave me an insight into two particularly relevant parts of service life. The first is the amazing way that military training, operations and social life enables you to create highly functional and closely bonded teams who can operate well in excess of the sum of their parts. That, in itself, although not always recognised at the time, is a joy and one of the great pleasures of service life. Bomber Command achieved this both through operational evolution and design.

THE RAF'S YOUNGEST BOMBER PILOT OF WW2

*For my family and the families of all Bomber Command aircrew,
particularly those who knew and flew with my uncle.*

THE STORY OF

FLIGHT LIEUTENANT

BRIAN
SLADE DFC,

LANCASTER PILOT

AND PATHFINDER

THE RAF'S YOUNGEST BOMBER PILOT OF WW2

GRAHAM WATERTON

AIR WORLD

AIR WORLD

THE RAF'S YOUNGEST BOMBER PILOT OF WW2
The Story of Flight Lieutenant Brian Slade DFC, Lancaster Pilot and Pathfinder

First published in Great Britain in 2024 by
Air World
An imprint of
Pen & Sword Books Ltd
Yorkshire – Philadelphia

ISBN 978 1 39908 017 0

Typeset by SJmagic DESIGN SERVICES, India.

Printed and bound in the UK by CPI Group (UK) Ltd.

Pen & Sword Books Limited incorporates the imprints of Archaeology, Atlas, Aviation, Battleground, Digital, Discovery, Family History, Fiction, History, Local, Local History, Maritime, Military, Military Classics, Politics, Select, Transport, True Crime, After the Battle, Air World, Claymore Press, Frontline Publishing, Leo Cooper, Remember When, Seaforth Publishing, The Praetorian Press, Wharncliffe Books, Wharncliffe Local History, Wharncliffe Transport, Wharncliffe True Crime and White Owl.

For a complete list of Pen & Sword titles please contact:

PEN & SWORD BOOKS LIMITED
George House, Units 12 & 13, Beevor Street, Off Pontefract Road,
Barnsley, South Yorkshire, S71 1HN, England
E-mail: enquiries@pen-and-sword.co.uk
Website: www.pen-and-sword.co.uk

or

PEN AND SWORD BOOKS
1950 Lawrence Rd, Havertown, PA 19083, USA
E-mail: uspen-and-sword@casematepublishers.com
Website: www.penandswordbooks.com

MIX
Paper | Supporting responsible forestry
FSC® C013604

Contents

The second was our ability to enjoy ourselves in both the comfort of our messes and in the grimmest of situations. RAF Bomber Command aircrew could do both, often in the same day. Some of my fondest memories of mess life was having fun and frankly behaving badly, and I wondered whether my uncle and his chums did the same. I was not to be disappointed.

It has been Brian's pilot's logbook that I first read in our attic that has guided me through his time in Bomber Command. Every entry in his neat hand leading me to explore his part in the progress of the war, the events that made the bombing campaign so controversial and, most enjoyably, to get to know some of the characters he flew with.

For many years I imagined him with red and black pens, filling in each detail of every time he flew. My entirely romanticised image drawn from films like *The Dam Busters* was of the fresh-faced, smiling, young man I'd peered at by torchlight, in leather flying jacket and boots sitting at a desk in an airfield billet, with a glass of whisky and a cigarette penning his adventures. It was never like that but nor was it always the dangerous, terrifying and gut-wrenching work of operations. There were parties, drinking, laughter, high spirits and practical jokes – the accepted and customary behaviour of young fighting men. Many just wanted the excitement and sheer joy of flying and they were given the opportunity, at a frighteningly young age, to fly huge, modern, sophisticated aircraft, packed full of state-of-the-art technology. A schoolboy's dream.

I intended to write, as far as possible, from a neutral perspective, avoiding the temptation of viewing events from this side of the English Channel only. I haven't succeeded as time and again when my research followed my uncle and his friends into the air I was unashamedly on their side and wanting them all to return regardless of the results of their actions. I was, and remain, in awe of their resolve and determination to play their part. If you did not already know you will soon also read of the ghastly suffering imposed on civilians in Germany, Italy and many other occupied countries and the reasons why, as the only tool available to Churchill's War Cabinet, Bomber Command led the fightback against an undoubtably tyrannical regime. I think it is now impossible, as the wartime generation have now all but gone, to understand fully what it was like to experience conflict on this scale, whether as civilian or combatant. It was total war and in Europe its effects were impossible to escape.

I do not intend to directly confront the morality of the Allied bombing offensive, which has been much more hotly debated since than it was at the time. This is a story about the crews, the work they did and how they did it, but I am aware that to eulogise them may seem unsympathetic to the civilians who suffered so terribly. However, if we consider the bombing offensive to be savage and uncivilised, we dishonour the unstinting commitment, bravery and sacrifice of the crews. I have no answer to that dilemma. The results of their work were often brutal but very few were brutalised by its execution at the time. There were many, though, who were deeply affected for many years afterwards.

There are a number of subjects that are important to the story but beyond the scope of this book other than a few passing mentions. First is relevant to the Allied strategic bombing campaign and the second to the day-to-day running of a wartime RAF station. The United States Army Air Force started its bombing operations in July 1942 and before the end of the war had 200 airfields each manned by more than 2,000 personnel. The USAAF's contribution to the strategic bombing offensive of occupied Europe was considerable but little affected the day-to-day activities of Brian and his crew mates.

The Air Transport Auxiliary (ATA) women who delivered aircraft, the Women's Auxiliary Air Force (WAAF) on every station and the civilian women who sustained the 'industry' of war in the UK, were a different matter, as they, every day, affected the lives of aircrew. A third is the essential part played by the ground crews. I regrettably pay scant attention to their significant contribution to this story.

This is not intended to give readers the knowledge or the opportunity to take sides or make judgements but if it gives them a little more understanding about Brian and the other Bomber Command crews and what they did, I will have achieved something. There are many first-hand accounts of crews' experiences, both recorded and written, and I have listened and watched clips of these now old men sitting comfortably in their armchairs remembering with rheumy eyes those days they were lucky to survive. Their cracking voices slowly retelling the highs and lows of their times in the air and the friends they knew and lost. Brian cannot tell his story so I will try and tell it for him.

By the standards of the day, Brian's experiences in his three years with Bomber Command were not remarkable, as throughout the war the 125,000 others did something similar. The individual motivations that led these young men to step forward may have been very different but for Brian joining Bomber Command was his route to flying. Others, by volunteering, avoided the hazard of being pushed somewhere they did not want to go. There were of course, some idealistic romantics but many simply chose what they believed was an easier option; fly in, drop bombs, fly home.

It proved to be anything but. Few understood the risks, and all would have to muster very different levels of courage to carry out their work.

At the time he volunteered, I believe Brian had simpler motives and there are two reasons why his story is different to most others.

Firstly, he survived significantly longer than most, logging more than 1,000 hours in the air, 300 of them on operations. He was clearly luckier than many, but he was also a very capable pilot and supported by good crews. Bomber Command's remarkable crew self-selection process worked well for him. Whether he was a good judge of character, or they were, I will leave you to judge.

Secondly, he was different because of his age. While there may have been a handful of younger bomber aircrew, I doubt there was a younger pilot. He was given his nickname, The Boy Slade, by his first squadron because he looked so young, but even those who named him were ignorant of the truth about his age.

He was flying a 14-ton bomber, its crew of five, full of fuel and a load of high explosives over Germany well before he was old enough to drive a car. I received no reply when I wrote to his school asking whether 15-year-old schoolboys in 1940 wore shorts. I suspect they may have considered my request suspicious by modern standards, but I had then, and it remains, an image of a shorts-wearing boy walking out of school and within months pulling on the blue-grey long trousers of an RAF bomber pilot.

Whatever rendered my grandparents incapable of celebrating their son's service was initially a mystery. What prevented them similarly stunted the memories and celebrations of countless bereaved families, all part of the psychological shock suffered by the post-war generation, but my distance from that generation now allows me, with great pride, to tell his story.

I have researched and written, not only to satisfy my curiosity about his life but also for my family, who know so little about him and the times he lived in, to understand what happened without the controversy and tragedy that has suppressed past generations.

His portrait hangs proudly in my house.

Introduction

ollowing the Armistice in 1918 that brought the First World War to an end, Europe rebuilt itself. Crippled by reparations, Germany and its people suffered debilitating hardship and its leaders were neutered by the terms of their surrender. Limitations on the growth of their defence forces, an imposed war guilt, the austerity of its people and the frustrations of its ruling class were a hotbed for the political instability that enabled the 'right' to gain a foothold throughout the late 1920s and, eventually, the Nazi Party, led by Adolf Hitler, to take control, in 1933.

All nations party to the Armistice Treaty in 1918 agreed to reduce their military forces for ten years. The British armed forces, particularly the Royal Navy, started slowly to expand from 1931 and as soon as it became obvious that the Nazi Party was heading into power, the Armistice agreements were formally ended and rearmament started; albeit in the United Kingdom, its progress was slow. In Germany, as well as extensive industrial expansion and gradual but significant rearmament, Hitler reintroduced conscription. This increase in Germany's rearmament became perfectly obvious in the mid and late 1930s but Britain and most of Germany's neighbours struggled to keep up.

Another of the Armistice conditions was to limit any future German territorial ambitions. This became a preoccupying frustration to Hitler who, signalling his intentions in his 1925 political manifesto, *Mein Kampf,* wanted more 'living space' to satisfy his aspirations for his country's expansion and the creation of a third German Empire, the so-called '1,000-year Reich'. Accordingly, he regained the Saarland on the French-German border in a 1935 referendum and, with that, access to its rich coal deposits. He remilitarised the Rhineland in 1936 in violation of the Versailles Treaty, which had created this demilitarised buffer between France and Germany. The annexation of Austria followed in March 1938 (the *Anschluss*) and the Czechoslovakian Sudetenland in October of the same year. In March 1939 he occupied Czechoslovakia. Whenever possible, Hitler entreated his generals to brief their men that every step they took into these countries became the boundary of their new empire. It was clear where all this was heading.

Throughout this period, weakness and appeasement from the rest of Europe fuelled Hitler's ambitions and did nothing to prevent the invasion of Poland on 1 September 1939. Britain, who with France had assured Poland of its support, had no choice but to become involved and Britain's prime minister, Neville Chamberlain, declared war on 3 September. At the same time, Russia, then an ally of Germany, invaded Poland from the east.

Although nothing was done to directly help the beleaguered Poles, within a few days a British Expeditionary Force (BEF) was despatched to bolster the defence of France and the Low Countries, widely believed to be the next obvious area of German expansion. The absence of the expected large-scale bombing by Germany and the relative inactivity of the BEF led to this nine-month period becoming known as the Phoney War. It was not, though, 'phoney' for others in Europe. Poland was still resisting both the Germans in the west and the Russians in the east, as were the Finns, having been invaded by Russia. The Royal Navy, the French navy and the German navy, the *Kriegsmarine,* were also engaged in a battle for the Atlantic.

In early 1940 Hitler turned his attentions to Norway and Denmark, both to try and protect Germany's source of iron ore and to provide it with Norwegian ports enabling better access to the Atlantic rather than the easily monitored and restricted Baltic bases. The Allies, of course, wanted to prevent that as well as securing a land link to Finland in the north. But on 7 April it was the *Kriegsmarine* that started the build-up to the invasion of Norway and Denmark.

By the night of 9 April, Denmark had capitulated. The Norwegian army was reinforced by a poorly organised and equipped contingent from the British, but by mid-April, central Norway and all Norwegian ports were in German hands. In the north the Royal Navy inflicted severe damage on the *Kriegsmarine* at Narvik and Norwegian forces supported by British, Polish and French reinforcements fought to retake the city. As the situation for the BEF in France worsened, the British took fright and Allied forces were withdrawn from the Narvik area, leaving the Norwegians alone and by 10 June Norway was entirely under German occupation. One of those evacuated from Narvik would end up serving with Brian, but more of that later.

A month before, on 10 May 1940, Germany started the operation it had been planning for months: the invasion of France and the Low Countries.

All schoolchildren would have been aware of the German expansion in previous years but as Brian and his peers were preparing to take their School Certificate exams, what was to happen on the other side of the English Channel and above the south of England over the next two months would galvanise the country.

The British Expeditionary Force under the command of General Lord Gort had expanded by May 1940 into ten infantry divisions with supporting armour, artillery and aircraft, including fighter and bomber squadrons, who were moved to airfields in northern France. This bomber force was effectively No. 1 Group RAF with twelve squadrons of light bombers: ten of single-engine Fairey Battles and two of the twin-engine Bristol Blenheims. It was renamed the Advanced Air Striking Force and was there in a tactical role to directly support the BEF.

The BEF was broadly deployed along the Franco-Belgian border and spent much of the Phoney War preparing a number of fixed defensive lines to extend the Maginot defences to the west. The Allies' strategy for this inevitable war was to defend that line for a year or two, build up military strength and then push the German forces back into Germany. They were entirely unprepared for what came next.

On 10 May 1940, German forces invaded France and the Low Countries and advanced with hitherto unknown speed across Belgium, making a bold and completely unexpected flanking advance through the Ardennes. As early as 16 May, the withdrawal of the BEF commenced and by 21 May the force was outflanked and surrounded on three sides. On 23 May, Gort ordered it to withdraw to Dunkirk, the only port now available. This withdrawal was supported by the RAF fighter squadrons based in France who were outnumbered by the Luftwaffe fighters and both sides suffered heavy losses. The Advanced Air Striking Force also experienced significant losses. The Battles and Blenheims were shot to pieces, not only by the more advanced Luftwaffe fighters, but also at low level by light anti-aircraft fire. Much of the RAF activity took place inland, out of sight of the soldiers on the beaches awaiting evacuation, with the result that they often inaccurately accused the RAF of 'not turning up'.

A combination of a fierce rearguard action by the British Second Corps and the much-debated hesitation from the German Panzer divisions gave a vital three days to plan and prepare for the evacuation of British, French and Belgian forces from the beaches of Dunkirk.

Between 26 May and 4 June, a total of 363,417 troops were evacuated by the Royal Navy and a flotilla of boats of all sizes from the UK, the latter often crewed by their civilian owners.

Further evacuations of those Allied troops to the south who were not trapped by the German army took place throughout June, July and August. By 14 August, a total of 558,032 people had been evacuated, 368,491 being British personnel, including the ground-based elements of the Advanced Air Striking Force. The vast majority of the BEF's equipment was lost; 66,426 men of the BEF were killed and 41,338 were missing or taken prisoner.

The remarkable outcome of the Dunkirk evacuation was rightly lauded in the press and lifted British spirits above the gloom of the battering received by the BEF and the dismal performance of the Advanced Air Striking Force, which must have been as shocking to Bomber Command as it was dispiriting to the aircrew. Some of the best and most experienced aircrew, particularly pilots, were lost and their tactics often proved to be wholly inadequate. Would Bomber Command draw anything out of the wreckage of France?

On 22 June, France buckled and signed an armistice. France's humiliation was complete when Hitler forced it to sign that agreement in the same railway carriage in the Forest of Compiègne in which Germany's defeat was sealed at the end of the First World War. Hitler now had access to the ports of northern France, from where his U-boats and surface fleet could dominate the Atlantic, as well as airfields from where he intended to impose air supremacy.

Now, Hitler's ambitions could extend to the invasion of Great Britain. He wanted the latter to surrender, or at least to declare neutrality, and the invasion, code-named Operation *Seelöwe* (Sea Lion), was seen only as a last resort. Either way he needed complete air and naval superiority over the English Channel and the south-east of England. Hitler turned to his Luftwaffe to force Britain to a negotiated surrender by destroying the effectiveness of the Royal Air Force.

In July 1940 the Luftwaffe started its campaign to eliminate the RAF by first targeting shipping, ports and creating a blockade. In August they swung their attentions to the RAF itself with attacks on airfields, infrastructure and aircraft production. In time they targeted more strategic infrastructure and political targets, and in the end areas of high population. A battle not only to destroy the RAF but also to weaken Britain's resolve before an invasion. However impractical the plans for Operation *Seelöwe* were, and in hindsight doomed to fail, the threat of invasion was clear and present.

The Battle of Britain was pivotal. It lasted just over three months, and for those involved it was never one sided. Day by day the tactics of both sides evolved as each sought an advantage.

The pace of the campaign meant that squadrons and groups were developing tactics on the hoof, which was difficult for Fighter Command, commanded by Air Chief Marshal Hugh Dowding, to control and unsurprisingly his two senior group commanders clashed on tactics; an unresolved situation that ultimately led to Dowding's removal in November 1940. As ever, it was the pilots and their ground crews who daily performed their exhausting aerial jousting against their adversaries who were, at that level, equally motivated and equipped. Fighter Command, however, had a number of advantages. The first was geography; they were fighting over home ground. The Luftwaffe fighters, having flown from their airfields in France and the Low Countries to meet up and escort their bombers, had, by the time they arrived over the south-east of England, only a very short time to fight before having to refuel. Fighter Command, in contrast, was able to refuel its fighters and have them in the air again quickly as the battle was being fought over their heads. Although numerically quite close, the impression was, certainly in the minds of the Luftwaffe pilots, that the RAF had an endless supply of fighters.

As July and August 1940 progressed, a steady stream of Luftwaffe raids of light and medium bombers to a variety of targets most often accompanied by fighter escorts, crossed the Channel day after day. A further advantage and the key to Fighter Command's ability to intercept these raids was the early detection and prompt communications to the fighter bases with accurate enemy locations. The pre-war domestic early warning radar was called the Chain Home system. This, with a network of air observers and through a structure of command centres, became known as the 'Dowding System'.

Before the Battle of Britain, it was not unusual for the average interception operation to have a less than 30 per cent chance of seeing, let alone engaging, any enemy aircraft. The Dowding System improved that percentage to 75 per cent and, for periods, to 100 per cent. Once again, this led to Fighter Command appearing to be much more effective than its number of aircraft would suggest. It did, however, put huge strains on the pilots, their ground crews and the system's ability to manufacture and supply new fighters and to train replacement pilots.

The leader of the Luftwaffe, Reichsmarschall Hermann Göring, was originally convinced that it would take only four clear days to destroy the

RAF, but he was spectacularly mistaken and, in frustration, in the middle of August he ordered his Luftwaffe to put in maximum effort. These multiple raids were met, time after time, by the Spitfires and Hurricanes of Fighter Command. Every fighter squadron was tested throughout that summer, with both sides taking significant casualties, but by the end of August the daily raids started to reduce.

In September it was clear to the Luftwaffe that it was not degrading the RAF as much or as quickly as had been expected and it resorted to an increase of strategic bombing, mainly at night – the Blitz. By 31 October 1940, the Battle of Britain was won, and Fighter Command had inflicted the first significant defeat of the war on German forces.

The casualty figures at the time were sobering and there is no disputing the resolve and bravery of the young crews. The number of kills were exaggerated by both sides and even now there are various estimates, but it seems that over the duration of the Battle of Britain, some 112 days, 1,012 RAF aircraft were lost, and 537 aircrew killed. The percentage survival rate for Fighter Command pilots was 50 per cent. The Luftwaffe lost 1,918 aircraft and 2,662 aircrew.

On 24 August 1940, a small number of German bombers that were off course from their intended target of RAF fighter airfields, bombed the Spitalgate area of east London. The following day, under direct orders from Churchill, the RAF reciprocated by bombing Berlin with a significantly larger force of mainly Wellingtons and Hampdens.

The errors of a few Luftwaffe pilots followed by impetuous reactions from Churchill and Hitler was a bizarre start to what would become a lengthy and destructive strategic bombing campaign.

Bomber Command also had its role during the Battle of Britain; the largest contribution being the bombing of the 3,500 barges, tugs and motorboats being amassed at the Channel ports in preparation for Operation *Seelöwe*, which was postponed on 17 September and the invasion fleet dispersed. The remainder of its activity was small-scale operations, many in daylight, with its small and medium bombers sent to Germany, Holland and France on industrial targets, frequently oil, naval targets and infrastructure such as airfields and storage depots.

Bomber Command learned some hard lessons while carrying out these small-scale, daylight operations. Firstly, some of the elderly bombers were not up to the job; secondly, daylight was not the time for slow bombers when the Luftwaffe fighters so often had air superiority over the targets; and thirdly, their tactics were as outdated as the BEF's defences in France.

Having suffered such heavy losses in some of the early daylight operations, particularly against naval targets, Bomber Command switched to almost exclusively night-time operations and for the next few months would conduct mainly ineffective bombing raids on a number of targets in most of the occupied countries and Germany. Throughout this period the Royal Navy was fully engaged in its defensive role, protecting mainland Britain, its colonies and interests in the Mediterranean and ensuring the vital trade routes principally across the Atlantic, remained open.

The British Army, wounded but rebuilding at home, was in defensive mode; unable, convincingly, to go on the offensive until the North Africa campaign the following year and nowhere near ready for operations on mainland Europe. Fighter Command had been victorious in the Battle of Britain and Coastal Command, with the Royal Navy, defended the UK's coastal waters. Of any part of the three services, it was RAF's Bomber Command, created for strategic offensive action, that was one of the few sectors of the British armed forces that could now fight back, however poorly it was prepared.

The scene was now set for thousands of young men to volunteer for the RAF. Brian Slade was one of them.

Chapter 1

Early Days

Brian was born on 25 July 1924 in Tring, Hertfordshire, on the edge of the Chiltern Hills, 30 miles north-west of London. His father, Bernard, was also born in this small rural town, though Emily, his mother, came from Watford, where they were married in 1923. After a few years they moved to another Hertfordshire town, Hemel Hempstead, and squeezed into a cottage just off the High Street in the Old Town.

In 1911 the population of Hemel Hempstead was 6,500 and by 1921 it had grown to 6,850. Its slow growth mirrored that of most similar-sized towns as in the intervening period the First World War took 393 of its young men and that generation took time to rebuild.

Printing was to become an important local employer. One of the earliest paper mills was established in the early 1800s at Frogmore Mill, which was soon overtaken by the John Dickinson Company at Nash Mills and Apsley Mills, where the river and the canal provided power and transport. By the end of the 1800s they were significant employers and by the 1960s with the creation of the Dickinson Robinson Group became the world's largest stationery company. Both Brian's sister, Norma, her husband to be, his father and many other friends and relations worked for John Dickinson at the Apsley Mills.

During the First World War, one of the John Dickinson mills was converted to munitions manufacture but in the Second War produced aircraft parts and ammunition. The company also used its traditional expertise to support the war effort by producing cardboard fuze caps, mapping paper and, later in the war, 'anti-radar paper'.

The production of 'anti-radar paper' has a particular resonance to this story. It was made by laminating vast rolls of paper to a foil backing, then cut into small strips and packed into bundles. In the spring of 1943 so many of these paper strips were needed that the bundles were packed in their thousands not only at Apsley Mills but also by a group of women volunteers in a disused garage in the nearby town of Berkhamsted, where I went to school. These paper strips would be given the code word 'window' and would be introduced into the war much to the delight of all bomber crews, but more of that later.

Hemel Hempstead at the outbreak of war was a small, prosperous, confident and aspirational community, with a proven patriotic streak familiar with sacrifice – much like countless others across the country. As loyal a 'Middle England' town as you could find. Throughout the 1930s the town and its residents watched the country prepare for war and was ready to do its bit. The Slades were Hemel people.

By the time Brian won a scholarship and started at Hemel Hempstead Grammar School in 1935 the Slades had lived in the town for about six years. The school was opened in 1931 and they, along with the rest of the town's inhabitants, watched it being built about half a mile from the Old Town. Its motto was *Esse Quai Videri*, the translation of which baffled more students, including Brian, than it inspired, namely, 'To be, rather than to seem to be'. With its imposing mock Palladian central portico, this new educational establishment was an entirely appropriate building for this up and coming town.

Brian worked towards his School Certificate, or 'SC', for which students had to gain six passes including English and Mathematics, and students typically took these exams aged 16. Patricia Daniels was a contemporary of Brian's:

> I came to the school in 1935 and left in 1940 … There wasn't a rigid division between scholarship and fee payers or between Class 1 and Class 1A but most of the scholarship pupils were in one form. There was no real streaming but you got the impression that one class was rather more intellectual than the other. We were the only mixed grammar school in the area …

Another of Brian's contemporaries, Derek Collier, remembers:

> Brian … Was my Tudor House vice captain … Not a big chap but a clever little footballer …

A school friend, Tony Horton, said: 'He was a year above me and I knew him very well … he was a bright boy …'

Although the period between 3 September 1939 and Brian leaving school in July 1940 was known as the Phoney War, preparations for combat had been taking place for some time and were visible to all. Operation Pied Piper was the mass evacuation of children from urban areas, there was large-scale building of public air raid shelters, the imposition of blackouts and the issuing of gas marks to all. Air raids were expected, and no one was exempt from preparing. The winter of 1939–40 was also the harshest for forty-five years.

However protected British children were from the realities of the war by their parents and teachers, they heard plenty of stories from refugees of what was really happening on mainland Europe. Mary Horton (née Letto), a contemporary of Brian's but younger, arrived at the school in 1938. Experiencing this at first hand, she recalled the following:

> One important feature of the school during the war years was the diversity of the pupils … Children came to Hemel Hempstead from all over the UK and from Europe. These European children were mostly Jewish. They didn't want to talk about their experiences at first but opened up later and had earth-shattering stories to tell.

Keith Miles, also at the school at that time, remembered:

> The first reaction to the outbreak of war was the appearance of sticky brown paper crosses on all the window panes. This was followed by walling up the cloistered arches of the girls' cycle shed with sandbags to form an air raid shelter … It was on one such occasion when, with the whole school out on the sports fields, a low-flying, twin-engined German plane passed over – I believe that it went on to strafe a train in Boxmoor station.

The two issues of war and weather that preoccupied both the school and the town were neatly addressed in the opening sentences of the editorial in the school magazine, *The Magpie*, in April 1940:

> The second term of the war period has passed away uneventfully so far as major events were concerned. Failure of the coke supply through the terrible weather conditions made it necessary to close the school for three days and the epidemic

of rubella has seriously affected attendance, even members of the staff being involved.

As the 15- and 16-year-old pupils of Hemel Hempstead Grammar School were preparing for their School Certificate examinations in the warm early summer weather of 1940, Churchill's speeches may not have been ringing in their ears but they would have certainly known about and most likely seen the start of the Battle of Britain above their heads. However stirring for their parents and febrile the national atmosphere, it wouldn't have had much relevance to most schoolchildren but for Brian, even as he was taking his School Certificate, he planned to leave school … and he could.

Chapter 2

Why Join the Royal Air Force?

After the First World War the 1918 Education Act raised the school leaving age to 14. Although Parliament in 1939 debated to increase this to 15, that was postponed due to the approach of war. In 1939, as a 15-year-old, he was legally free to leave school regardless of his parents' wishes.

The Military Training Act of 27 April 1939 required all British men aged between 20 and 21 who were deemed fit enough to take six months' military training. This created a reserve ready to be called upon when needed. When the war started only 895,000 men were available and further legislation was provided by the National Service (Armed Forces) Act that made all men between 18 and 41 liable for conscription.

All that was irrelevant to this 15-year-old schoolboy, even one with a bright educational future.

At that time the age limit for full entry into the RAF was 17 years and 3 months, and 18 for flight crew training, although 16 year olds could become apprentices. Known as 'Halton Brats', they were trained at RAF Halton, near Tring, where, you may remember Brian's father, was born and spent his childhood.

It is clear that Brian had wanted to leave school for some months. He contributed to the April 1940 edition of *The Magpie*, the school magazine, with an article entitled 'Recollections', which started: 'As my school career draws to a close and the time for me to leave approaches.'

How much he discussed this with his parents or revealed his true intentions is unknown but Brian, according to his sister, wanted to fly and fly as soon as possible. If he had followed the RAF apprentice route he would not have been eligible to start aircrew training for two years and not likely to be flying operationally for more than three. So he did what a number of impatient, headstrong young men did … he falsified his age, but in Brian's case by a full two years. On his birth certificate it records his birthday as 25 July 1924. His Royal Air Force Volunteer Reserve Service Records show that date as 25 July 1922 and his occupation as 'Student'. Quite what sort of student he imagined he was I shall never know but it was clearly intended, and indeed succeeded, in fooling the reader that he had completed secondary education.

Brian was also able to persuade his father to support that falsification. On Brian's Service Records underneath his date of birth 'per Birth Certificate' had been crossed out, confirming that no birth certificate had been submitted. Clearly father and son colluded. Brian's father, as his nominated next of kin, would have been required to confirm in writing his son's date of birth, albeit falsely. I would imagine that, however easy it would have been to acquire a copy of the birth certificate, the authorities had neither the time nor the inclination to risk losing a volunteer with his background. They believed Brian and they believed his father.

Derek Collier noted that:

> … [Brian] sat his School Certificate examination in 1940 and
> that year, at the age of 16, left school immediately – without
> his parents' permission – falsified his age as being 18 and
> volunteered for flying duties with the Royal Air Force.

Locally, around Hemel Hempstead, Brian was often seen in uniform. Derek mistakenly observed:

> His first posting was at RAF Halton, near Tring, where the
> pilots became known as 'the Halton Brats'.

Tony Horton, another school friend, said:

> He left school without taking his matric so he could get into
> the air force. He was a bright boy and a pushy lad so he got into
> the aircrew. He left school … so he could get into the RAF.
> He probably went in as an apprentice at the age of 15 or 16.

Both Derek and Tony were wrong as he did not join as an apprentice or serve at Halton. His enlistment was all down to him falsifying his age, a fact he withheld from everyone including his school friends. They all simply assumed he was an apprentice, the only way into RAF uniform at 16.

Patricia Daniels recalls:

> Most of the boys in my year joined up. By 1942 we were all 18. You saw them drifting around town in uniform … Brian Slade was in a parallel form (to me) … He left school at the same time as me and within weeks I saw him walking around town in uniform. I thought how did he manage that? The story is that he got his father to sign the form (and thus was able to join up though under age). I met him in 1942 when we were both stationed in Norfolk. He was a serving pilot by then and halfway through his tour of duty so he must have done 15–20 tours already. He was flying Wellingtons then.

Although mature for his age, Brian didn't look 18 and had to learn very quickly to act older than his years, fearful of being found out. I suspect that during his training, he told no one. His age must have had an impact on his next few years. At 5ft 5½in he wasn't tall, had a particularly boyish face and, being short of his 16th birthday, he could not have looked 18. How many times over the next year did RAF administrators look up from their clipboards at this fresh-faced schoolboy and ponder his real age? Many times I suspect but 1940 was not the time to turn down young, willing and able men, desperate to fly. Having described himself as a student, I wonder what answer he gave when asked what was he studying.

Where was the motivation for a schoolboy to do this? What influenced Brian to make that decision? There are potentially many but in Brian's case the reasons are easy to grasp.

It has been well understood for centuries that prevailing social conditions influence young men 'to take the King's shilling'. Before 1900, they saw a life in uniform as a way out of the social deprivation of the times: with unemployment the recruiting sergeant's friend. Those looking for an escape from poverty could at least see regular meals, shelter, clothing and pay when civilian life may have offered none of these. Most contemporary research identifies that at that time economic and social factors were much more important to recruits than patriotic ideals, but these drivers applied less to Brian's generation and indeed more recent recruitment research has revealed they have had less and less influence in more recent times. Brian was a bright and well-educated boy, and came from a relatively comfortable family life, nothing to run away from but an easy target for the fashionable RAF.

It is clear that parental influence was very relevant for many of these young volunteers. Just over twenty years earlier their parents went through the First World War, with few families unaffected. In 1914 Bernard was 15 and Emily 11 and they both will have witnessed the huge call to arms with more than 10,000 a day joining up in late 1914 and 1915. By the end of the first year of the First World War alone, more than 1.2 million had joined up, all of whom were volunteers, and they would have seen countless relatives and friends troop off to France. So what did Bernard do? He was nearly 19 when on 3 November 1917 he enlisted and joined his regiment, the 17th Lancers. After basic training and time at his regimental depot, he was sent to France. At that time his regiment was part of the 7th Cavalry Brigade used as a mobile infantry during the German spring offensive of 1918 and the later August counteroffensive. On 7 August he wrote to his mother, telling her:

> Now don't let this upset you at all but by the time you get this
> I shall have been in a great battle, I am writing these lines on
> the eve of it, as it were. I shall get through mother dear never
> worry, I ought not to have told you, but my conscience tells
> me to, so don't worry or fret and don't repeat this outside the
> family.

The following day the Battle of Amiens started and over the next three days the allies advanced more than 8 miles, a huge distance in a campaign where small gains were the norm. It was though at considerable cost, with 19,000 Allied soldiers killed. At some stage over the three-day battle Bernard was shot and after treatment was sent back to the UK. By 11 November the war was over and Bernard was medically discharged on 18 February 1919. So far his story was one replicated many thousands of times but what happened next, less so … he re-enlisted and joined the Royal Army Service Corps as a staff car driver, spending time in the British Army's occupation of the Rhineland until his final discharge in March 1920. I have a rather wonderful photograph of him at the wheel of his 4-litre Vauxhall 'D' Type staff car. He had a love of large flashy cars for the rest of his life.

I don't know how much of that he shared with Brian but if nothing else his son would have been left in no doubt that military service was not just acceptable but encouraged. For that generation it was what you did. Family influence was clear but what else may have affected his decision?

From the recollections of his school friends, it is clear that even at school they saw the preparations for war and the effects of war. They heard stories not only from their elders but also from their contemporaries, from the refugees who had witnessed at first-hand what was happening on mainland Europe.

BBC radio broadcasts were the only non-printed media available and were listened to avidly at home and abroad. The war was a huge test of the BBC's independence and it did broadcast good and bad news, although it ceded to the government's requests not to give too much detail of losses that could benefit the enemy. The evening news at 2100 hours became required listening for those wanting to keep up to date with news of the war. That broadcast and the next morning's printed headlines would be the conversation topics at work and I suspect at school on most days.

As the Phoney War ended with the invasion of the Low Countries and the evacuations from Dunkirk the war became real and as increasing numbers were being conscripted there was a genuine wave of patriotism fuelled, as we will see, by the real possibility of a German invasion.

There was another key reason that so many joined the RAF and it was ironically influenced by the lack of government funding for the service in the decade following the First World War, when the Royal Navy and army were the largest beneficiaries. The story of the RAF's inception is a long one but it was its new Chief of the Air Staff Hugh Trenchard, appointed in March 1919, who had to manage its underfunding.

A soldier, Trenchard rose through various commands and roles within the Royal Flying Corps and commanded the French Wing under direct control of the army and its commander, General Douglas Haig. The creation of the RAF was a painfully long-winded process. Originally mooted in 1916, it was dogged by political shenanigans, inter-service squabbling between the navy and the army and not least the ambition of trying to achieve a single air force while its embryonic components were trying to fight a war in 1917 and 1918. Trenchard's position on the creation of this separate service was ambiguous to say the least and his various roles, resignations and reinstatements added to the petty arguments over such things as ranks, uniforms and flags, which all combined to impede progress.

Post-war, Trenchard, although he would never be free from inter-service rivalries and political meddling, now commanded an independent service and set about reorganising the wartime RFC and Royal Naval Air Service into a peacetime independent RAF but with a very restricted budget. Post-1918, the newly formed RAF fell from being the foremost world air power with 188 operational squadrons to having, in March 1923 when the Secretary of State for Air reported to the House of Commons, only sixteen aircraft in the UK and no serviceable aircraft in India. By 1920 there were only seven UK-based squadrons but Trenchard spent those early years continuing his fight with the other services, who for operational reasons cast jealous eyes on this new service and its funding.

Although things improved for the RAF in the 1930s, it remained ill equipped for what would confront it in 1939. It would, though, be better prepared for the rapid expansion ahead due to the infrastructure that Trenchard created in the 1920s. With limited funds and a government with no appetite for the expansion of the operational capability of the RAF, Trenchard planted his service's foundations. He created Cranwell, the officer pilots' college, a senior officers' staff college and the apprentice colleges at Halton and Cranwell as well as various research establishments. The Auxiliary Air Force and the University Air Squadron were also his creations, as was funding for air displays and competitions such as the Schneider Trophy (of which more later), which exposed the RAF to an already engaged audience. He was also a firm believer in the strategic use of bombers and we will look more at this in the next chapter.

All this led to very high standards of training and gave both a structure to the RAF and raised its public profile. This, combined with the growth of flying as an exciting civilian pastime, made the prospect of joining up very appealing to thousands of young men.

David Denchfield left the grammar school in 1936 and his memories of that time summed this up:

> This was the time when the flying bug bit, and I read all I could of the exploits of the pilots in the Great War. My schoolwork suffered a bit and aeroplane drawings sprouted all over my school books. I began building models out of whatever I could find or scrounge. It was tough work with no decent glues or paints. During 1935 my school reports were suggesting that if I was to get the School Certificate required to enter the RAF, which was now my dream, then I needed to get my head down to far better effect. So during 1935/6 there was much burning of the midnight oil and I am pleased to say that it all paid off as I gained the School Certificate

and exemption from Matriculation ... Dad served with the Inniskillings from the Somme through Passchendaele to the retreat of March 1918 before advancing back via Ypres before being wounded just before the end. It left an impression and a 'never again' attitude.

Brian's father would also have exerted a similar influence. Having been brought up in Tring, Bernard Slade would have seen the growth of RAF Halton from 3 Squadron exercising their biplanes in Tring Park in 1913 to the establishment of the aircraft apprentices school in 1919 by the burgeoning RAF. Indeed, in 1922, having just left the army, he briefly shared accommodation in Tring with two RAF men from the camp. The combination of Bernard's observations of the early RAF near Tring and his time in France in 1917 and 1918 may have led him to advise his son to steer well clear of the army and could well have set the seeds of flying with the RAF in Brian's head. There were many cold, wet, hungry soldiers who had gazed enviously from the filth of their holes in the ground at the aircraft above believing that its occupants had slept in a bed, wore clean clothes and had eaten a hearty breakfast. Many fathers would have preferred their sons to fight and die that way.

Young men of the time were obsessed with flying, pilots were seen as dashing and glamorous and when the need arose Trenchard's exciting RAF easily gathered in willing recruits. Pre-war, the RAF looked to public schools for their intelligent young men but they would cast their net wider once the war started. Brian, it turns out, was fairly typical of those who volunteered for Bomber Command, intelligent, well educated, studious, attentive, well motivated and physically fit.

Did Brian, a 15-year-old schoolboy, a cheerful happy go lucky character, a bit of a joker, constantly smiling and 'always whistling', feel the rising national patriotism or have a sense of 'doing good'? Possibly, but he will not have felt the inevitable peer pressure that the older 18- and 19-year-olds felt. After all, at his age he was safe from conscription for another two or three years.

There will have been some difficult conversations at home when Brian first mooted the idea of giving up his scholarship education and not only volunteering but also falsifying his age in order to start aircrew training. Bernard's support for those ambitions will have created tension between him and Emily. Her position in a 1930s house, and however much she argued to keep her only son out of harm's way, would have been subordinate and Bernard's view would have prevailed. She never let Bernard forget that.

There will have been many reasons in the background that influenced him but the wartime atmosphere and the fog of patriotism that swirled across the country merely provided the justification for his decision. I can't believe this carefree 15-year-old had a refined moral compass that directed him to fight, or a deep resolve to right the wrongs of the world. There were many young romantic idealists inspired by 'the few' but as a 15-year-old, albeit a bright one, it's more likely that, with the direction and encouragement provided by his father and, as for many of his generation, influenced by Trenchard's inspiration, he volunteered in innocence and naivety looking for fun and adventure, and most importantly to fly. Regardless of the reasons, he will have had absolutely no idea of what that entailed and where it would take him.

Chapter 3

Training 1 – Learning

22 August 1940 – 26 October 1941

It has always taken time for the architects of military strategy to equip their forces with the resources to execute their theories. The fact that Bomber Command wasn't ready at the outbreak of war in 1939 to effectively justify its existence was not only due to the time it took for new aircraft, bombs and technological advances to appear but also that aircrews were not trained to use them in the way those strategies required. During the slow process of preparing Bomber Command for the inevitable war, it arrived inconveniently and embarrassingly early.

The Royal Air Force Volunteer Reserve was created in July 1936 to supplement the Royal Auxiliary Air Force, which since 1924 had been tasked to provide aircrew, principally pilots, in the event of war. In 1939 the existing Royal Air Force recruiting system could not have coped with wartime requirements and the Air Ministry therefore used the established RAFVR procedures as the principle means to recruit, enlist and train future airmen for the RAF.

A further problem was the rapidly changing nature of the aircraft, the size of their crews and the trades required. In the early 1930s, for instance, pilots did the navigation and there was no requirement for an airborne engineer. Bombers went from a crew of two to three and four, then to five or six for a Wellington and ultimately to seven for a heavy bomber. Slowly the Trenchard system of basic training, trade training and operational training that assessed, selected and weeded out during the training cycle, was expanded and developed to cater for these operational requirements.

Even the existing RAFVR recruiting and training infrastructure was tested to the limit when war broke out as significantly larger numbers of servicemen were required. The number of recruit centres, receiving wings, reception centres, initial training wings, and flying schools increased quickly and many changed their roles, designations and locations as the War Office and the Air Ministry struggled to organise an efficient system for getting these men administered and trained. Added to that, the war at home was now having a real effect on the civilian population and the country's infrastructure. So stretched was the training system that many recruits were sent home to wait until more training establishments were created to handle the demand, the so-called deferred entry.

Commonwealth aircrew had for some time been partly trained at home and then in Britain but soon after the outbreak of war a great deal of training had to be done abroad under the British Commonwealth Air Training Plan in Canada, Australia and New Zealand.

Looking at the many RAF establishments that Brian had to attend and considering the number of recruits, the administration required to record and assess each recruit and move them around the country, the travel documentation, the temporary accommodation etc., it was a miracle that the vast majority ended up in the right place at the right time with the right kit; and I suspect many didn't. An extraordinary feat of organisation but a baffling and confusing journey for each recruit … particularly if you are a 16-year-old schoolboy. It seems that Brian's passage through the system was relatively speedy as many spent up to a year waiting for a training vacancy to arise.

Brian submitted his application papers on his 16th birthday on 25 July just as the Battle of Britain started. His official enlistment date was 22 August, a week or so after the last members of the BEF were evacuated from France. As the Battle of Britain raged in the skies above the south-east of England, he was sent to Blackpool to join No. 9 Recruit Centre, twenty-eight days after his birthday. Seaside towns were popular for these proliferating RAFVR establishments as they had such an abundance of available short-term accommodation. Within the first day or two Brian would have been issued with a uniform and associated kit, given a haircut, a medical and dental check. He would have been inoculated and issued with all his service documents including his two dog tags and most importantly his airman's pay book. There was a basic intelligence and maths test to get through and a formal attestation that included signing an Oath of Allegiance, after which he was issued with the small, blue leather-bound New Testament. In Brian's, on the inside page is a neatly handwritten prayer in red ink:

The Angel of God
To whose only care
Brian is committed,
Enlighten, defend and
Protect him from all
Sin and danger during
This his service for
His Country.

I have seen a few of these issue Bibles, indeed I have my own, but have never seen one of that vintage with a prayer. As far as I know the Slade family were not overly religious. I wonder who wrote it?

It was here at Blackpool that the initial assessment was made by an Air Crew Selection Board, which identified him for aircrew. I can only imagine how important that was to him. To have been told he was not fit to fly would have been devastating. He was in Blackpool for September and early October and would have been gripped by the news of Fighter Command's success in the Battle of Britain, the bombing of Cripplegate, the retaliatory raid on Berlin and the start of the Blitz. What he wouldn't have known was that as the Battle of Britain swung towards Fighter Command, Hitler postponed his invasion plans.

On 11 October he was packed off to Devon to report to No. 1 Receiving Wing at Babbacombe on the edge of Torquay. Here further administration, further medical tests, more uniform and then after a few days a short trip down the Devon coast to join No. 4 Initial Training Wing at Paignton on 19 October. This was the first phase of pilot training – ground school. The course was about three months and in addition to the more basic training such as drill and PE, the majority was classroom work. Brian will have covered a number of more technical subjects including aeronautics, engines, meteorology, navigation and signals. He would have learned Morse code, how to fire a rifle and first aid. The drudgery and apparent pointlessness of basic military training was accepted by most recruits but for these embryonic pilots in the distance flying training beckoned. Towards the end there were more assessments and aptitude tests to take. These tests were critical to Brian. Should he pass, it would lead to pilot training at one of the many elementary flying training schools and he did. On 5 March 1941 he was posted to No. 16 EFTS at Derby. At the end of the next two-month course it would be decided whether Brian would be a pilot or a member of the flight crew. There was only one outcome he wanted.

At that time, as the RAF recruiting and training systems slowly developed, these EFTSs were often civilian-run flying schools now contracted to train RAF pilots in their basic skills. Burnaston Airfield was built in 1937 between Derby and Burton-upon-Trent. It was taken over by the RAF on the outbreak of war and early on the majority of the instructors were civilians from Air Schools Ltd based at Burnaston. Later experienced RAF instructors and 'resting' fighter pilots were posted there to instruct. Many students were housed in spare accommodation at the nearby Repton School and the standard training aircraft at the time was the Miles Magister.

The 'Maggie' was a two-seater open cockpit aircraft supplied in large numbers by the makers, Miles Aircraft, to the EFTSs (its civilian name was the Miles Hawk Mk III) and by the end of 1939 more than 700 were in service and overall 1,290 were provided. It was built of a spruce frame covered in plywood and fabric and had a low wing so an ideal basic trainer for fighter pilots (who would move on to Spitfires and Hurricanes with the same low wing) as well as bomber pilots. It had a de Havilland Gipsy Twelve engine and was capable of 130mph and a ceiling of 18,000ft. The instructor sat in the rear seat the trainee pilot in front, both protected by a small Perspex windscreen. It must have been mighty cold flying in an open cockpit in March as aircrew clothing at that time was basic, with only a one-piece flying suit (the Sidcot suit) and sheepskin-lined boots, leather gauntlets and a leather flying helmet and goggles. Not much had changed since 1918.

On 6 March 1941, Brian sat in a Maggie for the first time with his Instructor, Sergeant Shufflebottom, to learn the basic cockpit layout. On 12 March he learned how to taxi and on the next day 16-year-old Brian flew for the very first time with Sergeant Shufflebottom at the controls.

Over the next month Brian and his sergeant instructor had fifteen lessons, most of which were less than an hour long, partly due to the cold weather. On 7 April, less than a month after his first flight and after only a total of eleven hours and five minutes together in the cockpit of a Magister and at the age of 16 years and 8 months, he went solo; a flight of ten minutes. The dream of becoming a pilot was now a reality but there was a great deal yet to learn.

The following week Brian flew for the first of many times with Flying Officer Hamilton-Bowyer as his instructor. Hamilton-Bowyer was a fighter pilot who as part of a detachment from 245 Squadron had flown sorties over Dunkirk during the evacuation and was now on training duties. The pattern of most training flights were a thirty- or forty-minute flight as second pilot with the instructor demonstrating followed by landing, the instructor jumping out and the student repeating the exercises solo. They covered endless 'medium turns, take off into wind, power approach landing', progressing to 'steep turns, climbing turns, spinning, low flying, gliding approach landings, abandon aircraft, restart engine and fire action'. Towards the end of this basic training most time was spent on cross-country flying and map reading, and although instrument flying was practised, there was no night flying.

After a further three weeks and a total of sixty hours (thirty-one of which were solo) Brian was assessed as 'average' by his instructor. There was another very important decision that was taken before a pilot could complete his training.

Would a trainee become a fighter or a bomber pilot, or a pilot at all? The pre-war selection system was soon to run out of candidates and in any event was based more on a candidate's background rather than his aptitude. There was not an oven-ready system of assessments and appraisals to judge candidates as pilots or their potential for any given trade such as navigating or bomb aiming. So a system of continual assessment was established for them to prove their aptitude through the successful completion of the various exercises. It was unsophisticated but effective. The fall-out rate was high but there was plenty of volunteers.

For almost the entire duration of Brian's training, the Luftwaffe would be bombing Britain. From 7 September, London was bombed on fifty-six out of fifty-seven nights. The capital was by no means the only target to receive multiple raids as Plymouth, Southampton, Birmingham, Sheffield and Belfast also suffered that fate. The most notorious took place on 14 November when the Luftwaffe targeted Coventry in the most concentrated raid of the Blitz. About 570 people were killed and more than 850 seriously injured. Some 1,500 homes were destroyed and about a third of the city's factories were destroyed or severely damaged. The Luftwaffe was no novice in the art of strategic bombing. It had carried out equally devastating attacks on a number of cities in Poland during the invasion and on Rotterdam on 14 May as it invaded the Netherlands and, of course, many of its commanders and pilots cut their teeth with the Condor Legion in support of Franco during the Spanish Civil War in 1936–37. It is worth noting that most of their bombing was done with high explosives and incendiaries and the targets were marked by radar-assisted aircraft.

These early bombing raids were devastating for the communities affected, whether Coventry, Guernica, Warsaw or Rotterdam, but what they all had in common was how little effect they had on the morale of the wider populous; if anything, it hardened their resolve. The Blitz comprised about 140 raids on about 17 British cities and killed just over 40,000 people, more than half of which were in London. Over the coming years the Blitz was used regularly to justify and motivate those required to retaliate.

On 13 October Hitler postponed Operation *Seelöwe*, although the Luftwaffe continued the bombing campaign until 11 May 1941. With air superiority lost and at a major naval disadvantage, he almost certainly knew *Seelöwe* would fail, and indeed it is difficult to have ever seen it being successful. It was, though, perceived by the government and all those responsible for home defence as a real threat and its postponement gave the British government as much of a boost as Fighter Command's success.

Throughout the period of the Battle of Britain and the Blitz, the Royal Navy was fully occupied. As soon as war was declared, Britain became dependent upon supplies from America rather than from Europe. The transatlantic resupply convoys were vulnerable to German attacks by surface vessels and U-boats. Germany had rebuilt its navy throughout the 1930s and was particularly proud of its large battlecruisers; as early as June 1940, two of these capital ships, *Gneisenau* and *Scharnhorst*, sank the British aircraft carrier HMS *Glorious*.

Those two, with the other two German capital ships *Bismarck* and *Prinz Eugen*, were destined to attack the North Atlantic convoys. On 24 May 1941 *Bismarck* and *Prinz Eugen* were engaged in the Denmark Strait as they tried to escape into the North Atlantic, resulting in HMS *Hood*, one of the Royal Navy's most important battleships, being sunk. Infuriated and determined, the navy pursued and sank *Bismarck* three days a later. After many more engagements the three remaining German capital ships would end up in Brest, in occupied northern France, for repairs.

Brian was to see, rather too closely, these behemoth German warships later in early 1942.

The last two months at Derby had trained Brian to be a pilot but typically 25 per cent were told that their 'services were no longer required'. There were some that during the EFTS process would demonstrate they were not up to flying an aircraft but could fly *in* an aircraft in a different capacity. Due to specific trade shortages, they were encouraged to head to Bomber Command but to continue their training as a navigator (or observer as they were called in the early years), air bomber or air gunner. That was not only a process of continual assessment but also part of their final 'grading' when they passed the flying test. That grading to a large extent determined their future – Fighter Command, Bomber Command or another trade within it. Increasingly there was no choice, it was a demand-led decision over which they had no influence. To some though, being denied their future as a pilot was just too much. One such was the combative young Canadian, Walter Thompson.

Thompson, who flew with Brian and became a great friend later in the war – and whose character is encapsulated in his nickname, 'Punch' – having qualified as a pilot, did rather too well in his navigation exams and to his horror was posted to the Central Navigation School at RAF Cranage. After one day he concluded navigation wasn't for him and rather casually he left, returned to his training school and, having disobeyed the direct order his posting represented, was duly arrested. Preparations were made for his court martial. After some months, he and the paperwork ended up in front of the air vice marshal in charge of training, who after delivering the expected rollocking about disobeying orders was impressed with this pugnacious Canadian. He cancelled the court martial and dispatched Walter to a gunnery school as a staff pilot. This was not a time to lose committed pilots and, while not the operations he wanted, he was a pilot. We will meet Thompson again.

Operational squadrons broadly had fighters or bombers and as each type of aircraft developed so did the demands put upon their pilots and crews, and naturally enough men with different skills and personal characteristics gravitated to one or the other.

What was the difference between fighter and bomber pilots? Fighter pilots were individualists, more instinctive fighters, happy to be fighting for their own survival; while a bomber pilot is managing and leading a crew and a complex (relatively to fighters) machine where a combination of organisation, discipline, control and team work are required. More experienced fighter pilots talk of having an unshakable confidence, many believing that it was their opponent that would die, a belief in their own invincibility. Novice fighter pilots often perished before they acquired that belief. Bomber pilots on occasions needed that confidence and desire to survive a duel but also needed to accept that they may die. They needed to live with the possibility of their unseen demise and many found more comfort in accepting that. Most likely, they would. Don't imagine what might happen, just accept it might. It was only a matter of time. For some that knack came quickly, for others it never did and they were the vulnerable ones. Those who accepted their fate but worked hard to survive made good bombers.

I'll never know whether Brian had a choice. He desperately wanted to fly and he wanted to serve but what did he want to fly? His assessment at Derby was made at the end of April 1941; the Battle of Britain that rocketed the fighter pilots of 'the Few' into the public consciousness as heroes, was long since over, the bombing of London by the Luftwaffe continued and the provincial cities were raided again and again during his time at Derby, including Coventry, Liverpool and Birmingham. There was no ground war in Europe, so if a pilot wanted to get his own back, to fight back, to kill Germans, there was only one choice. Was he the type of young man that given a choice would have chosen the 'cool' option? I suspect he was and in the post-Battle of Britain RAF, bomber pilots were pretty cool.

After the Battle of Britain the demand for fighter pilots continued but the demand for bomber pilots soared. I don't know whether Brian had the leadership qualities required but perhaps his assessors knew. If he did then his fate was sealed, particularly at a time when replacement crews were required in such numbers. He was heading for bombers.

But how did Bomber Command come about? In France in the First World War aircraft provided their army commanders with eyes in the sky, initially just to observe and report the enemy, then to observe and adjust artillery and finally to deliver bombs. As aircraft became larger and heavier, smaller aircraft were used both to escort them and protect them from their attackers. Even though some imagined the use of aircraft to deliver bombs much further behind enemy lines to more strategic targets, they were essentially battlefield tactical weapons until June 1917, when German aircraft first bombed Paris and then others crossed the Channel and bombed London. Giulio Douhet, the Italian general and author of the influential book of 1921, *The Command of the Air*, was a strong and early proponent of air power and particularly strategic bombing. His theory, often paraphrased into 'the bomber will always get through', was quoted by many and believed to be an unassailable truth. Douhet's belief was based partly on the successes of those early German cross-Channel bombing raids, which killed about 320 people and were so inadequately defended. The evidence for Douhet's book had become obvious to others in the RFC, which reciprocated the German bombing of London by a number of raids on infrastructure and residential targets in Germany in 1918.

These raids, although ineffective, had a dramatic effect on senior military commanders and politicians, who were suddenly exposed to the possibility of an airborne force bypassing ground forces, crossing defended boundaries unhindered and attacking a nation's political and industrial infrastructure. Although the phrase 'the bomber always get through' was later proved to be a singularly false prophecy, at the time it was very influential. Sir Hugh Trenchard, architect of the RAF, was one who embraced the potential of a bomber force and during the 1920s and 1930s he developed the concept of an RAF with predominantly a strategic role. His RAF would be capable of delivering a large-scale bombing offensive and its secondary role would be to defend Great Britain from the enemy's similar capability. In those two roles, Bomber Command and Fighter Command were born. In 1936 he issued specifications for new four-engine heavy bombers but did not expect them be ready in any numbers until 1941. If the war started earlier they would make do with their smaller bomber fleet and Fighter Command would protect them until they and the country was ready. Fortunately technology would enable the RAF and Fighter Command to do just that but at a terrible cost to Bomber Command in the first two years of the war.

This expansion of Bomber Command from 1936 but prior to war attracted officers from many backgrounds within the RAF, and many officers who did not have the skills or mindset of the fighter pilot saw their talents being used better and their careers extended in Bomber Command, which was seen as a war winner and the future of the RAF. The qualities required of a fighter pilot were not always those required for a long RAF career but the leadership qualities of a bomber captain happen to be the same as required of senior officers.

After a week's leave, Brian was sent to No. 17 EFTS at North Luffenham in Rutland for a further week's ground training and then to RAF Kidlington in Oxfordshire to No. 15 Service Flying Training School (SFTS) to continue his training on a new aircraft, the Airspeed Oxford.

As tensions in Europe increased in the mid-1930s, one of the many operational requirements was the need for a monoplane training aircraft, particularly to train pilots and aircrew destined to crew bombers. Airspeed, who had a factory in Portsmouth, was tasked to satisfy this demand and by 1937 the first Oxford had flown. The demand was so great that throughout the war a number of companies produced Oxfords, including de Havilland in Hatfield and Standard Motors in Coventry. By the end of production more than 8,000 had been built.

It was a twin-engine, low-wing monoplane, reliable, easy to fly and similar to many of the bombers in service at that time. It could take a crew of six and some were fitted with a rear gun turret for training air gunners. Like the Magister, it had a wooden frame, covered with plywood and fabric but powered by two Armstrong Siddeley Cheetah × radial piston engines and capable of 188mph and a ceiling of 19,500ft.

The bombing of British city targets continued, with London suffering some of the worst nights of the war in March and April 1941 and with Liverpool bombed for seven consecutive nights at the beginning of May. Abroad the news was no better. The U-boat campaign in the Atlantic was causing significant damage to convoys from the US and Rommel's Afrika Korps was pushing the Allies back into Egypt.

Hitler's gaze was now turning east. Germany's invasion of Russia, named Operation Barbarossa, on 22 June opened up an European eastern front. The Wehrmacht was now engaged on many fronts and their impressive expansion in the east and around the Mediterranean would stretch their resources and their supply lines.

On 23 May 1941 Brian started his training on the Oxford, or the 'Ox-box', as it was known, at Kidlington. The first few flights were repetitions of many exercises he had done before but now on a different and much larger aircraft. By 28 May, and after only a further four and a half hours of training, he went solo. Over the following months, training intensified. He often completed up to four or five training flights a day. This included what must have seemed long navigation exercises that took him as far afield as Church Stretton, South Cerney, Leominster and Devizes. In late June he did some dusk flying and then on 1 July had two twenty-minute night flights as second pilot with his instructor. On 5 July he flew once more with his instructor and then had his first solo night flight of forty minutes. He did two more of those but would leave Kidlington with only two hours of night flying in his logbook.

He took his 'wings test' on 23 July and by the end of the month he had a further eighty-three hours (fifty-five as first pilot) in his log and a total of four hours' night flying. It's worth noting that pre-war, no night flying was taught by this stage but now the growth of night operations forced it into the syllabus.

On 30 July he was awarded his 'wings', officially known as a his 'flying badge'. His logbook notes that his assessment as a pilot remained 'average'. I can only imagine the sense of achievement he felt having qualified as an RAF pilot, which he achieved five days after his 17th birthday. On 9 August he joined Course 16 at No. 12 Operational Training Unit to fly Wellington bombers.

At the end of the 1930s, Bomber Command had fifty-five squadrons but twenty of those were reserve or 'pool' squadrons and a further ten squadrons of No. 1 Group went to France with the BEF in September 1939. Bomber Command at home was woefully under-resourced. Creating new squadrons from those disbanded after the First World War was easy but manning them both with aircrew and hardware was more complex. The aircraft manufacturers now had to raise their game but the provision of trained operationally ready crews was a major problem. The head of Bomber Command, Air Chief Marshal Sir Edgar Ludlow-Hewitt, recognised the issue and early in 1940 he reorganised his training group, then known as No. 6 Group, by disbanding fifteen squadrons based on eight different bomber stations to create the first eight operational training units. The system creaked with many changes of leadership and a new administrative and logistical structure evolving but, incredibly, by early April 1940 the OTUs were established and operative. Another example of how the events of 1939 accelerated, albeit chaotically, Britain's preparations for war, which had been ponderous throughout the 1930s. Their creation and resulting demand for instructors, however, reduced even further the pool of trained pilots already hit by the losses suffered in France.

No. 12 OTU, which was created from 52 and 63 squadrons (and a flight from 12 Squadron), used two airfields, RAF Benson and RAF Chipping Warden (where most flying was carried out) and they were a case in point. Although there was a proliferation of civilian airfields throughout the 1930s (due mainly to the growing popularity of flying), once again the threat of war prompted not only a number to be taken over by the RAF but also the impetus to build new airfields – some very quickly. Benson, south-east of Oxford was built in 1937–38 and opened in 1939. Chipping Warden, less than 50 miles north near Banbury, was opened in July 1941 only a month before Brian arrived.

His arrival at Benson on 9 August coincided with preparations being made to move the OTU to the new Chipping Warden. The formal transfer took place on 16 August but both stations were pretty chaotic as aircrew, ground crew and all the kit made the journey north. For the first few weeks they were living and carrying out ground training at Benson and travelling up to Chipping Warden to fly. At last, on 22 August he flew in a Wellington for the first time as a passenger from Chipping Warden. The next few weeks were further familiarisation, countless circuits and landings, instrument flying and navigation exercises with flights to other airfields. Already the demand from the operational squadrons for replacement crews was growing and the OTUs would have to respond. Pre-war, the RAF had exacting standards for both pilot and aircrew training and the timescale within which

23

to achieve those standards but now training courses were shortened and training staff, trainees and aircraft and ground crew were put under extreme pressure to produce crews quickly without lowering standards. For instance, three weeks after his first Wellington flight as a passenger and after fewer than seven hours flying as second pilot, he went solo as first pilot.

The rapid, demand-led expansion of the training system gave rise to, on the face of it, a fairly chaotic regime at the OTUs in 1941. Courses at 12 OTU lasted between six and eight weeks, and a new course started every two weeks, which enabled students who failed certain exercises or tests to be 'back-termed' to another course. Course failures were rare but some spent more time there than others as they progressed slowly through the syllabus. Brian's course had fifteen students, although later ones had up to fifty. It was not surprising that during this accelerated and pressured programme of training, mistakes were made, accidents occurred and crews and aircraft were lost.

Soon after his arrival and a few days before his first Wellington flight, a Wellington Mk Ic on a night cross-country training flight from Chipping Warden lost power in one engine and crashed trying to land at Upper Heyford. Remarkably, although all were injured the crew survived. A few days later a Mk Ic also on night training crashed, burst into flames and killed its four crew.

On 22 September another Wellington piloted by Sergeant William Onions had a seized port engine, which caused the propeller to fly off and strike the fuselage only feet away from Onions. It severed some hydraulic lines, causing the bomb bay doors to drop open, which increased drag, and as the speed dropped the pilot had little option but to crash land just north-east of the airfield. A few days later he had another scare when an engine failed. He survived both but later his luck ran out and he was killed over Cologne. Soon after, another Wellington overshot the runway at Chipping Warden and crash-landed, injuring two of the crew, but then the following day another Wellington crashed into it, writing off both aircraft. Later in October another Wellington on night training crashed on a local village, killing the pilot instantly, with the second pilot dying from his injuries the following day.

A few days later a Mk Ic piloted by Sergeant G.W. Bibby, who was on the same course and had flown with Brian, crashed into a hangar having misjudged the final turn into the flare path to land. The Wellington burst into flames but ten members of the ground crew fought hard to get the crew out and due to their courage only one of them, Sergeant Thomas Leighton RAAF, perished. Leighton, who Brian had flown with only days before, was their screened pilot instructor. Teaching young, inexperienced young men to fly these machines was a dangerous business.

I doubt Brian and his fellow trainees were deterred by these accidents but the reality of the risks were now manifest. A few of them were down to mechanical failure but the majority were pilot error and that news would filter back quickly to the trainees. It will not have escaped Brian that the better pilot you were, the longer you might stay alive. A fundamental lesson best learned early.

On 26 October, after about two months at Chipping Warden, his conversion to Wellingtons was complete and he awaited his posting to a squadron. The week before he did his first live bombing exercise over the bombing range at Wainfleet on the Lincolnshire coast near Skegness. He had now completed more than 220 hours of flying, 111 as first pilot, 70 of which were on Wellingtons, and having completed the grand total of four practise bomb runs it was now deemed he was ready for operations. It's often thought that as the demand for aircrew increased, they were poorly trained. That was untrue. While the training they received was good and the flying hours adequate, the conditions under which they trained were not in any way like operational conditions. Most navigation was done in daylight and although the country was in blackout, their familiarity with the areas over which they trained masked their navigational inadequacies. Bomb aimers and pilots did little bombing and no high-level bombing. It was only in his last few days at the OTU that on his four bombing range sorties, he dropped a total of sixteen bombs, one at night including one flare. There were neither the range facilities or the time for more. In peacetime a pilot joining his squadron would continue his training with hundreds of hours to be added to his logbook. Not now. The formal training might have been done but as the navigation officer in the 1945 RAF propaganda film *Journey Together* says 'training's only over when your dead'. Further training would now have to be done with their operational squadrons and over German-occupied Europe.

The eight pilots, two navigators and five air gunners on his course were now ready to join their squadrons.

His logbook displays his 'Summary of Flying and Assessments for OTU Course'. He seemed to be finding his métier as his assessment as a heavy bomber pilot was now judged 'above average'. In addition, the summary noted that his rating as a pilot/navigator was average and he was not recommended to attend a navigation course. For him that must have been the perfect result.

The country saw RAF aircrew as an elite within which pilots were the aristocrats. He was now to join that exclusive group who would over the next few years pay a high price for their status.

Unwittingly, his instructors had just put a juvenile in charge of a bomber. At that stage of the war, even if they had known, I'm not sure they would have stopped him. Brian had fooled them and now revelled in the fact that someone, somewhere was paying him to go flying.

Chapter 4

Wellingtons

A s a boy I spent much of my summer holidays on the local farm and much to my mother's annoyance, I took home one of the farm kittens. Her cry of 'just for one night' was, of course, ignored and we had Wimpy for twelve years. The name was my mother's idea, no explanation. That was that. I had no idea that J. Wellington Wimpy was a hamburger-eating character in the Popeye cartoons of the 1930s and adopted by crews as their affectionate nickname for the Wellington bomber. She had heard her big brother use the name many years before.

In the 1930s the United Kingdom Air Ministry needed to completely upgrade the bomber fleet, which had developed little from the biplanes of the First World War. The interest in pleasure flying for private individuals had led to Britain in the years after the First World War having the largest aircraft manufacturing industry in the world. That experience and expertise was now invaluable.

There was a particular requirement for a new medium bomber and as early as 1932 the Air Ministry issued a specification for a twin-engine medium daylight bomber from which Vickers produced some prototypes, resulting in an agreed aircraft going into production at the end of 1936.

Others were designed and came into service like the Handley Page Hampden and the Armstrong Whitworth Whitley but as they were phased out the more advanced Wellington populated most of the bombing squadrons as the workhorse of the war's early years. In total, 11,461 Wellingtons were produced and only about 30 per cent were destroyed during the war but not one is still flying.

It was designed jointly by the chief designer at Vickers, Rex Pierson, and the remarkable Barnes Wallis, who at that time was one of Britain's best airship designers and would come up with the famous bouncing bomb used in the dams raid in 1943. It was his design of the structure that made the aircraft strong, relatively light, providing good unobstructed internal space and was simple to mass produce using unskilled labour. Known as geodetic construction, it was a lattice of light alloy struts that created the curved shape of the body. The sections were produced by a number of subcontractors off site and assembled in the two main Vickers' factories.

The lattice framework was covered in Irish linen, which was clamped and hand-stitched into place and then covered with up to nine coats of dope that shrunk it to fit. Because the geodetic design flexed, a linen cover was required rather than a rigid covering. Although initially distrusted, this design proved excellent in combat and the fuselage could take multiple hits and significant damage without losing its structural integrity. On many occasions fires would remove the outer cover but the aircraft still flew.

The first mark produced in numbers was the Ic with two Pegasus XVIII, on which Brian did most of his training and flew with his first squadron. In total 2,685 Mk Ics were built mainly at the Vickers' factories at Weybridge in Surrey and Broughton near Chester. Later in 1941, his first squadron was one of the first to receive the improved Mk III with the more powerful Hercules XI engines. These aircraft were the most sophisticated in Bomber Command when they appeared and became trusted and loved by their aircrew; more than 1,500 Mk IIIs were built. The Broughton factory, more than half of whose workers were women, at its most productive was building twenty-eight Wellingtons each week.

The standard crew was pilot, navigator/bomb aimer, radio operator and two air gunners, and in the early days, a second pilot.

Conditions inside were basic but seen as a real improvement on the contemporary bombers of the time. One of the practical problems for the crew was that of keeping warm. The Wellington's maximum altitude was 18,000ft for the Mk Ic and 22,700ft for the Mk III, and its standard cruising altitude was 10,000ft. Most operations were flown between 10,000 and 15,000ft. At that height, sub-zero temperatures were the norm and in winter -30°F was common. Although the crew area for the pilot, navigator and radio operator had hot air heating, it was pretty ineffective as the men preferred to have the plywood bulkhead doors open. The poor air gunners in the front and rear turrets had the worst deal, having the most exposed and cramped positions with no heating. Although all wore sheepskin-lined boots and jackets, full leather flying helmets and gloves, crews resorted to extra layers of their own to combat the bitter cold. Later some electrically heated suits became available but not in the early days for Brian and his crew.

Oxygen for the crew was used when flying above 10,000ft as without there was a deterioration of performance and at worst apoxia; in extremis, death. A row of up to sixteen 750-litre oxygen cylinders were stored centrally in the fuselage and fed oxygen to each crew member's position. They plugged it in their flying helmet, which had an oxygen regulator.

While dressing for their operation all crew members would collect their parachutes and Mae Wests. Pilot's parachutes were fixed to their harness in a way that they could sit on them, and Wellington pilot seats were therefore unpadded. Other crew members wore 'observer-type parachutes' which fixed to their chests. These were cumbersome for the navigator and the radio operator and most hung them close to their crew positions, although some would wear them on the bombing run, when they felt most vulnerable. For the air gunners it was impossible to fit into their turrets and operate the guns with their parachutes on, so they hung them outside their turrets. Pilots knew that if they ordered a bale-out, they needed to keep the aircraft steady long enough for the crew to fit their parachutes and get to an exit. It wasn't always possible.

At the rear of the fuselage was an Elsan chemical toilet. Things would have to be desperate for that to be used and crew often took bottles to avoid having to make the journey aft. It was not unknown to get stuck on a freezing seat and spillages were common; a great job for the ground crew on return.

Getting into and out of a Wellington was an adventure in itself. The inherent structural strength of the geodetic design required openings to be at a minimum. The main hatch was at the front underneath the bomb aimer and entered by a short ladder, normally stowed inside. It was also the bale-out exit, although at the rear of the body on the starboard side was a triangular strip of fabric that could be torn away to offer another. The only way out for the rear gunner was to rotate the turret fully to one side and fall out backwards through the sliding door, but not before he had grabbed and fitted his parachute hung in the body of the aircraft on the turret bulkhead.

Once inside the front hatch it was a scramble up to the crew area for the pilot, radio operators and navigator. The front air gunner had a simple step up into his very cramped turret. The rear air gunner had to step up, pass the pilot, radio operators and navigator, down the fuselage along a plywood floor, step down from the roof of the bomb bay, climb over the tail spars and into his turret.

The pilot's seat is raised and on the port side of the cockpit. To his right was a pull-up collapsible canvas seat for the second pilot, known as the 'dicky seat', which would need to be folded up in order for the crew to

29

move through the cockpit. As you will read, the second pilot role ended in spring 1942 during Brian's first tour. The view for the pilot was good to the front and to each side through the Perspex panel cockpit windows. The window panel to the left of the pilot would slide back to open and the smaller triangular window in front of that would open an inch or so for ventilation but both would be tight closed from take-off bearing in mind the bitterly cold outside temperatures. Only about 3ft from the pilot's head was the port engine propeller tips; he could virtually touch them from that sliding window. The noise must have been deafening, indeed for some it was.

In front of him was a wide control panel with the standard set of pilot's instruments and gauges including airspeed indicator, altimeter, heading indicator, artificial horizon etc. The control column had a 'spectacle'-type hand wheel at the top with most engine controls including throttles to the left. The control surfaces were directly operated by a series of push pull rods that ran down the port side and elevator and rudder controls with wires from the foot-controlled rudder bar.

Among the various dials were the fuel tank gauges for the outer wing tanks, which in later marks had some basic armour plating and a self-sealing system, containing a total of 634 gallons. In each nacelle (the enlarged section of the wing containing the engine) was a further tank containing 58 gallons used as a reserve, so 750 gallons in total. This gave the Wellington a range of between 2,040 and 2,550 miles (depending on the mark). Extra tanks could be fixed into the outer bomb bays but the standard configuration was used for the vast majority of operations. Under each wing was a vent pipe to discharge unwanted fuel when needing to lose weight quickly prior to a forced landing.

One of the innovations on the Wellington was a basic automatic pilot situated beneath the cockpit floor. It was pneumatically powered and gyroscopically controlled, giving aileron and elevator control. When a second pilot was flying, the first pilot could take a break but for most of Brian's operations he was the only pilot so the automatic pilot potentially gave him a chance for a brief rest. However, it wasn't trusted and rarely used.

Behind the pilot was a structural bulkhead, the port side half of which was covered in plywood, behind which was the wireless operator's seat with his radios and other various navigational aids. The starboard side had a plywood door on which was an axe intended for the crew to cut themselves out should that be necessary. To the wireless operator's left on the side of the aircraft were a line of pilot's instruments. The type of radios and other equipment changed regularly as technology improved throughout the war, though their purpose remained standard. First was an intercom system linked to one of the other radios that enabled crew members to speak to one another. This was essential, firstly because the air and engine noise even at cruising speeds meant normal conversation was impossible. Secondly, the air gunners were required to observe the whole time and needed to communicate instantly if trouble was encountered or as they spotted landmarks to assist the navigator. Add to that the noise of anti-aircraft fire or attacking night fighters and the intercom became essential.

On the floor behind the operator was a small short-range transceiver used to communicate with the control tower before take-off. From about the time Brian started flying Wellingtons two new radios had been introduced: a long-range transmitter for W/T (wireless telegraphy) for communicating with their home base with a morse key fixed on the desk and a shorter-range radio capable of voice communications up to about 10 miles, the latter having a DF (direction finding) and homing capability. Later equipment included the Standard Beam Approach to assist landing and the Gee radio direction-finding system for aiding navigation. The wireless operator, as well as all the technical communications equipment to look after, was responsible for the effective distribution of oxygen to the crew. He had plenty to think about.

Behind the wireless operator's cubicle was the navigator's desk and chair. Navigators in the early days were called observers, a throwback to the First World War. As operations became more sophisticated and the distances involved became greater, they became a separate trade and had specific training at an air navigation school, which continued at the OTU. Between the navigator and the wireless operator on the Mk III was a bulletproof screen as part of another bulkhead to protect the wireless operator and pilot from a night fighter attack from the rear.

The navigator's desk was fixed but had a sliding seat chair. He too had a row of instruments to help him with his navigation – a compass, airspeed indicator and clock.

Above him was the handle to rotate the DF aerial that protruded above the fuselage, often protected by a Perspex cover. Behind that was a half-sphere Perspex 'astrodome' used occasionally for star navigation but, as Brian and his navigator would discover later with 115 Squadron, it had other more critical uses.

The navigator needed to move forward quickly past the radio operator and pilot, down two steps to the flat padded board on which he would carry out his secondary role of bomb aiming. When there his heels would be virtually under the pilot's controls and his head underneath the front turret. In front of him was the bombsight, below which were clear Perspex panels enabling him to see down and forward.

As the navigator had studied charts and plotted the route he would be aware of the obvious physical features on the ground, river bends and junctions, large buildings, linear features like railways etc. He had also been briefed in detail by the 'met man' on the weather that would affect their route and therefore their ability to get their bombs anywhere near the target. It was this homework that made him the right man to spot the target, finally control the aircraft and deliver the bombs. On the final bombing run he would be directing the pilot from his prone position while peering through his bomb-aiming sight.

In poor visibility, particularly when under fire from ground defences, it's hardly surprising that bombs very rarely found their target.

Both the gun turrets were difficult to squeeze into and cramped. Although covered they were extremely cold, so cold that frostbite was not unknown. As well as operating the guns, the air gunners were key observers for the pilot and navigator. In the later marks the turrets were made by Nash and Thompson, a company started by Archie Fraser Nash who before and after the war made stylish motor cars.

Turrets were hydraulically controlled by a central control stick that could be rotated by twisting the stick on its vertical axis, and the guns could be raised and lowered by pushing or pulling the stick forward and back. The guns were .303 Browning machine guns and initially had 1,000 rounds in boxes within the turret from which the belted ammunition was fed direct to each gun. Further ammunition was stored in the fuselage. Spent cartridges in the rear turret were ejected outside but in the front turret, because there was a danger of them interfering with the engines if ejected, they were kept within the turret. A number of improvements were made to these turrets, including better sights and powered ammunition feed systems allowing 2,000 rounds per gun. Up to 8,000 additional rounds could then be stored in the fuselage. The .303 was the standard calibre for a whole range of British Army weapons, which made for consistency of manufacture but was never really suitable for the role in bombers. It was a major frustration for future senior commanders that they could not persuade the Air Ministry to equip new bombers with heavier machine guns or cannon to match those found on most night fighters.

The air gunners continued their training at the OTUs. In terms of pure accuracy training, they were often taught to shoot clay pigeons with shotguns in order to learn the principles of 'lead' and 'swing' (called deflection), as were fighter pilots. The method that was discouraged was 'hose piping' by swinging the stream of rounds onto the target by watching the tracer, which was very wasteful on ammunition. The recommended technique was short accurate bursts using the ring sight to gauge how much lead to give the target.

The bomb bay extended from the bulkhead behind the pilot's seat, under the navigator's and radio operator's seats to the rear of the fuselage. The ceiling of the bomb bay was a plywood sheet, which was also the crew cabin floor. The bomb bay was 23ft long and divided lengthways into three separate bays. The number of bombs depended entirely on the bomb load for that operation but the total load was limited to 4,500lb (4,000lb for the Mk III). It could hold a variety of bombs from the 4,000lb blockbuster, known as a 'cookie', nine of the standard 500lb and eighteen 250lb bombs as well as 3 × 1,500lb anti-shipping mines. The smallest ordnance was the 4lb incendiary carried in pre-loaded small bomb containers (SBCs). Each one contained three canisters of twenty-seven incendiaries and the bomb bay could carry six SBCs, giving it the ability to drop 486 incendiaries. The empty containers came home and would be refilled for future use.

There was a fire extinguisher system in each engine operated by switches on the pilot's control panel and hand-held extinguishers in the fuselage, which Brian's crew would soon be using.

For the first two years of the war the Wellington worked alongside the Hampden and the Whitley. The four-engine bombers started to arrive as Brian finished his training but out of 530 bombers typically available to Bomber Command at that time, only thirty-five were four-engined. For a further twelve months the Wellington was the mainstay of Bomber Command.

Chapter 5

115 Squadron – Part 1

'Despite the Elements'

6 November 1941 – 10 July 1942

After finishing his Wellington training at Chipping Warden Brian headed to Norfolk in late 1941 and his first operational posting, having first spent a few days back in Hemel Hempstead enjoying another opportunity to tell stories and show off his wings. As thousands of other recruits and trainees criss-crossed their way around the country, Brian (paid the princely sum of 12s 6d a day as a sergeant pilot), in uniform with suitcase and travel warrant in hand arrived at Downham Market station and on to the transport for RAF Marham between Swaffham and King's Lynn.

East Anglia was an obvious location for airfields, having relatively flat open countryside, and, as the prospect of war in Europe increased in the 1930s, geographically closest to mainland Europe. The paucity of large conurbations was also an advantage that led to many airfields having an intimate connection to the surrounding rural communities from where local staff were often employed. Marham, initially a grass aerodrome, was handed to the Royal Flying Corps in 1916 and then closed in 1919 soon after the end of the First World War. That original all-grass airfield was smaller than the standard 1,000-yard diameter area but had the traditional semicircle of buildings including hangars and a control tower to one side. Work started in 1935 to enlarge Marham to the dimensions required for heavy bombers and it was reopened in 1937. This was simply a larger area of grass to give a maximum runway length of about 1,750 yards and the additional necessary buildings and infrastructure built to accommodate two squadrons, as did most Bomber Command stations.

During Brian's time at Marham there were as many as 2,800 personnel. The two squadrons totalled about 1,100, a station headquarters and ancillary staff, about 350 other RAF or RAFVR personnel, 236 WAAF and the station was defended by 130 men of the Bedfordshire and Hertfordshire Regiment, 121 men of 282 Light Anti-Aircraft Battery and 41 members of 317 Searchlight Regiment.

From its inception on 1 December 1917, 115 Squadron was destined to be a bomber unit. Once trained and equipped with the RAF's first 'heavy' bomber, the Handley Page O/400, it was deployed in August 1918 to Roville-aux-Chênes, some 20 miles behind the front line. The O/400 was a large biplane with a crew of two and powered by two Rolls-Royce Eagle engines. It carried 2,000lb of bombs and by the end of the war, some three months later, the squadron had completed fifteen operations. Most were 'strategic' targets such as major rail junctions and aerodromes but rarely more than 40 miles beyond the front.

As most squadrons were, it was disbanded in October 1919, but it reformed in June 1937 at Marham, initially with Handley Page Harrows. By May 1939 it had re-equipped with Wellingtons. When Brian arrived in November 1941 the station was shared with 218 (Gold Coast) Squadron, which re-equipped with Short Stirlings a month later. Both were part of No. 3 Group and often took part in the same operations, shared accommodation and messes and the crews would have known each other pretty well.

A Bomber Command squadron at that time typically comprised two flights (normally named 'A' and 'B') and was commanded by a wing commander. A flight comprised eight to ten aircraft and was commanded by a squadron leader. At that time 115 Squadron had about 136 aircrew and 362 other personnel. That's 498 people to keep about eighteen aircraft operational. Other senior positions were the squadron adjutant, responsible for the day-to-day running of the squadron, and the squadron intelligence officer (SQUINTO). There were also three 'trade' leaders for navigation, gunnery and bomb aimers, who were normally senior flight lieutenants or pilot officers and responsible for the maintenance of high standards for their trade speciality within the squadron.

No. 115 Squadron at that time was commanded by Wing Commander Trevor Freeman DSO DFC and bar of the Royal New Zealand Air Force. On arrival, Brian joined 'A' Flight commanded by the very experienced Wellington pilot and another Kiwi, Squadron Leader R.J.K. Hogg, who was also new to the squadron having arrived on the same day as Brian from 15 OTU at RAF Harwell but had completed his first tour with 75 (NZ) Squadron from RAF Feltwell and had also flown Wellingtons in North Africa in 1941. It was normal for a new pilot to be twinned initially with an experienced pilot and Brian's mentor was Sergeant Jim Holder, with whom he was now to fly his first operation after six training flights and fewer than five hours' squadron training.

Brian was 17 years and 4 months old.

Sergeant Albert Ernest Holder, for some reason known as Jim, was born in Aylesbury not that far from Hemel Hempstead. His brother Reg was a radio technician at RAF Honington, some 30 miles south, and occasionally they would talk on the aircraft radio as Jim approached Marham on his return from an operation. Reg was Jim's best man when he was married the previous May.

On 23 November, Wellington Z1070 joined thirty-six other aircraft, four of which were from 115, to bomb Dunkirk. Jim Holder was the skipper, with Brian as second pilot sitting in the collapsible 'dicky seat' alongside. It was a pretty high-powered team that night as Wing Commander Freeman took one aircraft and Squadron Leader Hogg was in another. The specific target at Dunkirk is unrecorded and the weather was poor with cloud cover over the town but at debrief crews from only seven of the thirty-six aircraft indicated that they had bombed the primary target; a level of inaccuracy that was typical for the time. Not a great first mission but it could have been worse as all aircraft returned.

Three days later, with three other squadron aircraft, the Holder/Slade crew took off to bomb Emden, a town on the north German coast close to the Dutch border, but soon returned with engine trouble. The following night, as part of ten from 115 Squadron, they joined eighty-six other aircraft to bomb Düsseldorf in the industrial Ruhr Valley, and all ten returned safely. Brian had now flown three operations with Jim Holder and I'm sure was desperate to fly as first pilot, but instead he was sent off on a week's leave.

While he was on leave, on 7 December, the Japanese navy bombed the US Naval base at Pearl Harbor, Honolulu. America was now in the war and few underestimated the repercussions of that surprise attack on the neutral United States, but in Europe Bomber Command's work continued.

On 11 December Brian was back at Marham and once again 'second dicky' but this time with his boss, as he notes in his flying log: 'W/Cmdr Freeman DSO, DFC and Bar, as First Pilot.'

The highly decorated Wing Commander Freeman was one of many New Zealanders serving with the RAF and regularly flew with new pilots for their first trip or two. After his time with 115 Squadron he was posted to establish and command the RNZAF station in Odonga, New Georgia in the Solomon Islands, to support US forces in the Far East. He was killed on air operations on 17 December 1943. After the operation on 11 December with Freeman, Brian was moved over to 'B' Flight, which was commanded by Squadron Leader Ian Grant AFC, and flew circuits and landings with him on 15 December. If the flights with Freeman and Grant were an informal assessment, Brian presumably impressed, as on the next squadron mission on 16 December he was to captain Wellington X9831 on his first bombing sortie as first pilot. However, before he could skipper his own aircraft, he needed his own crew. As it happened his crew had arrived, ready made, a week earlier.

It's interesting to look at how crews were put together as Bomber Command evolved a novel form of crew self-selection. The early bombers often had a crew of only two or three and replacing them was done from the regular postings from the OTUs into the squadrons, a peacetime system that continued into the first few months of the war. Inevitably as the larger medium and heavy bombers were lost the replacement of entire crews of five, six or seven were needed and a system of creating and posting oven-ready crews was required. During their time at the OTU, having spent time together all course members would meet up and self-select their future crew mates.

This system is appealing to military historians because its apparent random and disorderly nature was the antithesis of Trenchard's well-organised and structured pre-war RAF. It wasn't though quite as haphazard as many have described. The final part of aircrew training was the two-month period at their OTU where the various trades came together in order to polish their individual skills, and more critically flying with a variety of other course members learning to work as a crew and in the process learning about each other. They got to know the grafters and the lazy and found people they trusted and who could work under pressure. They started to recognise that just liking somebody, however appealing that may seem, was not enough. Finding those they had confidence in, were good at their job and they got on with, made for a good crew. Over the two months they flew with a large number of the others on their course (there was only fifteen on Brian's course) and not surprisingly friendships and bonds were formed. That final crewing up meeting wasn't a 1940s version of speed dating as it is sometimes characterised as but merely the formalising of a two-month process of flirting.

The early OTU system wasn't really conducive to crewing up until course sizes grew. That was principally led by the proliferation of the heavy four-engine bombers, and consequentially, their losses. The larger the OTU, the earlier crewing up was done and the better it worked. The course was typically six to eight weeks with a new intake every two weeks. There was no fixed end date, trainees leaving when they had completed the required exercises successfully. Brian's course of eight pilots, two navigators and five air gunners could only have formed two incomplete Wellington crews. As there was course overlap, crews were formed from different courses and on occasions would be broken up when they arrived with their squadrons. It was a rather chaotic system for the smaller OTUs that improved as numbers grew; 12 OTU would have courses of between forty and fifty within a few months.

Crewing up had a number of advantages, not least that it was quick, simple and needed little administration. A system that required assessments of skills and temperament and then to match five individuals into a team would be overcomplicated, long winded and not necessarily effective. One advantageous consequence of this apparently arbitrary system was almost certainly accidental. It nullified the pre-war class-dominated rank and trade structure and helped cope with the arrival of much-needed aircrew from the dominions and other Allied countries. Before 1939 there was a standard route to become a pilot. Public school, university officers' training corps (OTCs) or the Royal Auxiliary Air Force would lead to officer training at Cranwell, a commission and, if having the aptitude, becoming a pilot. If you weren't an officer you could not become a pilot. All other trades, particularly on the ground, were predominantly filled by NCOs and other ranks. After 1939, with a dire shortage of aircrew, background and class soon became subordinate to ability, which suited many aircrew from the colonies who found the old class-ridden RAF structure intolerable. Once the barrier of non-officer pilots was broken and the 'in air' hierarchy of the pilot being the skipper regardless of rank was established, it was the crew that became the priority. Although life in officers' and sergeants' messes clung to an earlier RAF, the process of crewing up, to a significant degree, neutralised the pre-war social baggage to produce men from all backgrounds and of all ages who when crewed up reacted better to the stresses and pressures of working in tight interdependent teams. Wartime demands were changing the grass roots RAF into a meritocracy. The system also made squadron life more tolerable for novice crews, who found a more welcoming social norm in both sergeants' and officers' messes instead of the traditional social divisions.

Once their time at the OTU had finished the majority would be posted to their squadrons as complete crews and the remainder as individuals. For Brian's crew, there was a bit of both. Four of Brian's eventual crew met and crewed up at Lossiemouth, a significantly larger OTU than 12 OTU. Ken Dodwell, Jack Reynolds, Sam Lowry and John Burbidge and were all posted to 115 Squadron around 8 December 1941. John was the eldest at 30, Ken and Sam were both 21 and Jack was 20. It was at Marham where they first met Brian and started to get to know him. More importantly, Brian needed to get to know his crew, their characters, their backgrounds and their skills. So what were they like?

Ken Dodwell was born in July 1920 in Newham, brought up in Northwick Park in north London and educated at John Lyon School for Boys in nearby Harrow. The school was established by the governors of Harrow School in 1876 for local boys and in the 1930s was another grant-aided school, much the same as Hemel Hempstead Grammar School. Ken joined the RAF in June 1940 and wanted to be a fighter pilot as many did, but his eyesight let him down having damaged his eyes while boxing as a young man at school – he was a great all-round sportsman. While he waited at home for a vacancy on a training course, he witnessed at first-hand the Battle of Britain and could see the glow of fires in London's East End docks some 10 miles away. After initial training in October 1940 he went to Canada in January 1941 in a Royal Navy-escorted convoy via Nova Scotia. He was sent to 31 Air Navigation School in Port Albert, Ontario, to learn the dual skills of navigation and bomb aiming. He returned in July and started his course at No. 20 OTU in September.

John Gilbert 'Jack' Reynolds was born in London but his parents later moved to Broadstairs in Kent. Jack was a trainee analytical chemist and 19 years old when he joined up, the day after Brian on 23 August. They may well have met as they were processed through the same reception wing at Blackpool at the same time and both were recommended for pilot training. While on his basic training course at Aberystwyth he had a month at the nearby isolation hospital at Tan-y-Bwlch but soon afterwards his flying training started at 17 EFTS at North Luffenham. However, his course was transferred and finished at 6 EFTS at Little Rissington in the Cotswolds, not an uncommon occurrence in the chaos of the early training system. Jack was a shy young man, a bit of a loner who Ken Dodwell described as an introvert. However, having sown his pilot's wings on his tunic Jack was then posted up to the Scottish coastal RAF station at Lossiemouth, where he met the Australian Samuel Keith Lowry.

Sam came from a farming family in the small rural settlement of Karramomus in the rich, fertile country of the Goulburn Valley, about 100 miles north of Melbourne, Victoria. Sam had initially joined the 59th Battalion of the Royal Australian Army but was discharged having volunteered to join the RAAF. He enlisted in Melbourne on 15 September 1940 and after basic training embarked from Sydney on the three-month journey by sea, arriving in Belfast at the end of August. After the normal few days at a reception centre, he was sent to Lossiemouth to join 20 OTU to finish his training as an air gunner. This robust young Australian occupied the rear turret, arguably the toughest seat in a bomber, and became a favourite with Brian's family.

John Burbidge, their tall, slim and moustached wireless operator, was the eldest at 30, having been born in 1911, and was also posted in from 20 OTU. He was raised in a large upper middle-class family from north Kent and educated at Beckenham County School for Boys (by the end of the war it was a grammar school), which he left aged 16 and worked in the London Borough of Bromley's education department. His father was a local government civil servant, from whom he received an overly rigid and formal upbringing. In September 1939 he escaped from the formalities of family and work life and went to the south of France on holiday with his girlfriend, who shared his love of classical music. From there they observed from a distance as Germany invaded Poland and war was declared. John's greatest friends from his rowing club sent him a telegram telling him to come home as they all intended to join the RAF. Although not accepted for aircrew training initially by June 1940, John and every member of his rowing eight had enlisted into the RAF. His trade training took him to No. 2 Signals School at Yatesbury and a month at bombing and gunnery school before heading north to Lossiemouth, where he met Sam, Ken and Jack.

Having arrived at Marham, those four knew very little about Brian and it was Ken Dodwell who gained some inside information about their 17-year-old pilot.

'Luckily, it turned out that Brian and I were a good combination. He with his flying skills and although no one was officially told of their flying category, someone from "the office" told me he had been given an "above average category". Not many had that, he was a natural.'

40

Brian and Ken soon became good friends, although Brian was still very cagey about his age. There was a moment when he felt he could confide in Ken, although not even his trusted navigator got the whole truth. Ken recalls:

> I recollect that my pilot, Brian Slade, had put a year on his age to get into the RAF and was therefore only seventeen years of age when accepted for pilot training. He said when he joined the service that he was in fact eighteen years of age, which at the time was the earliest age for entry. He'd been to grammar school and then straight into the RAF, a fairly typical occurrence at the time.
>
> I recall that the authorities tended not to ask too many questions if they thought you were the right type and keen to fly. He got the nickname 'Boy Slade'; he was a 'chirpy' boyish character and sometimes I had to constrain him. For instance flying low over the Norfolk countryside, 'beating up' farms and stampeding cattle. And me with my newly acquired navigational skills.

The handsome Ken soon had a very pretty girlfriend called Jean, who was part of the Women's Auxiliary Air Force detachment at Marwell. Perhaps it was Jean that tipped Ken off about Brian's flying category. Ken and Jean were married after the war and I was very fortunate to meet her when she was 97. When I met her, their son John recalled a conversation with his father about Brian when the crew were about to take off on a training flight and one of the WAAF-driven airfield tractors passed them on their dispersal. Brian flagged her down, she let him jump into the seat and, with her help, drove up and down the edge of the grass runway. At the end of Brian's joyride he leapt off beaming with delight. His crew were puzzled as to why he should be so excited. Little did they know that not only had he not driven a tractor, he had never driven a car as he was too young to have a licence. He then climbed into their Wellington and took off with his baffled but none the wiser crew. Not even Ken knew the whole truth about his age as Brian wisely considered that his crew would not be happy to know that their pilot was a 17-year-old who couldn't drive a car.

Derek Collier, Brian's school friend, recalled: 'There is a story, not confirmed, that on one occasion he flew a Wellington Bomber in a tight, low circuit around the pointed spire of St Mary's Church in Hemel Hempstead to say hello to his parents and sister who lived there.' Having spoken to Jean, she confirmed this little stunt and recalled that Ken was none too happy. Brian and Ken had one more thing in common in that they shared the same birthday, their age though was very different; the 21-year-old navigator being four years older than his 17-year-old pilot.

It took a while to secure a permanent front gunner and meanwhile they flew with the young New Zealander Sergeant Hugh Dalton and Sergeant Brown, who both went on two operations with them before they found their permanent man for the front turret: Ken Swann, also 21, who you will hear more about later.

Hugh Dalton had quite a journey before he could join in the war. He was born near Opunake in the fertile, dairy farming region of Taranaki and, having left school at 15, worked on a number of farms, including his fathers, before he joined up in September 1940. Having completed his basic training at the ITW at Levin, he decided that Bomber Command was for him. His training could go no further in New Zealand and so in September 1940 he embarked on the troopship *Aorangi*, crossed the Pacific to Vancouver and then to wireless school at Calgary. From there he completed his training at the Bomber and Gunnery School at Manitoba before crossing the Atlantic as part of one of the many convoys arriving in the UK in September 1941. He arrived at Marham in December after nearly sixteen months of training and almost four months of that at sea. He was one of the many thousands who came from the Commonwealth to fight for the Allies.

As Ken Dodwell described, he and Brian got on well and became great friends, sharing a room for several months at Marham. Ken saw more than the above average pilot and soon recognised that the cheery, boyish persona masked a technical ability, a pilot who knew how to use and get the best out of his aircraft. Although a crew relied on each other to do their job, ultimately the survivability of the aircraft was to a large degree dependent on the ability of the pilot. It's possible that Ken Dodwell and the older John Burbidge recognised other qualities in this 17-year-old but I suspect they just liked this cheerful grammar school boy who, as long as they could keep him under control, was damn good at flying a Wellington. If they saw any leadership qualities in Brian it was what he did by example. With good humour, he went to work, did it well and that was keeping them all alive. In Ken, Brian saw a technically good navigator and a mature character who, along with John, would be steady when times got tough. And in time, he would need them to be. Over the next few weeks and many training sorties their trust in each other grew.

No. 115 Squadron was fortunate at the time Brian joined them. They were one of the first squadrons to receive the Wellington Mk III, now powered by the Bristol Hercules engine, which generated 1,375hp – a considerable improvement on its predecessors. Ken Dodwell recalls:

> This development was met with relief from aircrew … we were delighted at the prospect of being able to carry a 4,000 lb bomb load and full tanks of fuel (and at the same time being able to take off clear of the hedge at the end of the runway with ease!)

The first Mk IIIs arrived at the end of November but it took some months to completely replace the Mk Ics and until then both types were used on operations. By March 1942 the squadron had almost completely converted.

Can you imagine what it was like to have a brand new aircraft? It was an aircraft they were familiar with having trained on the Mk Ic, but most of those were well used and although well maintained were getting tired. Then they got the new Mk III – not just a new design but brand new, straight from the factory new, packed with all the newest technology. With only a few hours on the aircraft logbook, it would be clean and smell and feel new. New turrets that the air gunners loved to get their hands on. Sam Lowry in the rear turret now had four machine guns rather than two and clean unscratched Perspex. There were new radios for the wireless operator, John Burbidge, and for Brian those new Hercules engines providing so much more power. I suspect they could not wait to take their smart new bird into the air.

These new aircraft were often delivered single-handedly from the factories by pilots of the Air Transport Auxiliary, many of whom were women. The ATA was created in 1939, initially under the control of British Airways but soon administered by the RAF, and it became responsible for the delivery and ferrying of new and repaired aircraft throughout the network of factories and RAF stations. Based at White Waltham Airfield, pools of pilots from diverse backgrounds were spread across the country. They were often those who did not qualify to be operational pilots by dint of physical disability, poor sight and age, or because they were women. They volunteered from many different countries, including the United States. They were not taught to fly on instruments, so flew in daylight, map and compass on their laps and always single-handed even when delivering bombers. They provided a remarkable service and freed up many other pilots to fly with the squadrons.

A further critically important improvement was the introduction of the new navigation aid, named Gee. No. 115 Squadron pioneered the testing of Gee, which started in early 1941, and further tests both in training and occasional operations were carried out by the squadron throughout the summer. As you will read later, good navigation was fundamental to finding the target and it was hoped that by improving navigation, improved bombing accuracy would follow.

Gee was a radio system based on signals from two ground stations. Two grid lines were displayed on a cathode ray tube on the navigator's desk and by calculation he could measure the time delay between the two stations and determine the aircraft's position. It was easy to use and more accurate than anything else available but it needed 'line of sight' to the transmitter stations and therefore its range, depending on altitude, was limited to about 400 miles. By early 1942 further large-scale testing was carried out and more and more squadrons were equipped, with the first large-scale operation in March 1942 on an operation to Essen. By the end of the year it was widely used across Bomber Command and where bomb aimers were dual role with navigators, as in Wellingtons, they would find themselves increasingly controlling bomb release while peering at a screen rather than through the Perspex at the front of the aircraft. The Luftwaffe soon learned to jam it and the battle of improvements and countermeasures continued over the next two years. As 115 Squadron had early experience of Gee, they were increasingly used as target markers, an early experiment of the Pathfinder techniques that became established later in 1942.

On 16 December, twenty-five aircraft bombed Ostend, nine from 115 Squadron with their two flight commanders, squadron leaders Hogg and Grant, leading the way, with Brian and his new crew in Wellington X9831 on their first operation together. Although one aircraft was lost overall, all the squadron's aircraft returned.

Brian and the crew were due a week's leave but knew they would be back before Christmas. Before he left Norfolk though, he found time to send out some RAF Marham Christmas cards. At 17 years and 4 months old, he was now an operational bomber captain with his own crew. If he went home, which I suspect he did, I can imagine he had a great deal to talk about to his friends and family. He had flown with his squadron and flight commanders, he had his first crew and he had flown his first operation as skipper. But what was it like to fly an operation … what was their job?

44

Chapter 6

Working Tonight?

W hile all operations were different, in late 1941 the routine of an operational day for Brian and his crew on 115 Squadron was reasonably predictable.

When they weren't 'stood down', crews would know by mid-morning if an 'op' was happening or, as many of them described it, if they would be 'working' that night. Rough details, a 'Battle Order', would be posted on squadron and mess noticeboards listing the participating aircraft and crews. On rare occasions they could be woken up as late as midday having worked the night before to be told they were flying again.

As far as the crews were concerned the targets were selected 'higher up'. Originating in Bomber Command Headquarters in High Wycombe, a complete operations order would go to the participating group HQs. A briefer version went to the stations and squadrons with enough information to enable the squadron staff and ground crew to prepare the appropriate amount of fuel, bomb load or mines and any special equipment. Later the target locations, routes and timings would come down from group and squadron staff would prepare the detailed orders ready for the briefings.

On an operations day, aircraft that were designated to fly that night would be prepared and loaded, and all equipment, checked and checked again by the ground crews while on their dispersal areas around the airfield.

Crews would often take their allocated aircraft out for an 'air test' or 'night flying test', NFT, as it became known prior to a night's work. Brian's logbook shows they would often test an unfamiliar aircraft, or one fitted with new equipment, or if it had been repaired and the ground crew wanted it checked, but they wouldn't test if allocated the same aircraft as their last operation. Crews became attached to certain aircraft; partly the simple issue of trust that everything worked and partly superstition, admitted or not. It was in the squadron's interests to allocate the same aircraft regularly to the same crews. Superstitions were rife, so one fewer thing for a crew to worry about. These air tests took typically between twenty minutes and an hour.

On return the ground crew or 'erks', as they were affectionately known, would do their checks, correct any faults and top up the wing tanks with fuel. Then the armourers would start to 'bomb up'. First the boxes of .303 ammunition for the machine guns was loaded. Then, long low trains of bomb trailers often towed by WAAF-driven tractors would snake from the bomb stores to the aircraft, frequently 'ridden' by the armourers cadging a lift to the aircraft's distant dispersal. A crew of three or four armourers would be allocated to two, three or maybe four aircraft and briefed on the detailed bomb load and fuze settings required. Later, cameras and appropriate 'flash bombs' were included.

The trailers would be manoeuvred by hand under the aircraft's open bomb bays and their hand-cranked winches would raise each bomb onto the bomb beams. Armourers were highly trained and took bomb handling seriously – mistakes were punished harshly. The precise details and layout of the bomb load would be passed to the bomb aimer for him to set up his bombing panel. An experienced crew, on hearing the details of the bomb and fuel load, would start to make calculated guesses as to that night's destination. The uneasiness would start.

A series of briefings started after lunch, normally in a large hall (which often doubled up as the station cinema). In the first with the squadron commander and his flight commanders (occasionally the station commander, if both Marham squadrons were involved), the squadron intelligence officer, a signals officer and a meteorologist would brief all the pilots and navigators. These two bore the leadership responsibilities, although the pilot, regardless of rank, was the skipper, and the navigator was quite often considered by the crew as the second in command. At this meeting the night's objective would be revealed for the first time. Tapes pinned to a large map marked the routes – where would the tapes end? This was all done behind locked doors for security. Both navigator and pilot would take copious notes, including take-off times, taxiing order, target locations, routes, altitudes, times over target, weather details both at home, over the route and target, bomb loads, photography details etc. At this point, and sometimes later at a separate briefing, the rest of the aircrew would join them to hear a shorter version, which included the radio operator getting his frequencies, Gee settings and Jbeam settings. Briefings ended with the bombing leader synchronising watches. As well as receiving routine information, it was often the moment, particularly for operations employing large numbers of aircraft or involving important targets, that a morale-lifting, inspirational oration would be delivered by their commanding officer, or he may read a message from group or Bomber Command. Crews would be reminded of the Blitz and the opportunity they now had to 'get their own back', they would be told of the successful results of previous targets and the effect that was having on the German war machine and civilian morale. They would be made aware, once again, of the importance of tonight's target. To the experienced crews, who had heard it all before, they were thinking of what was to come.

After the briefing, crews would then relax, write letters and eat, if they could.

The navigator, though, would go to the map or plotting room to mark up his charts with assembly areas, route headings and legs, timings, speeds, turning points, targets, flak positions, likely night fighter concentrations, and mark anything else of relevance including, of course, the routes back. Ken Dodwell, Brian's trusted navigator, recalls:

> Many times the first briefing was at 1 pm, the second at 3 pm, then the navigator would go to the navigation plotting room to mark the route … Brian, the pilot would come into the plotting room and look over my shoulder to get the picture of the route and where I had marked the flak or defended areas. The pilot and navigator were always close …

At the appropriate time they would crowd into the locker room, collect their parachutes and Mae Wests and ensure all personal items were left behind. Although they might be suiting up on a warm summer's evening, they pulled on their thick sheepskin-lined Irvin jackets over trousers and boots in preparation for the sub-zero temperatures ahead. Sandwiches and flasks for all were collected. The build-up of tension led some to bin them, a few ate them immediately to avoid future distractions and others ate them on board later as if it was a picnic.

There must have been an intense atmosphere in that locker room. Having been briefed, the night's target and routes would be known. For those on repeat visits, the strength of the defences would be remembered. Some would say nothing, deep in their own thoughts and hiding their fear. The senior crew members would also be nervous, knowing the horrors ahead but better able to hide their emotions with smiles and jokes. A place of frightened faces, nervous laughs, reassurances and dark thoughts. In those moments their courage was the conquering of their fears. For all crew members it was the worst time, the new did not know what to expect and the experienced did. All they wanted was to get in the aircraft, let the training kick in and the discipline and routine of the pre-flight checks shift the worries and calm the nerves.

An additional passenger was often picked up at this time, although some saw them as extra crew members – a carrier pigeon. They were the responsibility of the wireless operator and on many occasions saved lives. As an aircraft ditched in the Channel it was often too low to transmit a location. Assuming the ditching went to plan, the pigeon was released and amazingly on many occasions it would get home, the message would be read and the crew rescued all within a few hours. How unreasonable to think that in the confusion and sheer terror of a ditching or crash landing that the navigator was expected to provide a location to the wireless operator, who would write that in pencil onto a piece of paper, insert it into the small carrier tube and release the bird. However, quite often that was exactly what they did.

Dressed and ready, the crew would normally be driven out to their dispersed aircraft by WAAF-driven lorries in the late afternoon or early evening – a time for that last cigarette. Smoking was not allowed near or inside an aircraft but both rules were routinely ignored. Superstitious crews carried their personal mascots, and went through the same routines that had succeeded last time; having a pee on the tailwheel was a favourite custom for good luck. It would be an angry and nervous crew that took off without a regular mascot or a lucky routine completed. Once final checks by the ground staff were finished, the aircraft was 'signed over' to the crew, who would then carry out a checklist of drills that would result in the engines being started. By now the nerves were starting to settle. The reassurance of routine and ritual. They were accustomed to their aircraft, it smelt familiar, they knew its every detail by feel, reflex actions from endless training, and for the more experienced crews they were now in control. It was time to go to work.

Marham, being all grass without defined runways, would have been set up for the night's operations. The wind direction would dictate that layout in order that aircraft could take off into the wind. At night the runway would be marked by 'goose neck' paraffin lamps and the airfield runway caravan or trailer set in the right position. For security reasons radios were not used on the ground as excessive radio traffic risked warning the ever alert German 'listening stations'; even the use of radios on NFTs was discouraged.

In the dark, and once the pre-taxiing checks were done, the pilot, according to his timings and taxiing order, would start to move round the perimeter in a long queue to the runway. When final checks were completed, the pilot waited for the Aldis lamp 'green' light from the runway controller who manned the caravan, and would then increase power to the two Bristol Hercules engines with the brakes on. The aircraft shook and the engines roared; the pilot released the brakes and slowly the trundle turned to a sprint, the tail lifted and then, as 120mph was reached, he encouraged the 14 tons of Wellington, crew, petrol and bombs into the air. Most propeller aircraft have clockwise-rotating propellers (pilot's view), which for a variety of reasons make an aircraft veer to port during take-off and this requires a heavy right foot on the rudder pedal to keeps things straight. As Brian would discover in the future, having four engines increased the need for a heavy right boot and an extra pair of hands.

Assuming a prevailing wind, the aircraft would take off towards the south-west, in summer and early autumn climbing into the setting sun and, as winter took hold, an increasingly distant glow beneath the horizon. In winter they flew into the black night sky. At that time, in late 1941 to early 1942, aircraft took off as much as five to ten minutes apart. For safety, take-off times were more spread at night than day and their expected time of arrival over the target could be spread over an hour or even two. As we will hear, that would change and soon aircraft would be taking off every thirty to sixty seconds.

Early in the war, in daylight, aircraft would form up and head to their assembly area. At night it was often more of a free for all as they headed east. They would become very familiar with that route, soon seeing the familiar landmarks of the Norfolk countryside passing by; the shapes of woods, railways and bodies of water, many of which would be recognisable at night, until the coast was seen when they reached about 2,000ft. This would be crossed at about 3,000ft and the features of Southwold and Lowestoft would soon fade as they headed for the Dutch coast. Once dark, aircraft were pretty much on their own and expected to find their own way to the target. They would often not see another aircraft from the start to the finish of an operation. In bad weather Brian would be flying on instruments and the accuracy of their route out was in the hands of his navigator, Ken Dodwell:

> The procedure was that we would take off for the target about one hour before sunset, then down to Southwold (3 Groups assembly area) in daylight, and then across the North Sea to the Dutch Coast, hoping that by then it had become dark. We would have been climbing since take off, and therefore may be at 10,000ft when we went over the Dutch coast. Our very young Australian Rear Gunner would tell me when we had cleared the Dutch coast.

As soon as the aircraft was airborne and the appropriate cruising speed achieved, typically around 170mph, every one of the crew attended to their roles. In talking to each other over the intercom, many crews now abandoned their ranks and called each other by their role or even Christian or nicknames.

Navigation in the early days of the war was a combination of 'dead reckoning' and map reading from obvious visible ground features. 'DR' was essentially applying a bearing to the pilot's compass and then flying at a set speed for a certain time – a method used by seafarers for centuries. The margins for error were huge, with unknown wind speeds at certain altitudes playing havoc with intended courses. If no ground features could be identified then a three-star fix by use of a sextant from the astrodome could be carried out but conditions had to be perfect, and even then accuracy was poor. Soon technological advances would help the navigators.

Once the course was set it was incumbent on all who peered through Perspex to look for trouble, principally the pilot and the gunners. It was not unknown for bomber formations to be attacked over the Channel by night fighters, and flak ships were an ever-present danger off the Dutch coast. It wasn't always enemy fire they received over the Channel. Heavily protected Royal Navy convoys used the waterway and although their presence would have come up at the briefing, convoys were nervous about aircraft and shot first, then asked questions later. Having safely crossed the Channel, they were flying over enemy-occupied countries from the coast to the target and back. There was no safe space, no respite from the concentration required to scan the sky ahead. Bad weather and low cloud on the approach to the target must have been on occasions a huge relief.

When an attack from a night fighter or fire from the ground could arrive at any time, that high level of concentration was required for many hours. The longest missions for Brian came later when in Lancasters, when he flew to northern Italy and Czechoslovakia, trips that often lasted just over eight hours.

Missions of four, five and six hours were the norm in 115 Squadron. Later in the war crews occasionally resorted to drugs – either the bitter-tasting caffeine tablets or amphetamines such as Benzedrine, known as 'wakey-wakey pills', to help their concentration. Typically they took them on take-off or just as they started their bomb run to keep them awake on the way home. Although not widely available or regulated in private life, and banned within the services in 1939, their use was approved in November 1942 and they were issued by station medical officers. Caffeine tended to have a diuretic affect, which wasn't that convenient, and crews often resorted to bottles. The downside of these 'uppers' was that, if having taken one and the operation was cancelled, you couldn't sleep. The use of drugs to enhance concentration or improve 'wakefulness' was well known and the German drug Pervitin, now known as methamphetamine, was openly marketed before the war and used widely by the Wehrmacht, most notoriously by tank crews, among whom it was known as *Panzerschokolade*, and the Luftwaffe, *Stuka-tabletten*.

At their briefings, crews were reminded by the intelligence staff of where they could expect the most aggressive defences but the experienced crews knew where and when they were most likely to fly into trouble and when to be on the highest alert. That started as soon as they crossed the coast.

After the Blitz, senior Luftwaffe commanders had to prepare for retaliatory bombing of Germany and with all the Channel countries occupied they were now able to create comprehensive defences. This line of defences was created by the Luftwaffe officer Colonel Joseph Kammhuber and was known as the Kammhuber Line. Initially a chain of Freya radar would provide early warning of the bombers as they approached the coast with night fighters responding randomly, but Kammhuber developed a more regulated system with the aid of increasingly sophisticated radar.

By mid-1940 a network of night fighter defences was created, with Freya radar providing early warning and then a grid of overlapping zones known as the *Himmelbett* (four-poster bed) boxes. Each box was roughly a 20 × 15-mile rectangle and up to three boxes deep. They stretched from the Danish coast in the north to south of the French border. Each box was covered by initially one, but later two, narrow-beam Würzburg radar and searchlight systems, which enabled a ground-based operator not only to detect a target with one radar but also to guide a night fighter onto the approaching bomber with the second.

Searchlight technology was initially basic, with standalone lights providing little more than early warning and occasionally being a dazzling distraction for pilots, but by 1941 they were linked to the radar of the *Himmelbett* boxes, which as the bombing campaign against the cities intensified proliferated in the major targets such as the Ruhr Valley, Cologne, Hamburg and Berlin. Searchlight units were coordinated from a central radar and directed 'the master searchlight', which was capable of tracking a target aircraft and, once found, the unit's other searchlights up to a mile away would follow suit and the aircraft was 'coned' by multiple beams. Being caught by that master beam was terrifying. It was a bluish blinding light and if no evasive action was taken it was only a matter of seconds before the secondary lights locked and a few more before the anti-aircraft guns had them ranged and were firing.

As these anti-aircraft tactics became more effective, Bomber Command developed strategies and countermeasures, but these took time. There were tactics, though, for the pilot to employ. One was the 'corkscrew'. In the air, crews developed and adapted the basic manoeuvre circulated by Bomber Command, as a response to an attack by a radar-directed night fighter. This involved some violent manoeuvres in order to throw off the night fighter and create a more difficult target, typically a series of steep dives and climbs in random directions. This was often prompted by the tail gunner having seen the approaching night fighter and telling the pilot its direction of attack. The pilot would immediately open the throttles and dive in the direction of the approaching threat. The bomber would accelerate and after a few seconds would climb, then roll and repeat if necessary.

This manoeuvre put the aircraft under enormous strain as speeds in excess of safe tolerances were exceeded. From a cruising speed of just under 200mph, the first dive could reach 300mph, faster for the four-engine bombers. By climbing and rolling the aircraft, air speed dropped dramatically and hopefully the faster night fighter overshot his target. Pilots were gambling with relative risks. But there are many reports from German night fighter pilots that a corkscrewing aircraft restricted their firing opportunities and often forced them to swing away early to find an easier target. Throughout the corkscrewing manoeuvres, the pilot would attempt to give a running commentary to help his crew brace themselves for each twist and turn. There was also the danger of collisions as aircraft, particularly as they started their bomb run, were in close proximity both laterally and in altitude. This type of manoeuvre was also adopted when coned in searchlights, which became harder to evade once they were radar controlled.

Good pilots who had confidence in their aircraft, given the consequences of not evading that searchlight or night fighter, would throw every twist and turn they could into the evasion.

Bomber crews were legitimate combatants and legitimate targets of the ack-ack crews. Sparring was conducted impersonally at great distance. The night fighter was different. It was closer, only occasionally seen but more intimate, a dogfight, frantic and frightening. Survival was dependent on that delicious blend of individual skills and teamwork. Sorting out the chaos inside the aircraft afterwards was a small price to pay for survival.

Although the front and rear turrets were there for defence, gunners had to be careful in their use of their machine guns. If used too early the tracer could give their position away. The night fighters controlled by ground-based radar operators were only directed into the general area of the bomber. A bomber flying with no lights wasn't always easy to see and a stream of tracer by an over-eager tail gunner made their work easier. Many crews preferred to work on the basis of spotting the night fighter early, taking evasive action before it was in range and hoping it went off and looked for an easier target. Once again it highlighted the importance of a crew full of confidence and trust in each other's ability.

Taking evasive action was often practised with locally stationed fighters. This trained crews to evade an attacking fighter and tested not only the pilot's skill but crew co-ordination. The Spitfires would be practising their attack drills and the sessions became very competitive. Brian and his crew would be thankful for this training in a few months' time.

There was another controversial ruse employed by pilots principally to avoid searchlights and flak but to a lesser extent night fighters and that was 'weaving'. This was to avoid flying at a constant height and heading, and there were pros and cons. By swinging to port and starboard the pilot hoped to present a harder target, an obvious advantage. Searchlights found it harder to track their target and night fighters when confronted by a stable or a weaving target opted for the easier. It also gave the rear turret gunner a chance to see below and to the rear, a blind spot when flying straight and level.

The principle argument against came mainly from senior officers, who felt that it reduced bombing accuracy as a weaving aircraft, they suggested, could not be steady enough to bomb accurately. They also argued that it wasn't effective as enemy radar-directed searchlights would still find their target and 'lock on'. This became a subject of heated debate among pilots. As you will read, bombers were soon to be more concentrated and weaving in a crowded sky invited collisions. This constant battle of improvements and countermeasures on both sides continued throughout the campaign.

In the early days of 1940, when smaller numbers of aircraft were involved, the bomb run was often ill disciplined. Each aircraft would be expected to find their own way and, with no formal marking, to find their targets visually. The later bombers tended to find smoke-obscured targets and therefore bombed at the fires and flashes already created. By the time Brian was on ops at the end of 1941 procedures and technology were improving but accuracy remained a goal that was rarely achieved.

Aircraft take-off times were spread and consequently so were their arrival times over the target. It was not untypical for 200 aircraft to take well over an hour to complete their bomb runs. There were attempts to concentrate their arrival by travelling in closer proximity but this would not become the norm for some time. When it did pilots and crews needed to be very aware of all that was going on in an increasingly crowded airspace but they gained the protection those numbers provided. 'Staying in the stream' would become essential but nerve-racking. Many crews were not used to flying in such proximity and squadrons started 'formation flying' training flights. A bomber barrelling along at over 200mph displaces a lot of air and many crews reported feeling that turbulence from other unseen aircraft when they flew too close. To feel the aircraft shake and rattle from the buffeting of another aircraft passing close, and even to hear it but not see it, must have been arresting.

On a Wellington the navigator would have given the pilot the various headings and times to the target area but on the final run-in he would move forward, setting the bomb run course on the pilot's compass as he passed and take on the role of bomb aimer. For their first few months they would have used the manually operated Course Setting Bombsight Mk VIIA and then early in 1942 the Mk XIV was introduced, which was seen by crews as a huge improvement on its predecessor. The Americans had the much-vaunted Norden bombsight but would not sell it to the RAF at the outbreak of war due to security worries, although a spy within the Norden organisation had already passed the details to the Nazis. It was also poorly suited to night operations. The British Mk XIV proved to be just as accurate (or inaccurate) as the Norden, particularly under 20,000ft, although neither performed as well under operational conditions as in testing. Much of the key information could be 'pre-programmed' and its main advantage as far as the crews were concerned was that the pilot only had to keep straight and level for ten seconds before the bomb release, enabling him to carry out whatever evasive manoeuvres were required on the approach. It was the pilot who would open the bomb bay doors at the start of the bomb run and the navigator, acting as bomb aimer while peering through the sight and trying not to be distracted by flak, searchlights and other bombers, would give last-minute instructions to the pilot, and at the critical moment, press the bomb release. The crew would immediately feel the lift of the aircraft as it became 4,000lb lighter. If a camera was fitted, the flash bombs would be released at the same time and the camera timer switch started. Just before the flash bombs exploded the camera, turned on and a sequence of photos taken while the target area was illuminated. For the aircrew it was a nervous time as the camera-fitted aircraft had to keep level and steady for several more seconds before the camera was triggered. The bomb aimer would report to the pilot when the photos were taken, which depending on the altitude, could be up to thirty more seconds before they could breathe again and the pilot could turn for home.

On occasions, if the aiming point could not be identified the bomb aimer would declare a dummy run and instruct the pilot to circle and do the run again, never popular with the crew. This had the continuing risks of colliding into another aircraft or being underneath one when they released their load. On occasions the pilot would override that decision and order the bomb aimer to 'press the tit'. One of Brian's fellow pilots was struck by a bomb dropped by an aircraft above and flew home with a 4lb incendiary stuck in one of his wing petrol tanks. It was still live when the very nervous ground crew removed it.

That time over the target was intense; the navigator and pilot working hard to keep a steady track and get the bombs away while searchlights scanned and flak exploded around them. Crews often reported the concussion and smell from exploding flak and the rattle as fragments of shrapnel struck the aircraft. The air gunners would be on high alert looking for night fighters but also watching and avoiding the other bombers above, below and alongside them. They would also have a view of the target, the explosions, the percussive shock waves, the flash bombs, the fires …

This was exhausting, frightening and adrenaline-pumping work.

Once the bombs were gone (and someone had to check in the bomb bay with a torch that there were no 'hang-ups') not only were they lighter but the drag from the open bomb bay doors was gone so the aircraft handled better and was capable of a higher speed.

As soon as he could the pilot would turn for home, often with a drop in altitude not only to pick up some speed but also to avoid predicted flak fixed at a certain altitude or night fighters that may have been tracking him while on that bomb run. The navigator would be on his feet and back to his desk to help the pilot with the run home. They weren't out of danger but it was a relief to get rid of 4,000lb of explosives and that now counted as an operation, one more ticked off.

The return journey, normally on a different course, could be no less dangerous. The pilot and front gunner looking west were the first to see the Dutch coast while the tail gunner watched the lights and fires of that night's work fade into the east. Their homeward route tried to avoid heavy concentrations of air defences, and although the navigator and pilot had a freer hand on route and altitude, fuel was an issue. It was quite common for night fighters to hunt along the route of the returning bombers and they would even cross the Channel to find targets that may need to circle before landing. Although the Wellington had a limited range, crews may have been in the air for four, five or six hours and tiredness and loss of concentration became a serious issue. Nearly home and in sight of the familiar shape of the Norfolk coast, all those land and watermarks were reassuring as they looked out for the Norwich barrage balloons.

As they approached Marham they became within range for direct voice communications and could receive landing instructions, which initially meant joining a circling queue until they were individually called in to land. Landing priority was given to aircraft low on fuel or with battle damage or injured crewmen. If there was poor weather, fog for instance, then aircraft could be sent to clearer airfields and then flown home the next morning. Landing was a dangerous time; pilots were tired, aircraft could be damaged, diverted aircraft from other stations could be circling that would not know the local tricks. Radios might have been damaged and aircraft low on fuel might not have waited for their final landing instructions. The weather in East Anglia was often foggy and aircraft with hang-ups were landing with fused bombs on board. The airfield's fire engines and ambulances were out, as were the squadron staff and ground crews looking anxiously for the safe arrival of their crews. As soon as the aircraft was back on dispersal, it would be handed back to the 'erks' with any damage or problems reported, sometimes casualties to be treated, unused bombs to be removed.

Landing safely must have been a moment of intense release. Much chatter in the transport back for debriefing; reliving the night's scares, the sight of a blazing target or the loss of other aircraft. Their faces still creased from their face mask and goggles, red and tired eyes, sweat-flattened hair, weak but relieved smiles. Some exhausted, some still high, all thankful to be on the ground.

Debriefings were intended to be serious affairs, normally conducted by the station or squadron intelligence officers, most of whom were well aware that the crews were near exhaustion. What time were they over the target, could they see the target, what time did they bomb, did they get photographs, extent of the fires etc? Photographs would also tell part of the story. Most debriefings took half an hour or so but occasionally squadrons had reason to debrief rather more aggressively.

It was not uncommon for crews to get rid of their bomb load early or deliberately away from the target to avoid trouble and get home as quickly as possible. If crews were suspected of this each crew member could be debriefed separately while physically and mentally exhausted without contact with other crews and in an atmosphere of interrogation. Evidence from ground crew about returned fuel levels could indicate if they did reach the target.

Debriefings over, it was back to the mess for a traditional eggs and bacon breakfast. Post-op banter was enjoyed; they had survived but it was more than just another one done. While many of these young men did not want to fly and would have done almost anything to avoid it, most joined their crew mates and flew, albeit with fear and trepidation. Such was the strength of their collective camaraderie that the thought they might let their crew down went a long way to override their fear of not returning. Many though, revelled in the thrill of operations and then the buzz of having survived, and the collective post-op celebrations.

Always grateful to be back, the enjoyment of breakfast could be muted by empty seats. Squadron and flight commanders would have letters to write and mess staff would have personal belongings to box up. For some there was no reason to celebrate and breakfast was an act of refuelling prior to carting their exhausted bodies off to bed. Another one done, more friends lost. Adjusting to these regular losses had to be quick and one aircrew remembered that as soon as they woke up the next morning someone would visit the missing crew's accommodation and pinch what was left of their coal supply.

From the moment a crew member had seen his name on the noticeboard the roller coaster of angst began. The nerves felt before the briefing would be ramped up when the target was known. A calming lunch, then the detailed preparation, crew room dressing, banter, leg pulling, heightening tension. The anxious wait for transport out to dispersal, trembling fingers light the last cigarette, the calming familiarity of final pre-flight checks and a roaring rattling take-off. A steady smooth climb and increasing apprehension as the coast was crossed, the stomach-churning sight of distant searchlights and the terror of being caught in their dazzling white light. The sight of other aircraft going down, the smell and concussion of heavy, accurate flak, the dread of night fighters, the seemingly endless, heart-pounding anxiety of the bomb run, the relief of bombs gone and turning for home with screaming engines, fighting exhaustion and flagging concentration and then the sight of home, landing … utter relief. Find dispersal and kill engines. Now quiet, climbing out bashed and ragged. The adrenaline-surging ups and the emotionally draining downs of a night's work. Day off, repeat: relentlessly tiring. As you will read, not everyone could deal with it.

Chapter 7

115 Squadron – Part 2

After his leave Brian was back at Marham and on 23 December he had a training sortie with Pilot Officer Ron Runagall as first pilot, another on Christmas Eve and Boxing Day but nothing on Christmas Day. Then three more as first pilot before on 28 December he took X9831 again with thirteen others from 115 Squadron to bomb Wilhelmshaven in a force of eighty-six other aircraft. It was a very successful operation with significant damage done to this Baltic Sea port and his longest to date; six hours and five minutes. One aircraft was lost but again all the squadron's crews returned. It was not uncommon to have two primary targets and on this occasion one of the squadron's Wellingtons bombed Emden and reported later having seen a bomber go down in flames.

For 115 Squadron there had been seven operations in November and four in December. Compared to the coming months this was relatively few but there had been casualties. Brian arrived on 6 November and on the 11th the first of two training accidents in the squadron occurred. Sergeant Gordon Dutton took a routine flight to carry out a fuel consumption test and the station doctor, 31-year-old Flight Lieutenant Harold Mellows, went along for the ride. It is unclear whether an engine problem had prompted the test but the subsequent board of enquiry reported a starboard engine failure as a result of mishandling by the pilot. However, another source suggested that there was a fault with an exhaust and that carbon monoxide leaked into the cabin. Either way, the aircraft crashed near Swaffham, Norfolk, killing all six on board. Mellows is buried in Marham Cemetery.

Another tragic accident took place about two weeks later. Sergeant Bruce was on a routine low-flying training exercise with his regular crew. He took with him three members of his ground crew team for a joy ride, or 'air experience' as it was officially known. Why is not clear but at some point they struck a line of railway trucks 2 miles north-west of March on the Spalding line, crashed and all nine occupants were killed. Taking 'erks' on training flights was seen by some as an important part of their role, not just to see their aircraft in the air but to understand that their competence on the ground was critical to the crew's peace of mind. There needed to be a bond between crews and ground staff and squadrons were very aware of it. They weren't the first and wouldn't be the last ground crew to be killed on training flights.

There were also operational losses. On 15 November during an operation to Kiel, Sergeant Alan Homes's aircraft came down, killing the crew of six. These were the first fatal incidents that Brian and his crew had to face within the close-knit community of an operational squadron. They will have known all these men, not well perhaps but known them nonetheless. They would have to get used to such losses. On the same raid Pilot Officer Stock was forced to ditch in the sea off Whitby after fuel issues but fortunately all the crew were picked up by a Norwegian naval vessel.

For the squadron, January was quiet with only five operations comprising ten sorties and none for Brian. There was, however, a lot of flying. He made twenty-one training flights in January, practising formation flying, air gunnery, bombing and navigation. Sadly, there was another training flight accident. On 15 January Sergeant Donald Faith was piloting Z1563 on a cross-country night flying exercise and experienced severe icing, causing a totally 'glazed' windscreen. The resulting crash killed the six crew.

Brian's next operational flight was on 12 February. He and his crew, in Wellington X9831, took part in a very different operation with 241 other aircraft and it appears that their bombs were some of the few that got close.

The German battlecruisers *Gneisenau* and *Scharnhorst* were commissioned in 1938 and 1939 respectively. In a navy that preferred battlecruisers to aircraft carriers they were the pride of the *Kriegsmarine* and they were unleashed into the North Atlantic in early 1941 to cause havoc among Allied shipping, which they did.

Both went into the Brittany port of Brest in March 1941 and as *Bismarck* had been sunk on May 1941 and *Prinz Eugen*, which had accompanied *Bismark*, was also under repair in Brest, it meant that the three remaining German capital ships were effectively out of action. While under repair in Brest they attracted constant attention by Bomber Command, whose airmen referred to *Scharnhorst* and *Gneisenau* as 'Salmon and Gluckstein' after the London-based tobacco retailers. Between July and December 1941, more than a thousand bombing sorties were directed at the ships, which were damaged regularly but never terminally. German High Command concluded

59

that all three must make a dash up the Channel to the safety of their home ports and for the opportunity to complete repairs. Just before midnight on 11 February, with the desired bad weather forecast, the meticulously planned Operation Cerberus started and the three battlecruisers with their extensive escort of six destroyers slipped out of Brest to be joined by twenty-six fast E-boats and extensive Luftwaffe air cover of 250 fighters.

Under the cover of low cloud, all three ships and their escorts arrived in the Channel by 0130 hours and, despite a navy submarine, RAF patrols and a resistance agent in Brest all tasked to monitor their movement, the German fleet was undetected until mid-morning, when they were spotted by patrolling Spitfires from Biggin Hill. Earlier intelligence suggested this breakout was likely and from 3 February a significant force remained on standby with a detailed plan, Operation Fuller, in place to attack the convoy when detected.

'The Channel Dash', as it became known, was a tragic fiasco – a combination of bad planning, bad weather, little inter-service co-ordination and bad luck, and it was deeply embarrassing for all in command, but particularly the Royal Navy. As soon as the convoy was spotted on the morning of 12 February, Operation Fuller was activated and the convoy attacked as it approached the narrowest part of the Channel; first by the coastal battery at South Foreland, then Royal Navy motor torpedo boats, followed by RAF Beaufort torpedo bombers. All failed to bother the three giant capital ships. Soon after, six Fairey Swordfish biplanes from 825 Squadron, Fleet Air Arm, based at RAF Manston in Kent (those used on the attack and sinking of *Bismarck* in November 1940) attacked and as their Spitfire escorts distracted the Luftwaffe fighter escort, all pressed on, flying at 50ft as they approached their targets. All were shot down. Lastly five destroyers attacked, launching torpedoes, which all missed. Throughout that afternoon, in deteriorating weather, 242 Bomber Command aircraft attacked the convoy in three waves.

The three aircraft from 115 Squadron that joined the attack were specifically tasked with bombing the convoy. Two of them, flown by Sergeant Reynolds and Pilot Officer Ron Runagall, took off from Lakenheath and joined the second wave, and Brian took off from snow-dusted Marham at 1630 hours as part of the last wave of thirty-five aircraft. Of the 242 aircraft, only 39 found the convoy and released their bombs, 15 aircraft were lost and 20 damaged, mainly by the intense flak. Brian's logbook entry was typically understated:

FEB 12 Wellington X9831 Pilot-self 2nd Pilot-crew
Operations as Ordered.

Attacked Convoy – Bombed Flak Ship
Engine trouble 900' over Battleship!

It was reported that none of the aircraft that dropped bombs were close but 'one bomber dropped bombs approximately 98 yards off *Scharnhorst*'s port side'. Ken Dodwell remembered the mission well:

> ... on 12 February we had operated a daylight mission against the German Battle Cruisers Scharnhorst, Gneisenau and Prinz Eugen. This was done on DR navigation (Dead Reckoning).
> There were no other aids. We were the only crew in the squadron to find them as the flying conditions were terrible. We broke cloud cover over the flak ship at 500ft. The crew could hear us descending and began firing at us. As soon as we broke cloud one of our engines was hit, there was little opportunity to 'line up' the bombing run. Our bombs missed by 25 yards.

The three battlecruisers made it safely into German ports, even though both *Gneisenau* and *Scharnhorst* hit recently planted British mines and were damaged. Although seen as a tactical victory for the German convoy, the three great capital ships had little effect on the remainder of the war. *Scharnhorst* was sunk in the Battle of the North Cape on Boxing Day 1943 on its first sortie out of the Baltic. *Gneisenau* was badly damaged by Bomber Command in Kiel and *Prinz Eugen* was torpedoed off the Norwegian coast, both being confined to the Baltic and rendered ineffective for the rest of the war.

Unlike Ken in his memoir, Brian clearly didn't seem to think that losing one of his Wellington's two engines to fire from the convoy warranted a comment in his log other than '*engine trouble*' but it was also noted in the squadron's Operational Record Book that they had lost an engine to flak and managed to get home on one. That operation was their last until 25 March. This six-week hiatus in operations was not for lack of targets. It signalled the gestation of a significant change in strategy and the arrival of a new head of Bomber Command instructed to implement it.

61

Chapter 8

Bomber Command – A New Direction

In early 1941 cameras had been added to a small number of bombers in order to provide photographic evidence of the effectiveness of the campaign on mainland Europe. While there had been pressure on the Air Ministry to bomb larger towns and city targets, from no less a voice than Churchill, Bomber Command continued to prioritise industrial targets, particularly the oil industry, and then later those related to U-boat and aircraft construction. Results were poor and even when larger urban targets were chosen, bombing was scattered and the damage limited.

The results of this photography were retained for post-operation target analysis, and disclosed to only a few in Bomber Command and the Air Ministry. Doubts about the effectiveness of the campaign led to a formal survey of this evidence commissioned by the government's chief scientific advisor, Frederick Lindemann, and carried out by his assistant, David Bensusan-Butt. The resulting Butt Report was presented in August 1941 to the War Cabinet and therefore Churchill himself.

The results were shocking: the RAF's bombing was inaccurate and ineffective. Bensusan-Butt's analysis looked at 100 separate raids on 28 targets over 48 nights in June and July. Crew debriefs led them to understand that of those raids, only two in three aircraft ever reached the target. Butt's analysis of the photographs taken by those that did bomb revealed that only one in three aircraft bombed within 5 miles of the target. Over the Ruhr it was one in ten. Furthermore, he looked at the effects of moon and cloud, which showed that in good moonlight (full moon) that increased to one in four but in no moonlight (new moon) it fell to one in sixteen. When you added cloud to a new moon he recorded no hits on target at all. He ends the summary of his report with:

Thus, for example, of the total sorties only one in five get within five miles of the target, i.e. within the 75 square miles surrounding the target.

The loss of life and aircraft for such a poor return in damage done caused the RAF's strategic bombing campaign to be challenged not only by the Air Ministry but in the War Cabinet. Bomber Command's future was now in doubt. Senior staff in Bomber Command refuted the report and defended their early tactics but their heads had been in the sand. If they had done this analysis themselves, and they had the evidence to do so, they ignored the results. The early operations to target the German navy and shipyards had in the main been failures. Daytime raids were costly as the early bombers had little defence against Luftwaffe fighters and the night-time raids on specific industrial targets, particularly the German synthetic oil production sites, caused very little damage. Precious crews flying old and unsuitable aircraft were being sacrificed for no advantage and now the evidence was clear.

The justification that it was the only way of supporting Russia (who were engaged in a bitter campaign on the Eastern Front) coupled with it being Britain's only way of retaliation on mainland Europe were acknowledged, but while this pressure on Germany had to be maintained it had to be executed in a different and more effective way.

Sir Richard Peirse (then commander-in-chief of Bomber Command) was summoned to a meeting with Churchill at Chequers. The result was that the bombing offensive was effectively halted over the winter months of 1941– 42 and a new strategy formulated. Peirse was relieved of his command.

After Peirse was removed and before a new commander-in-chief was appointed the role was filled on a temporary basis by Air Chief Marshal Jack Baldwin and on 14 February he received what would become one of the most contentious instructions of the war, Directive No. 22, which stated:

> You are authorised to employ your effort without restriction, until further notice, in accordance with the following direction.
> It has been decided that the primary object of your operations should now be focused on the morale of the enemy civil population and in particular, of the industrial workers …

The new plan put forward the concept of bombing the forty-three largest German cities. All had industrial areas but were also home to more than

15 million people, many employed in the German war effort, which was at the height of its production. Although small raids on specific targets may be required, the main thrust of bomber activity would be towards industrial targets, particularly those situated in the densely built-up areas of German cities. It was felt this would have the joint effects of stalling industrial production either directly or through killing their workers and occupying significant resources in the defence of Germany, as well as deeply affecting the morale of the German people.

At the same time as the issuing of Directive No. 22, the War Cabinet received advice from Lindemann, now Baron Cherwell, which supported this strategy. His memorandum became known as the 'de-housing paper' and advised that the best use of this blunt instrument that the Butt Report exposed was to demolish city housing. Churchill who shared with Lindemann an intense dislike of the German hierarchy and its people, although always sceptical of an enlarged bomber force targeting areas as the only way to win the war, was entirely supportive of this new initiative. After all, it was still the most effective, indeed the only offensive action he could take.

With a new strategy and Peirse sacked, Bomber Command needed a new, permanent head. Air Chief Marshal Sir Arthur Harris took up his new role on 21 February, which he kept until the end of the war. Although often labelled with the nickname 'Bomber', he was known as Bert by his close friends and 'Butch' by the men he led. Their nickname was used with affection and over the coming years this hugely controversial figure broadly maintained the respect of the airmen under his command.

Harris is a key character in this story. Although considered and prepared to listen to advice, he was never one to shy away from difficult decisions and he bore the brunt of the criticism of the bombing strategy, particularly in the last two years of the war and for decades afterwards. He was, though, a product of his early years in the RAF and a follower of Trenchard's convictions.

A grammar school boy, Harris, having fallen out with his parents who wanted him to join the army, emigrated to Rhodesia but in 1914 felt he needed to join up. In the 1st Rhodesian Regiment he saw at first hand an early use of the bomber when the only German aircraft in South West Africa (now Namibia) dropped artillery shells. In 1915 he returned to the UK and, having been refused entry by the cavalry and the artillery, he joined the Royal Flying Corps, a clear reflection of the scepticism with which this recent creation was held by recruiters. After training and an initial posting, ten months after joining the RFC he was given command of 38 Squadron but was soon posted to France with 70 Squadron, where from above he witnessed the muddy battlefield of Passchendaele. It affected him deeply, convincing him there must be a better way to wage and win a war.

Between the wars he served at home and abroad in India and Iraq, where he and others developed the use of aerial bombing. He converted transport aircraft to bombers, insisted on his crews being able to operate at night, trained them hard in navigation and started to use target-marking techniques. He impressed his superiors and contemporaries alike; many of the latter like Alec Coryton and Ralph Cochrane would later become his group commanders. Back in the UK, he served under and became friends with Charles Portal at RAF Worthy Down and, following further tours in the Middle East, he commanded 210 Squadron in the UK. There he met Australian Don Bennett, who again would not only command a group but it would become the Pathfinder Force. Further promotions and key jobs, (notably commanding No. 4 Bombing Group when Air Chief Marshal Sir Edgar Ludlow-Hewitt commanded Bomber Command) and an eight-month stint in Washington DC elevated him further until in September 1939, while convalescing after a duodenal ulcer, he telephoned Portal to ask for an active role and Ludlow-Hewitt was delighted to give him the command of No. 5 Group, a heavy bomber group with ten squadrons of Handley Page Hampdens.

It was here his leadership style was cemented. He immediately highlighted the inadequacies of his aircraft and regularly commented to Ludlow-Hewitt how strategic bombing would shorten the war but they needed new equipment and new tactics; he clearly understood the shortcomings of Bomber Command. He visited his squadrons regularly (which he rarely did when commanding Bomber Command) and was genuinely engaged in their issues, their suggestions and interests. They liked him and his reputation for hard training, discipline, an affinity and understanding of their jobs and an encouraging and sympathetic ear developed their affection for him. He was clearly a forceful and confident character, occasionally short-fused with a direct and blunt personality and much feared in High Wycombe, but grudgingly respected for his energy and drive. He did, though, always have his aircrew's welfare permanently balanced against his drive to bomb Germany to submission even when it became his obsession. His crews respected that and thought highly of him right to the end, unlike many of his group and station commanders.

Harris had been incensed when Ludlow-Hewitt was sacked in 1940 for trying to improve Bomber Command's training structure but as a consequence the pack above him was once again shuffled, which would lead him to the top of Bomber Command. His arrival had a similar effect on Bomber Command as Churchill's had on the country. New, optimistic and positive leadership provided purpose and confidence for the crews who were pushed night after night to take escalating risks.

Over this same period a number of new aircraft and new items of equipment were being introduced. The improved Wellingtons and larger four-engine 'heavy' bombers like the Lancaster, Halifax and Stirling were starting to replace the old Manchesters, Hampdens, Blenheims and Whitleys. With this ability to deliver more bombs came advances in navigation systems to assist in accuracy and other technical advances to improve overall effectiveness.

With Bomber Command's inability to accurately analyse their own results exposed, the Chief of the Air Staff directed the creation of an operational research section (ORS) at High Wycombe, which between the end of 1941 and August 1943 grew from seven researchers to fifty-five scientists and ten assistants. They were under the leadership of Dr Basil Dickens and were there to assist Bomber Command achieve 'maximum effect from available resources'. Harris would increasingly come to trust and depend on their analysis and predictions, particularly in the use of the new navigation aids.

No. 115 Squadron had been trialling the new Gee navigation system, which having proved itself was being rolled out to many squadrons. As well as equipment, tactics were examined. For instance, in the past the longer it took to get all the bombers to complete their bomb runs, the more vulnerable they were to the local air defences both in the form of flak and particularly the *Himmelbett* night fighters. They had time to attack the first bombers, return to their bases, refuel and rearm and return to re-engage. Harris insisted that squadrons should train intensively to concentrate aircraft over the targets for the shortest possible time.

Although Bomber Command had always maintained throughout these early night-time raids that they were targeting industrial targets and denied they ever bombed residential areas, the crews knew and had often reported that when they had missed their industrial targets, bombs and incendiary markers that fell on residential areas created huge and disruptive fires. Now this was to become policy, not accident. As 1942 progressed it was not uncommon to find specific orders sent down from Bomber Command to the stations and squadrons. For example, on 16–17 June on a raid to Essen the following formed part of the orders sent down to the crews: 'If there is little or no cloud in the target area, Bonn or any built up area outside the Ruhr is to be targeted.'

Harris ordered the use of large numbers of incendiaries as well as some larger high-explosive bombs. Mixed bomb loads within aircraft and within each wave became the norm. Large explosive bombs shattered and weakened buildings, incendiaries started fires and smaller bombs hampered access to deal with them. It was a calculated response to the strategy of property destruction. Pound for pound, incendiaries were significantly more destructive to residential properties than high explosive.

Although traditional raids on single industrial targets using 200 to 300 aircraft took place after Harris arrived, his approach, directed by the War Cabinet, soon developed into the tactic of using large numbers of aircraft on single area targets ... what became known as 'maximum effort' and ultimately, the '1,000 bomber raids'.

At this point it's worth looking briefly at the involvement of the United States in the war. From the late 1930s and including the outbreak of war in Europe the US staunchly remained neutral, although it had long since declared itself an ally of Great Britain. From September 1939 onwards the cost of Britain's war preparations spiralled and it was not able to pay for the raw materials it was receiving from the US. Although President Theodore Roosevelt wanted to help and public opinion was generally pro-British and against Nazi Germany it was not easy at that time for the US to help. Its Neutrality Act of 1939 allowed the sale of war materials but only on a 'cash and carry basis', which did not help Churchill respond quickly to the threat in early 1940. The Johnson Act of 1934 did not allow the US to provide credit to those countries that had not repaid the loans provided during the First World War, which included Great Britain. It was also a belief held by the US military at the end of June 1940, in other words after the collapse of France and before the end of the Battle of Britain, that Britain would almost certainly surrender to the Germans, so helping them would be futile and a waste of American equipment. Although Roosevelt's hands were to a degree tied, in September 1940 he provided fifty obsolete destroyers in return for the US leasing certain British bases. Only a few months after this Churchill had to admit to Roosevelt that Britain could no longer pay for the supplies being convoyed across the North Atlantic. In December 1940 Roosevelt came up with a plan known as Lend-Lease, whereby Britain would not pay in cash but would settle the debt as part of their contribution to the post-war economic order in Europe.

The US attitude changed gradually throughout 1941 as it became involved in the Battle of the Atlantic, having established a base in Iceland from where its navy was engaged in convoy protection and was suffering casualties at the hands of the German U-boats.

The defeat of Germany remained the priority of the 'Grand Strategy' agreed between the Allies even after the attack on the Pacific Fleet by the Japanese on 7 December 1941, much to the relief of their European allies. On 11 December 1941, Germany declared war on the United States and that was reciprocated on the same day by the US declaring war not only on Germany but also Italy.

The US now pledged its support for the strategic bombing of Germany and put in place plans to station its air force in many British bases, which resulted in the arrival of the Eighth Air Force Group in August 1942. It was equipped with the B-17 Flying Fortress, which was extensively armed, armour plated and consequentially heavy, which limited its bomb load. After a few joint operations that were broadly unsuccessful, the agreed strategy was that Bomber Command would continue with its night-time operations and the USAAF would carry out daylight missions, although there was considerable liaison between the two when selecting targets. The B-17s in their early missions were easy targets for the Luftwaffe and casualties were high until the Americans introduced the P-51 Mustang in early 1944, a long-range fighter that gave the bombers an escort well into Germany.

Just 2.5 miles from Hemel Hempstead is the village of Bovingdon, where an airfield was built in 1941–42 as a bomber station for the RAF. However, in August 1942 it became a base for 92 Bombardment Group USAAF, which was redesignated as a combat crew replacement unit, a training station with a similar role to the operational training units and the heavy conversion units of Bomber Command, of which we will find out more about later.

This led to the residents of Hemel Hempstead meeting many American servicemen from September 1942 until the end of the war. I wonder if Brian ever met any of them when he was on leave? I know his sister, as a 14-year-old schoolgirl, well remembered seeing them around town.

By the start of 1942 the Japanese were moving through the Far East inflicting defeat on both American and British forces. Closer to home, the Germans occupied most of Europe with only the neutrals of Switzerland, Ireland, Sweden and Spain escaping their attentions. As German forces prepared to push towards Egypt, the British were forced out of Greece and

Crete. Germany's invasion of Russia saw them closing in on Moscow and at that point they were all conquering.

To many in the War Cabinet and Air Ministry and to virtually all in Bomber Command, there was only one way to execute aggressive action against Germany and that was to bomb it with greater numbers of aircraft, with a greater tonnage of bombs and with greater accuracy. Soon the concept of a land invasion of Western Europe by the Allies would be developed and planned but until then, as far as mainland Europe was concerned, it was Bomber Command's war.

Chapter 9

115 Squadron – Part 3

After their attack on the German capital ships, there followed six weeks of training, including a week at RAF Wyton, near Huntingdon, doing blind approach training. This was a new system to help pilots land in poor visibility and at night. In just over a year Brian would become very familiar with the airfield at Wyton.

This period of Bomber Command introspection gave crews more time to fly training sorties and increase their logbook hours, mainly learning to use new equipment and familiarisation flights for new crews. While he was at Wyton and doing more training, the squadron conducted four operations to the Ruhr Valley, one of which on 8 March saw another casualty when Pilot Officer Runagall and his crew were only one of seventeen who failed to return to Marham from Essen. Ron Runagall was only 20 years old and his crew of six had an average age of 23 years and 6 months. Ken Dodwell felt that they were the most experienced crew in the squadron with two DFCs and a DFM, and having completed well over twenty ops they were the crew others went to for advice. Ken noted that they did push their luck as they liked to return home flying low over Luftwaffe fighter airfields to machine gun any targets they could see; sadly they may have done it once too often and he felt they most likely crashed into the North Sea after a fighter attack.

By March, the other squadron at Marham, 218, had completed its conversion to Short Stirlings and one of its aircraft on an Essen raid had a hang-up when two of its 1,000lb bombs failed to drop and they had no choice but to bring them home. On landing, they exploded, killing two of the crew and seriously injuring the flight engineer. That incident and many like it only encouraged crews to dump their loads if having to return early; full bomb bays led to nervous return journeys and careful landings.

After nearly six weeks of leave and training at last they appeared on the 'on ops' roster. On 25 March Wellington X3602 took Brian and his crew to Essen, one of the most heavily bombed cities in the Ruhr Valley. It involved 254 aircraft, 17 of them from 115 Squadron and the largest force to attack a single target to date. It was not a particularly successful operation, although most of 115's crews reported that their bombs or flares were on target. All the squadron aircraft returned, although nine aircraft overall were lost.

Brian clearly enjoyed both a mission involving so many aircraft and, as visibility was good, an excellent view of proceedings, but maybe he was just pleased to be 'working'. His logbook records:

Operations as ordered – Essen. WHIZZO!

The following day Brian started some leave but that night the squadron returned to Essen and another two crews were lost, Sergeant Taylor and Pilot Officer Soames. That month, four squadron crews were lost.

Throughout April, May and June Bomber Command was busy implementing the new strategy. It meant a lot of training for all squadrons as well as an increasing number of operations. During those three months the squadron trained on seventy-seven days and flew operations on forty-one. In May alone, on six occasions aircraft were prepared and crews were briefed only for the operations to be cancelled at the last moment. A very busy period for Marham and for Brian who, over the same three months, flew on forty-three days, including twenty-seven operations.

In his log he listed the crew for March 1942 as:

Capt. Self
2nd Pilot Sgt. Reynolds
Observer Sgt. Dodwell
W/Op. Sgt Burbidge
Fr. A/G. Sgt Swann
Rear A/G. Sgt. Lowry (RAAF)

In fact, Ken Swann had arrived at the squadron at the end of February but didn't join the crew until the end of the March, and the two temporary front gunners moved on, Brown to another crew and Dalton was soon on his way back to New Zealand. Ken, a devout Baptist all his life, was born in Norwich and educated at the City of Norwich School only about 30 miles from Marham but his route to get there was circuitous and painful. His grammar school was nearly moved to the West Country to avoid the possibility of being accidental bombed by the frequent Luftwaffe raids on the many East Anglian airfields; the skies above that school would have been thick with aircraft in Ken's last year. Like so many others, he wanted to be a pilot and tried to volunteer in September 1939 but was told there were no vacancies for pilot training and was persuaded to join up as a wireless operator/air gunner. In February 1940 he started his trade training, followed by his operational training with 11 OTU at Bassingbourn and then a posting to 99 Squadron at Waterbeach, near Cambridge. Air gunners were a diverse bunch. Some were wannabe pilots but were judged early in their training to have neither the required aptitude nor the technical skills for navigating or wireless operating. Many, like Ken, were not offered the opportunity for pilot training through lack of course availability, even though they had shown the aptitude. Some, though, saw the pilot as a driver, the technical trades as passengers, but it was gunners who did the fighting and many would not have had any other seat in the aircraft. You will meet one such shortly but Ken, I suspect, was a gentler soul who during his first tour discovered much inner courage and resolve.

The target for Ken's eighth operation with 99 Squadron on 15 November 1941 was Kiel. The weather was terrible, they took off just after 2100 hours but their Wellington soon iced up and had to return, eventually crashing about 6 miles north of their airfield. Having not ditched their bombs, they crashed with a full bomb bay, including a 1,000-pounder. Ken was thrown out as the aircraft crashed but as he was crawling away he remembers the bombs exploding. Every member of the all-sergeant crew were injured and Ken woke up in Ely hospital with a fractured skull, a damaged right eye, a broken arm and leg and cracked ribs. He was moved to No. 2 Aircrew Convalescence Depot at Hoylake in Scotland. It was here that he reconnected with Mollie, an old friend he had met in the Silver Road Baptist Church. Her fiancé had recently been killed in action and, having heard that her old friend Ken was convalescing, she wrote to him. After only three months, Ken was declared fit for aircrew duties and sent down to Marham, perfect for seeing his mother and Mollie in Norwich. Ken was three months short of his twenty-second birthday at the time of his first operation with Brian. Considering Jon Burbidge was 30, it is remarkable that the average age of Brian's crew was just over 21.

On 2 April 1942 their target was the Renault factory at Poissy, just outside Paris. This factory was in full production making lorries for the Wehrmacht. This raid went slightly against the new strategy but it was seen as an important target. Brian noted in his logbook:

– 3 Direct Hits!

The raid was deemed successful and only one aircraft was lost from the fifty that were used. Nine squadron aircraft went out that night, six to Poissy and three to Le Havre, and all reported some degree of success and returned safely.

For the rest of April, the city targets were prominent, with five to the industrial Ruhr Valley. The others were three to Cologne, one to Hamburg, two to Rostok and one to the outskirts of Paris.

Cologne was an important target, highly industrialised and a closely packed city centre with densely populated residential areas, and as such was heavily defended. Over the war it was targeted no fewer than 260 times by Allied bombers. On 5 April Brian in Wellington X3602 joined sixteen squadron aircraft and 263 aircraft in all that had the Klöckner Humboldt Deutz AG (an engine manufacturer that switched to military equipment, notably artillery) factory as its main target. In the event, bombs were scattered across the city. Five aircraft were lost. Brian's log reports:

> Operations as Ordered Cologne – Heavy intense accurate predicted flak. Very Shaky do!!!

On 6, 10 and 12 April they bombed Essen but on 8 April their target was Hamburg. There were 272 aircraft involved and the thirteen from 115 had a mixed night. Nine managed to drop their mixed load of bombs but four experienced severe icing and could not climb to a bombing altitude. One crew was 'coned' on their bomb run and another had a sick tail gunner when his oxygen supply failed. However, they all got back but the raid overall was seen as a failure and icing and electrical storms created havoc across the force. Brian's log described the operation thus:

> Operations – Hamburg. DNCO. Severe icing and static – Returned to Base.

The three Essen raids involved six, ten and twelve aircraft from 115 Squadron. Their bomb loads increasingly reflected their role and were now mainly flares and incendiaries, with one or two carrying a single 4,000lb high-explosive bomb, known as a 'cookie'. Icing, electrical storms and cloud cover hampered the raids and although many of the squadron crews reported good results at their post-op debriefs, overall the three raids were not seen as particularly effective. Of the 662 aircraft, only twenty-four were lost but there was bad news for Brian as one of the them was from the squadron and it was his early mentor and friend Sergeant Jim Holder and his crew. Jim was 27 and left his young wife, Winifred. They had only been married for eleven months.

On 13 April, four squadron aircraft went on a minelaying job, known as 'gardening' to the crews, but the next two ops for Brian on the next two days were to Dortmund. Twelve squadron aircraft were briefed for the 14th and nine for the 15th and all returned, but of the 360 aircraft used in all, thirteen were lost. Once again the weather was difficult and the bombing less than accurate. The flak was intense and terrifying, with many of the crews reporting flak damage to their aircraft and Sergeant Harris's tail gunner being wounded. Ken Dodwell remembers these five last Ruhr Valley raids very well:

> There were many missions that scared me in particular, mostly those to the Ruhr Industrial area. This was one of the most heavily defended areas in Germany, known as the Ruhr Valley. On five operations, one after the other we returned with damage to the fuselage, mostly holes from shrapnel with some holes very near to where I was sitting. One piece of shrapnel embedded itself in the ply wood floor exactly below where I was sitting. It had hit an aluminium strip reinforcing the plywood floor. This bent upwards and splinters from the floor shot up my trouser leg. The shrapnel had just lost its momentum; otherwise it would have pierced my backside! The next day a member of the ground crew presented me with the piece of shrapnel.

Brian did not comment on every raid and most of his entries are quite matter of fact, but he did make comments on all five of these:

> Operations as Ordered – Essen – Very Nice Hectic Welcome!!!
>
> Operations as Ordered – Essen – Usual Effort – Bags of Everything
>
> Operations as Ordered – Essen – Usual Show
>
> Operations as Ordered – Dortmund – As per usual – Many holes
>
> Operations as Ordered – Dortmund – 10/10 cloud in Target Area

The first of these to Essen was also noteworthy. Ken Dodwell again:

> The worst operation over Essen was when we were 'coned' by all the searchlights. It was when the master searchlight got you that you knew you were in trouble. All the other searchlights would point at you, and then every gun in the area would take aim. The good side to it was that most of the other bombers nearby would get a free run and thank you later, if you made it back to base. The reality was that most people who were 'coned' were shot down. On this particular occasion Brian Slade took retaliatory action by throwing the aircraft all over the sky. We did a severe 'corkscrew' to deceive the radar, and continually changed height and direction so that the shells burst where you were a moment before. I would hear the shell, from my position on the aircraft, bursting above the noise of the engines. During close calls I could even smell the cordite from the explosions all around me.

It is difficult to imagine what it was like to be in this aluminium-framed tube holding fuel and high explosive with a covering of linen and the odd piece of plywood the only protection from anti-aircraft shells exploding all around you. Then having to hang on in the dark while your pilot tried dives and swerves desperate to keep out of trouble. It was worse for the crew as there was little they could do but hang on; at least Brian was able to influence the outcome. From those logbook entries it appears those raids did little to dent his confidence.

Chapter 10

115 Squadron – Part 4

In an RAF bomber in the Second World War, although each member of the crew had a role, the ability to work together was fundamental to survival. Brian's crew had now completed a dozen or so operations together. A respect for each other's ability grew with each flight, each operation and in each incident where their individual and group skills were tested. Those improving skills would be tested a number of times over the next three months.

On 22 April they took off on another trip to Cologne. Thirteen aircraft carrying the usual range of SBCs, cookies and GP bombs. All but two of the sixty-four Wellingtons that took off returned.

This was an experimental raid with all aircraft fitted with Gee and ordered to use it as a blind bombing aid. It is thought that only about fifteen aircraft's bombs found the target. Most of the aircrew mention in their debrief the use of 'TR1335' and one of the squadron aircraft returned early as theirs was u/s (unserviceable). TR1335 was the term now used to describe Gee as radio equipment, a simple and late effort to disguise the new technology from German intelligence as there was Air Ministry paranoia about the security of this new navigation device after a Gee-equipped Wellington was lost over Germany in August 1941. In fact it was a 115 Squadron aircraft piloted by Sergeant Wallace on an operation to Hanover.

On four consecutive nights between 23 and 26 April, operations were flown to bomb Rostok, a relatively small German town on the Baltic coast connected to the sea by a wide navigable estuary known as the Unterwarnow. Rostok had two key targets. Firstly there was a Heinkel aircraft factory in full production, secondly the central part of the town, which had a high proportion of Medieval timber-framed buildings. A notorious and highly successful raid to the similar town of Lübeck had been carried out about a month earlier. There the majority of the bombs used were incendiaries calculated to create extensive fire damage.

The last of these raids did not involve 115 Squadron but virtually all squadron aircraft were rotated though the first three, with Brian taking part in the second and third on 24 and 25 April.

As with Lübeck, the attacking force on all four nights was split into two groups; the first and smaller group concentrating high explosives on the factory and the second, the majority, using incendiaries on the town centre. Like Lübeck, Rostock was not heavily defended and being on an estuarine coast was a relatively easy job for the navigators.

On 23 April, 115 Squadron dispatched ten aircraft led by Wing Commander Freeman and Squadron Leader Grant, eight aircraft loaded with either 1,000 or 500lb General Purpose (GP) high-explosive bombs and two with incendiaries. Although two crews aborted, the remainder reported dropping accurately and all returned safely. The second raid sent six squadron aircraft, five of which, including Brian's, were loaded with GP bombs, and a single aircraft with incendiaries. Brian reported in his debrief that his bombs fell in the built-up area of the old town and he observed very large fires, including an entire street ablaze. All crews returned without casualties, reporting accurate bombing and seeing many fires.

The following night twelve squadron aircraft were briefed for the third Rostok raid, again with the majority loaded with GP bombs. Crews once again reported accurate bombing and in Brian's debrief he reported 'the whole town was on fire'. The success of these raids was judged by the photographs taken by the bombers after their bombs were released. Brian noted in his logbook:

> April 24th – Operations as Ordered – Rostok. 3 Photographs

> April 25th – Operations as Ordered – Rostok – Many fires
> seen 150 miles away – 3 photos

The returning squadron crews were met with the news that one of their number, 21-year-old Yorkshireman Sergeant Alfred Fone and his crew in X3633 had not returned. The aircraft was attacked and hit by a night fighter on its way out to Rostok, crashed with its full bomb load and exploded. The local people close to the crash site in Denmark near Bevtoft collected and buried the remains of the crew, against the initial orders of the German officer in charge. Those same people erected a stone memorial to the crew in 1947.

The first two Rostok raids were not seen as particularly successful as neither the Heinkel factory nor the town centre suffered significant damage. However, the third achieved direct hits on the factory and the fourth did considerable damage to the town itself.

These raids on Lübeck and Rostok are seen as Harris moving into the new strategy of attacking and damaging residential areas as well as industrial targets. It was after these four raids that the Germans used the expression *terrorangriff* (terror raid). Goebbels (Hitler's Minister of Propaganda) recorded in his private diary 'community life in Rostok is practically at an end'.

About 1,765 buildings were destroyed and 513 damaged. In total 130 acres of Rostok was destroyed, 60 per cent of the town centre. The raid killed 204 people and injured 89. Clearly, the death toll would have been much higher on the destructive third raid had so many residents not left after the first two.

Before the end of the month the squadron undertook two more operations, the first on 27 April to Cologne and the second two days later to the aero engine factory at Gennevilliers, on the northern edge of Paris.

The Cologne raid involved only ninety-seven aircraft, a small number compared to what was to come in a month's time. It targeted a small industrial and residential area and in good conditions was judged a success. Squadron Leader Grant led thirteen Wellingtons from 115 including Brian, and overall only one aircraft was lost. However, as they discovered on their return, that casualty was one of their own, Sergeant Harris. It's not known what brought Leslie Harris's aircraft down but it crashed near Cologne, killing Harris and three of his crew. However, their rear gunner, Sergeant Jerram, managed to get out and, having parachuted safely, was captured and ended up a prisoner of war (POW) interned in Stalag 375 at Kopernikus in Poland.

The Paris raid was less successful as the main factory went unscathed, although some bombs did destroy an industrial building at Port de Paris. The sixteen squadron aircraft all reported mixed results. A number of crews reported bomb strikes on the factories and frustratingly Brian reported that his string of bombs straddled the target. Three Wellingtons were lost out of eighty-eight aircraft and once again they returned to hear that one of their aircraft was missing, piloted by Sergeant Reynolds. There was a suggestion that it might have been shot down but it is almost certain that it collided with another Wellington of 57 Squadron from Feltwell. It seems they both came down in the Parc de Maisons-Laffitte about 6 miles north-west of the target. On each of the last three operations, an aircraft and crew had been lost, a total of sixteen members of the squadron.

Overall April was busy with operations on 18 nights and 187 sorties. The squadron strength varied but most of the time 2 flights of 9 aircraft were available with about 140 crew allowing for leave and sickness. That month they lost four aircraft and twenty-two crew.

A few days later there was something to celebrate as Sergeant Ivor Charles Brian Slade was promoted to the rank of pilot officer on 1 May 1942. At 17 years and 9 months, he was still three months short of the official entry age for aircrew training to start. Now he would move into the officers' mess. He, of course, would have known most of the officer pilots and crew already but a more familiar face would soon arrive as his wireless operator John Burbidge was promoted two months later.

Like all newly promoted young officers, Brian was placed in a strange position as now he was separated from the non-commissioned members of his crew who had become his closest friends, like his roommate Ken Dodwell and Sam Lowry. Those crew friendships were maintained but now his 'in camp' social life revolved around the officers' mess. Brian was lucky as both the officers' messes where he was to spend most of his operational time were substantial and comfortable brick buildings situated on station, unlike others that were temporary buildings or requisitioned country houses off base.

These young officers' ability to adapt and fit in to mess life had little to do with their social backgrounds. Unless they had been brought up in a service family, mess life would be foreign to most. Full of custom and tradition with its own unique hierarchy, many struggled with its rules and behaviours. Now they had mess staff, their meals were served to them and many had batmen to bring them tea in the morning and clean their uniforms. It was those same batmen who were responsible for packing up the personal possessions of those who failed to return.

Only very senior officers had family accommodation close by, so a mess would have a variety of ranks and ages but it was predominantly occupied by young junior aircrew. Although there would have been organised events like Christmas lunches and squadron farewells, they would find any excuse for a party where heavy drinking, singing and mess games were the norm, indeed encouraged both to allow them to release the pressure of operations but also to keep riotous behaviour on station. To a bunch of young, intelligent and high-spirited airmen, the tacit encouragement led to an inventive range of pranks and practical jokes not always appreciated by the recipients but which kept morale high even in the worst of times.

The Slade crew were due a week's leave at the beginning of May and Jack Reynolds (Brian's second pilot) left to continue his pilot training. The era of Wellington crews carrying a spare pilot was almost over. The demand for replacement crews and particularly pilots grew week by week. Second pilots were now needed to captain their own aircraft.

As John Burbidge and Ken Swann got ready to disappear out of the station gates, Sam Lowry had to appear in front of the squadron commander and Brian and Ken Dodwell had a role to play. It seems that on 27 April Sam was put on a charge for causing damage to the landing and bedroom of a married quarter. On 1 May, Sam was marched in front of Wing Commander Freeman with the squadron adjutant in attendance, was admonished and fined £2 5s. An admonishment was the lowest form of punishment and was most likely a severe bollocking and the fine was the cost of repairs. Brian and Ken were there as witnesses but almost certainly would have given a character reference with the hope of reducing the award. Anything more severe would have left them without a rear gunner. What on earth was their single young Australian up to in a married quarter a few hours before they all took off on an operation to Cologne? The answer was simple. Marham, did not have any allotted women's accommodation so the WAAFs were housed in a fenced-off part of the married quarters. Sam's excursion to the forbidden WAAF accommodation was probably not a rare event on an operational station but at least he wasn't locked up. I hope they all had time to have a drink to celebrate Brian's promotion and Sam's near miss.

With seventeen operations completed together (a few less for Ken Swann as a late arriver), the Slade crew were now one of the most experienced in the squadron. Survival gave them all confidence. There were no distractions in Brian's life and no doubts about his ability. Countless veterans tell of new pilots who arrived unconfident and with doubts, who dwelt on their lot, who believed they were the next for 'the chop', which would develop into a self-fulfilling pessimism. I don't think Brian was like that. He believed in his ability and had confidence he could get out of any scrape. It 'wouldn't happen to him' was a message he always passed to his family.

They were now a pretty close team and despite being split between the two senior messes, had been used to spending much of their off-duty hours together. When possible they would go off station to the many local pubs in Marham and surrounding villages on leave. However, they often went their separate ways, but my mother told me how she loved Brian bringing his crew mates home to Hemel Hempstead, and Sam visited often. Ken Dodwell was spending most of his spare time with Jean, his wife to be, Ken Swann was off home to Norwich to see his girlfriend Mollie and Sam would soon be off to London to see his new Australian girlfriend.

When they returned from leave on 11 May, the crew were stunned to hear of a training accident involving Jack Reynolds.

As a young trainee pilot, he flew seventeen operations as Brian's second pilot. This quiet Kent man fitted in and they liked him, so he became a regular on the crew. On 11 May Jack and two other pilots, Sergeant Bachen and Sergeant Jones, were on a local training flight around Marham in Wellington X3602, coincidently the same aircraft used on their last mission together. That day the weather was poor with cloud and rain forecast. They became lost in misty conditions and as they came down out of the cloud to fix their position in the late afternoon, they hit a 200ft wooden radio mast, part of the Home Chain radar network, and crashed at West Beckham, near Sheringham, killing the three pilots.

Brian and his crew were now very familiar with losing people they knew, whether through training or operations, but as a member of Brian's first aircrew, Jack's death was close. They all would have felt the loss hugely. Brian and his crew carried Jack's coffin to his grave in Marham Cemetery.

The cemetery is some way from the church and occupies a gently sloping site, at the top of which is an area under the care of the Commonwealth War Graves Commission (CWGC). There is the conventional central stone war memorial flanked by two rows of the iconic, immaculately cared for graves. When I visited his grave in February it was a drizzly, misty day with low cloud.

Although there were operations that month, Brian's crew were not involved until 17 May, although they had three air firing and bombing training sorties earlier. That operation on the 17th was 'gardening'. In home waters it was relatively straightforward and safe for the Royal Navy to lay mines from boats to deter and possibly destroy enemy shipping, but a different approach was needed to mine enemy coasts, harbours and shipping lanes. An air-droppable mine was developed for the RAF to 'plant' or 'sow' from bombers. It achieved two main aims. Firstly, it could prevent free movement of enemy shipping, therefore channelling it into areas that were easier to monitor. Secondly, it required considerable German effort and manpower to defend these shipping hot spots and to minesweep.

Gardening was not popular with aircrews. It was seen as tedious and monotonous work but also dangerous. It was easy for both sides to determine the critical shipping lanes, which enabled the Germans to defend these key points aggressively. They used searchlights (minelaying was almost always done at night) with fixed and mobile flak ships.

Flak ships, or *Vorpostenboots*, were manned by the German navy and fixed ones were moored barges armed with a number of anti-aircraft cannon, others larger, mobile and more heavily armed. Some were the *Sperrbrecher*. These were often converted merchant ships armed with anti-aircraft guns and multiple anti-aircraft cannon mounted on raised platforms fore and aft. As well as the anti-aircraft role, they were also minesweepers equipped with powerful magnetic field generators that were capable of detonating a mine from distance.

They were unlit, unpredictably mobile and operated up and down the Channel coast. Having received a target's location from the air defence network, they were able to predict the routes returning bombers would take and it was not unusual for a night fighter to lurk close to the flak boats, who would flush out their next target. They were feared by the bomber crews.

As well as these key points being well defended, the 'gardening' aircraft had to adopt a particular approach. Mines had to be dropped accurately from the relatively low altitude of 1,500ft. The aircraft speed could not exceed 180mph or the parachute risked being ripped off as the mine was released. Consequently, this slow and low approach made them very vulnerable. Mines would be 'sown' in rows (the authors of the squadron ORBs often refer to these operations as 'planting vegetables'), which required a straight 12-mile timed run. Each aircraft could spend some time circling around the target waiting for their timed run. All in all, it is not difficult to see why airmen did not like these gardening operations but May started with another one for ten crews.

On 4 May, thirteen aircraft joined a force of 121 to bomb Stuttgart, more specifically the Bosch factory, but solid cloud prevented accurate bombing and the facility was not hit. A sophisticated decoy site set up by the local authorities and the Luftwaffe at nearby Lauffen used searchlights and anti-aircraft guns, and this fooled several bombers. The cloud cover rendered the city's defences ineffective and all the squadron's crews returned safely. On 5 May, another operation to Stuttgart was mounted, not involving 115 Squadron, but on 6 May, fourteen squadron aircraft went back for a third raid in three days but again it was ineffective, the factory was unscathed and the Lauffen decoy did its job again.

That operation claimed another two 115 Squadron aircraft. Flight Lieutenant John Sword's aircraft was hit and badly damaged, forcing the crew to bale out. Tragically, Sword and Sergeant Harold Batty both perished as their parachute webbing was insecure but the other four crew members, including Sergeant Brown, who was Brian's front gunner on three trips, survived and were taken prisoner, ending the war in four different POW camps. Flight Lieutenant John Sword was a farmer's son from Oxfordshire, near Heythrop. His family, originally from Scotland, also farmed land in Argentina, which they had bought around 1870. I suspect he might have had joint nationality as he is remembered not only in Heythrop but also on the War Memorial in the British Cemetery at Chacarita, a suburb of Buenos Aires. A significant number of ex-pats from all over the world, including Argentina, returned to serve at the outbreak of war.

You may remember that earlier in April, he and five other squadron crews, including Brian, completed a successful raid on the lorry factory outside Poissy, where he made six low-level runs over the target and took photos that proved their success. He was awarded the DFC, with the citation recording: 'This officer, who has carried out a considerable number of operational sorties, has invariably displayed courage and determination of a high order.' He left his wife Polly and their 4-month-old son John, who still works the family farm in Oxfordshire.

The other casualty that night was Flight Lieutenant Paterson's aircraft, which was attacked and badly damaged by a night fighter, but it seems that only three of the crew had time to bale out. The two New Zealanders, Nathaniel Paterson and his navigator Pilot Officer Patrick Leland, were both killed and the three who jumped, parachuted safely and ended up in a POW camp. It was an unwritten but expected duty that the pilot tried as hard as he could to keep a damaged aircraft flying straight and steady as long as possible in order to give the rest of the crew time to bale out. It is quite likely that Paterson did this and went down with the aircraft. His body was never found.

One of those who parachuted safely was an interesting character, one Edward 'Ned' Callander, and this was his thirty-ninth and, as it happened, last trip. Born in Dumfries, Scotland, he was raised with his elder brother and sister by their father; their mother having been admitted to Crichton Mental Hospital soon after his birth, where she stayed until her death. As their father was seriously mentally traumatised by his time in the trenches of the Dardanelles during the First World War, the burden of raising these three children was shared between father, various aunts and an elderly grandmother who became his legal guardian from age 11.

By all accounts Ned was a mischievous boy and hard to handle, and at 14 he had a run-in with the police for various petty offences including stealing a bicycle, groceries, some apples and money from his employer, a local grocer. It seems his grandmother lost patience with him and didn't speak up for him when he appeared in front of the Provost, who sent him to reform school for three years. The regime was tough; they wore uniform, marched everywhere and were taught a number of trades. After three years he left healthy, fit and a changed young man, and although he returned to his family briefly, he was soon off to London. While on a trip to Paris, he joined the French Foreign Legion, a common terminus for men with a troubled backstory.

After his basic training in Algeria, he served in Morocco and was promoted to Caporal, having become a tough, well-trained Legionnaire. Serving with the 13th Demi-Brigade of the Foreign Legion, he was deployed in the spring of 1940 as part of the significant Allied force that attacked the German-held port of Narvik in northern Norway. Many of the Allied troops were ill-equipped for fighting such winter conditions, but the Legionnaires, who had come from fighting in North Africa, did have a brief period of training in the Alps and were equipped for winter warfare. The Narvik landings attacked into heavily defended positions and the fighting was brutal with high casualty numbers. Ned gathered together the remnants of his unit and fought to clear the last German forces out of the town of Bjerkvik. He was awarded the Croix de Guerre for his part in the Battle of Narvik and his citation describes him as a 'living example of courage and endurance'.

Because of the occupation of France in 1940, Foreign Legion units could not go home and Ned returned to Britain, where he joined the RAFVR, trained at 15 OTU and then became an air gunner in 75 Squadron based at Feltwell in Norfolk. He completed a full tour of operations, which included collecting a DFM after a raid on the shipyards of Brest. He was clearly a good shot, as his citation describes:

> He is probably the finest air-gunner to have passed through this squadron and the experience gained during 4 years' service with the French Foreign Legion plus the great coolness, skill and courage he has displayed on all occasions merits his high recognition.

After a period as a gunnery instructor, he volunteered for a second tour and was posted to 115 Squadron at Marham.

Having survived his bale-out from Paterson's aircraft on the Stuttgart operation, he was captured and initially sent to Stalag Luft III, from which he twice escaped and was recaptured. The camp situated near Sagan, (now Żagań in Poland) 100 miles south-east of Berlin, was opened in 1942 and run by the Luftwaffe to house downed aircrew, initially British and Commonwealth, but expanded in 1943 to take the increasing number of captured USAF aircrew. It was built on sandy soil, the huts raised 2ft above the ground and seismograph microphones placed around the perimeter, all to deter tunnelling. Those measures did not deter countless escape attempts made by those wishing firstly to get back in the war but also to keep the local military busy in attempting to recapture them. Two particular attempts became famous due entirely to books and then films, namely *The Wooden Horse* and *The Great Escape*, but many other successful escapes were made.

After his second escape from Stalag Luft III, Ned was transferred to Stalag Luft VI in Heydekrug, East Prussia, from which he made his third escape in early March 1944 by hiding for fifty-six hours in a disused water tank. He was aware that the three 'Wooden Horse' escapees made it back to the UK via the Baltic ports of Stettin and Danzig by stowing away on ships. Ned tried to follow their example and made it to Danzig, where his fluent French enabled him to live among French POWs working in the dockyards while waiting to find a ship. However, his timing was unlucky as on 24 March the famous 'Great Escape' took place from Stalag Luft III and an infuriated Hitler ordered an extensive nationwide hunt for those escapees. Under the notorious *Kugal Erlass* (bullet decree) issued on 6 March, all captured POWs were to be executed. It is understood that a French dockworker alerted the Gestapo and Ned was recaptured and taken to Mauthausen concentration camp, where he underwent interrogation by the Gestapo. Eventually he was executed, aged 27, as were fifty of the seventy-six recaptured escapees from Stalag Luft III. He has no known grave but is remembered both on the Runnymede Memorial and on his home town's war memorial in Dumfries. A tough, brave and resourceful young man.

On 8 May, Wing Commander Freeman once again led fifteen aircraft to Warnemünde to attack both the town and the nearby Heinkel aircraft factory with only limited success, but all returned. As it was a small target, Freeman was determined to fly low to be as accurate as he could despite an abundance of local searchlights and light anti-aircraft guns. He made six bombing runs, was hit several times and lost one engine but made it home. He had also repeated his low-altitude approach on a raid to Essen and to prove his point achieved photographs on both occasions. He was awarded the Bar to his DFC after the Warnemünde raid, which stated:

> Throughout his operational career this officer has proved himself to be an outstanding and courageous leader who has inspired his squadron with that spirit de corps that is so necessary to success.

He must have been inspirational to his young crews and Brian clearly had the highest respect for him as he amended an earlier entry in his flying log to add Freeman's newest award.

On 17 May after some leave and Jack Reynolds' funeral, Brian and his crew took Wellington X3445 with ten others from the squadron to 'plant vegetables' off the Danish coast, specifically the Frisian Islands and Heligoland. Thirty-two Stirlings (carrying six mines per aircraft) and twenty-eight Wellingtons (carrying three) took part. The success of the mission is not recorded but seven aircraft were lost, one of which contained Sergeant Butterworth and his crew of four from the squadron. They were most likely shot down by a night fighter, which were active in the area that night.

Two days later, twelve aircraft including Brian's attacked the city of Mannheim on the confluence of the Rivers Rhine and Neckar. A total of 197 aircraft took part but the operation was deemed ineffective. Many of the crews reported delays in finding their target and making their bomb run, and a large fire south-south-west of Mannheim attracted the majority of the bombs into an area of forest and open country. The squadron crews' reports were mixed but several were confident they saw their bombs land in the town. For Brian's crew, particularly Ken Dodwell, it was a navigation success:

> As a navigator and bomb aimer the raid I feel most proud of was the one against a target in Mannheim. It was a relatively long flight in those days (5hrs and 30mins) ... I took up my position behind the bombsight for the 'run in'. On the run in our two gunners started shouting 'you're wrong, Ken, the target is 5 miles to starboard; the whole area is on fire!' to which I yelled back 'they're wrong!'
>
> I could see the River Rhine by the light of the moon ... Strangely, I noticed that all of the searchlights were in the doused position, or not shining upwards. They were making a dim circle around the outskirts of this large city. And above all, there was no attacking gunfire. They were giving us a free run not to expose their position. The enemy did not want to disturb the mass of Bomber Command bombing their fire 'decoy' in a forest some 5 or 6 miles outside Mannheim!
>
> The target came up, and still not a shot fired. As we were able to fly straight and level, we took a perfect photograph.

When printed, this showed our bombs straddling the target area, which became the only photograph in the Squadron.

At the next briefing the Squadron Commander questioned why they had all bombed a forest? He told them that only one aircraft in the Squadron and only 9 in total had photographs of the target.

He then turned to our pilot, Brian Slade, and said 'well done, Slade!' There was a voice at the back of the briefing room, in a complaining tone, that said 'what about the navigator?'

Quite understandably, Ken felt hard done by due to this lack of acknowledgment, but while Brian would have enjoyed the credit, it was more evidence that he had a skilled navigator.

Eleven aircraft were lost over Mannheim and although all the squadron's aircraft returned, Flight Sergeant Hyde had a serious scare as they were attacked and badly damaged by a night fighter that the tail gunner shot down. They made it back to Marham but crash-landed, thankfully without serious injury.

Buoyed by the successes of Lübeck and Rostok, Harris's strategy was taking shape and he now felt ready to put together a raid designed to do the maximum damage to one of the most important German cities. The target selected was Cologne.

At that time in 1942 Bomber Command could muster between about 400 and 600 aircraft for normal operations. To achieve the thousand aircraft Harris wanted he needed to tap into all his reserves from 2 OTU Group (Nos. 91 and 92) and with the support of their commanders, aircraft from Coastal Command and the Flying Training Command were pledged. Within days of Harris having the numbers, Coastal Command withdrew their support. This was the latest spat between the Royal Air Force and the Royal Navy over the control of maritime air power.

Every aircraft (including those in for routine servicing that would normally be rotated through the squadron) were prepared for operations. No crews were on leave, on standby or resting. Now Harris also had to use every training aircraft and man them with instructor pilots (many with considerable operational experience) and trainee crews. Some though, took off with trainee pilots. Eventually 1,047 bombers stood ready.

It is often suggested that the original target for this first '1,000' was Hamburg but although an easier place to find visually, being on a wide estuary, it was out of Gee range and too risky. This rumour drifted around but most of Harris's trusted advisors wanted and planned for Cologne; indeed for some weeks plans to accelerate the fitting of Gee in more aircraft were based on the concept of a target within Gee range. As Cologne sat close to the Rhine, a combination of Gee and an easily identifiable landmark improved their chances of accuracy. They, of course, needed good weather for that plan to work. The date was initially set for 26 May but a poor forecast for northern Germany delayed the attack for three days. In order not lose the benefit of the full moon, the raid was agreed for 30 May and Harris confirmed the target as Cologne. Early that afternoon the crews attended their briefings and were told for the first time that a thousand aircraft were involved. Up until then a raid with 300 aircraft was a big one. The news about Cologne rather than Hamburg would have been welcomed and met with great excitement. Firstly, it was closer and secondly, the met boys were convinced that visibility would be good.

One of Harris's particular tactics would then have been shared with the crews. He wanted a far greater concentration of aircraft on the bomb run. All thousand crews were to be through the target over a narrow front in one and a half hours. Although they trained to fly in formation, this level of flying in such proximity with so many other aircraft had not been rehearsed. Indeed, Brian had not practised formation flying since February. They would need to stick to rigid timings, headings and altitudes to reduce the possibility of collisions. It would need the highest standard of planning, briefing and execution by the aircrews.

One of the advantages of concentrating was the inability of the German night fighter network to react flexibly to such an attack. Their very effective system of *Himmelbett* boxes expected to see small numbers of bombers entering the box, where a controller could direct his fighter by radar on to one bomber after another. This system was swamped by large numbers moving through a single box, which these raids over narrow fronts achieved.

The ground defences of Cologne, based on searchlights and anti-aircraft guns (increasingly radar controlled), were familiar with a few hundred of aircraft typically over two hours. Their ability to handle 1,000 in 90 minutes was about to be tested. Contemporary analysis has suggested that while the percentage of aircraft lost was reduced by this tactic, the actual number of losses remained much the same. The positive advantage of the larger raids was that of increasing the likelihood of greater destruction on the ground – crew and aircraft survival was secondary but nonetheless crews, not unnaturally, liked the idea of overwhelming the defences.

As a 'maximum effort' operation, all available squadron aircraft were needed and it was a brilliant effort by the ground crew to get eighteen in the air. Brian and his normal crew were in Wellington X3724 this time, with incendiaries in SBCs. In order to achieve a highly concentrated bomber stream, aircraft were required to take off with very short intervals. 'A' Flight's ten aircraft took off in eighteen minutes and 'B' Flight's eight in fourteen minutes – so much faster than the ten- or fifteen-minute intervals on earlier operations. Brian was the last to take off at 0021 hours. Getting them all airborne quickly meant they could group together more easily into the required dense bomber stream. It was a very crowded sky over East Anglia and the North Sea that night.

Experienced Gee crews were used in a Pathfinder role, being first over the city and marking targets with their coloured target indicators. Most of the squadron crews reported their bombs falling accurately on various parts of the city and observed many large fires.

The raid was considered to be a resounding success for Bomber Command and Harris's new tactics. Of the 1,047 aircraft that took off, about 870 bombed. Some 1,445 tons of bombs were dropped, of which two thirds were incendiaries.

Brian's logbook was typically concise:

> Operations as Ordered – Cologne – 1,000 a/c in 1½ hours –
> Great Fires.

Brief and a typical Brian understatement. The statistics on the ground were frightening. There were a total of 2,500 separate fires, 1,700 recorded as large. Some 12,840 commercial buildings were destroyed or damaged, and 41,640 domestic properties were destroyed or damaged. It is a surprise to me that only about 470 people were killed, although more than 5,000 were injured. Between 135,000 and 150,000 people fled the city after the raid. All these figures represented a record for a single raid.

I should just explain these casualty and damage statistics. Most are taken from the reference book *The Bomber Command War Diaries* by Martin Middlebrook and Chris Everitt. These statistics have been meticulously gathered from German civilian municipal archives, which are recognised as infinitely more accurate than the figures that were available at the time either from official sources or from a complicit press. Aircrew, of course, would only know what they were told by their seniors or what they read in the newspapers. Both were no more than propaganda. For instance, the

Daily Telegraph on the day after the Cologne raid reported that 3,000 tons of bombs were dropped from 1,250 aircraft. German radio reported that 111 people were killed in the Cologne area. All wildly inaccurate. As with the general population, aircrew had no idea of the true casualty numbers but most who witnessed it at first hand, albeit from 15,000ft, had a clear idea of the destruction below.

Bomber Command losses were also a record. The attack went in with three waves with the most experienced crews in first, many acting as aiming point markers. The last waves were predominantly the training and novice crews and fortunately for them it was clear that the defences were overwhelmed as each successive wave suffered fewer casualties.

Forty-one aircraft were lost, twenty-nine of them Wellingtons. Twenty-two aircraft were lost over Cologne, sixteen by flak and four by night fighters. Most of the remainder succumbed to the radar-controlled night fighters on their way out or back. A testament to the discipline in the bomber stream was that only two aircraft were lost in collisions. Sergeant Edward's aircraft from the squadron was one of those attacked on their way back by one of the *Himmelbett* night fighters and crashed in Belgium near Wijgmaal, just north-east of Brussels, with none of the crew surviving. The navigator, Sergeant William Crampton, a married man from Lancashire, had previously been with 9 Squadron, where on 27 August 1941 his aircraft was shot down and Crampton made the perilous journey along the 'Pat O'Leary' escape line supported by the French Resistance and SOE operatives, through France, across the Pyrenees to Spain and then back to Britain to volunteer for his second tour with 115 Squadron. I don't think Brian would have known Edwards well as he had not long joined the squadron, but he knew his crew and their previous skipper, Sergeant Davie, very well. Edwards had taken over the crew after Davie had been posted to 20 OTU. The rear gunner was 30-year-old Sergeant Hubert Croston, a Lincolnshire man and a chum of Brian's, who he described as 'another good type'. One more friend gone. Davie, a Canadian, after that screening tour, joined 15 Squadron flying Stirlings and was shot down and killed with his crew on a gardening operation in July 1943.

The remainder of the 115 Squadron crews returned from Cologne and were back on the ground at Marham by 0510 hours.

The use of crews from the training units and the need for all squadron aircraft, including many novice crews, later came under scrutiny. Of the forty-one aircraft that did not return, only seventeen were from training units. Further analysis showed that of the twenty-four from operational squadrons, as many as ten were skippered by pilots on their first operation. Two more were flying Manchesters for the first time and two more had fewer than three operations in their logbooks. Five more had completed fewer than ten operations. The three squadron crews that crashed on take-off or landing were also piloted by first-timers. Even though it seemed that the squadron crews suffered more than the training units, this first thousand-bomber raid cruelly demonstrated that novice pilots and crews, wherever they came from, were the most vulnerable.

May had seen the crews of 115 squadron out on nine days taking on twelve different objectives. There were ninety-nine sorties, with four aircraft lost on ops and one while training. Seventeen members of the squadron were killed and seven became prisoners of war. A difficult month but there was to be no let-up.

As Bomber Command had assembled this large number of aircraft, it wanted to use them again before the OTUs' bombers were dispersed back to their bases. The moon and weather was still favourable and a second '1,000' was planned for 1 June, 2 days later. The target was Essen. It would be Brian's fifth trip to the home of the Krupps factories in Happy Valley. Previous losses and repairs reduced the total and 956 aircraft took part. Once again, a number of Wellingtons from No. 3 Group were equipped with incendiaries and flew a Pathfinder role. No. 115 Squadron managed to get eighteen aircraft in the air with a mix of bombs including five with 4,000lb cookies, while seven had SBCs with incendiaries and four carried flares. The eighteen aircraft all took off in just over an hour either side of midnight.

The bombing was scattered and although a number of crews saw fires through the cloud, the overall results were nowhere near as effective as the first raid on Cologne. It was, however, another impressive demonstration of Bomber Command's ability and vulnerability.

Of the 956 aircraft used, thirty-one bombers were lost, including Flying Officer Williams and his crew from 115 Squadron. This crew, in age terms, was a particularly senior one with an average age of 28 years and 3 months. Another loss of a precious aircraft and crew.

The ground crews worked their magic again and two days later they had fifteen aircraft for the next operation to Bremen. This raid only had 170 aircraft and was the first trip to the port for 8 months. The fifteen aircraft were all airborne in thirty-three minutes just before midnight. The orders from Headquarters described this as a 'Shaker' attack, which normally meant three phases: the first Gee-equipped aircraft with illuminators, a

91

second group with coloured target indicators and a third wave with HE and incendiaries. Once again there would be a gambit in the development of target-marking tactics to achieve greater accuracy; in this case it was to be illuminators and main force only. The order, which gave all the normal details, required six groups of two or three Wellingtons from three different squadrons, all Gee trained, to illuminate the target at intervals for the first eighteen minutes of the raid, each group having a specific time to bomb. The order also wanted the most experienced crews to lead. The first three aircraft to illuminate were from 115 Squadron. Squadron Leader Grant was first followed by Brian and Sergeant McKee. Pilot Officer Henry A'Court led the next two aircraft nine minutes later. The main force bombed from the second to the thirtieth minute.

These were not loosely organised raids. These experimental missions required detailed planning and complex orders, and in this case although only 170 aircraft, there were six different types from five different stations. However well organised and executed, there was so much that could, and did, go wrong.

The crews' reports were mixed, with Squadron Leader Grant reporting 'general confusion'. Nonetheless, the damage was considerable on the ground, particularly around the docks area. Overall eleven aircraft were lost, two from 115 Squadron. Pilot Officer Thomas Wood's aircraft went down but his wireless operator, Pilot Officer Pearce, survived and became a POW. The aircraft of Canadian Flight Sergeant Jack Hutchinson was almost certainly shot up by a night fighter and ditched in the North Sea; all were lost.

It was during this operation that Henry A'Court was awarded his DFC. Having seen his port wing shot up by a Junkers Ju 88 on the way out, he pressed on and completed his illuminating run but was then hit by flak in the starboard wing. With both wing tanks holed, his navigator, Pilot Officer John Worth, had to do some clever calculations to work out the most efficient course home. They managed to get the Wellington back but ran out of fuel just as they crash-landed back at Marham. John Worth was also awarded the DFC. A third medal was won that night in the same crew. Flight Sergeant Bill Bullock, the crew's radio operator, was able to stand in the astrodome directing the pilot away from the attacking night fighter. Then Bullock juggled the fuel cocks and for the last half hour held open the nacelle fuel cock to ensure what fuel they had got to the engine. They landed safely due to Bullock's 'resourcefulness and courage' and he was awarded the Distinguished Flying Medal. The ORB simply comments that

A'Court's aircraft was 'forced to crash land'. That doesn't quite do justice to the events of their night.

Henry A'Court completed thirty-three operations with 115 Squadron, then after time at an OTU became a Pathfinder Mosquito pilot, completing more than fifty further operations. He survived the war, becoming a pilot with British European Airways.

On 6 June they once again took off for an operation to bomb Emden, four including Brian with the flare/GP mix, some with incendiaries and five loaded with what the ORB describes a 'special 4,000lb HC'. Bearing in mind the others had marking bomb loads, these 'specials' could well have been the 'Pink Pansies' or the 'Red Spot' cookies that would become so popular with the Pathfinder squadrons in 1943. They marked targets for a force of 233 aircraft, which later was judged another success. All the squadron aircraft returned safely but overall nine did not.

Something went wrong on Brian's return as, although not mentioned in the ORB, his log records a landing at Alconbury, some 45 miles from Marham. This meant an early start as they had to fly back to Marham in time for their briefing and for the 'erks' to get the aircraft ready for a gardening operation that night.

That mining job went without incident but included in Brian's crew was a new pilot to the squadron. Sergeant Baden Fereday was on his sixth trip as second pilot but would have to wait another month for his next operation as skipper. We will hear more of his crew's adventures later.

Throughout the remainder of June, 115 Squadron carried out a number of raids; five of them gardening, with Brian's crew being involved in three. No squadron aircraft were lost. Harris clearly had another thousand aircraft raid planned as on 18 June he included this message in his orders:

> Owing to the urgent need for freshman to gain experience before the moon period, the maximum number of freshman crews to be included.

After the three mining jobs, Brian's crew just had training flights until 25 June but other squadron aircraft prior to that hit Saint-Nazaire and Emden. Coming back from Saint-Nazaire, Flight Sergeant Mooney had a scare when, with a flak-damaged engine, he just managed to get to Exeter, where he crash-landed safely. The shortage of crews was so intense that the following day Squadron Leader Cousens flew down, picked them up and returned them to Marham. Mooney's crew had recently lost their wireless

93

operator, Sergeant Eddie Killelea. Eddie had a penchant for singing and dancing and it was cruelly ironic that he was killed when a lone German bomber on one of the 'Baedeker' raids dropped four bombs on King's Lynn, one hitting the Eagle pub where he was drinking with a group of serviceman celebrating a friend's 21st birthday. Seven other airmen and many civilians were killed in the Eagle that night. Later in July, Mooney would be hit by flak on his way back from Duisburg and, unable to climb, the crew baled out and all spent the rest of the war in a POW camp. The previous week, Pilot Officer Malcolm Freegard's crew ditched on their way home after the second Emden raid and only a few weeks later they were attacked by a night fighter, also on their way back from Duisburg. Earlier that month, the novice Freegard had flown with Brian and more of his adventures in a later chapter.

Bomber Command now prepared for another thousand-bomber raid on Bremen on 25 June.

Bremen, a north German Baltic port, was an important target for the Allies. Although inland, it connected to the smaller port of Bremerhaven on the River Weser, which was fully navigable to the largest cargo ships. It was an important trading city and home to a number of industrial targets such as the Atlas Werke, Bremer Vulkan and DeSchiMag shipyards, the Focke-Wulf aircraft factory, Korff AG oil refinery, a steel mill, a major railway station and the Valentin submarine pens.

There had been a number of bombing raids to Bremen of varied success and Brian had been there before on 3 June. Although on that occasion various targets were hit including the submarine pens, the Focke-Wulf factory and a destroyer that happened to moored in one of the shipyards, a significantly larger raid was now planned. It was a warm still summer's evening when more than a thousand aircraft took off, including eighteen Wellingtons from 115 Squadron. Each group had specific targets and all 960 aircraft had completed their bomb runs in sixty-five minutes. The weather over the target for this third and last thousand-bomber raid was unkind, with all targets obscured by cloud for the entire raid, leading to fewer than 700 aircraft claiming to have bombed the target. Brian's logbook entry confirms this with the single word:

Operations as Ordered – Bremen – 1,000A/C - – - CLOUD – - -.

Not surprisingly, results were indifferent and many of the squadron's aircraft failed to find their targets, with three bringing their bombs home.

Brian was one of them as when Ken tried to drop them, due to a faulty bomb release, all the bombs 'hung up' and would not drop. Another landing with a full bomb bay – not good for the nerves. Pilot Officer William Croxton was hit on his way home and was reported as having landed in the sea but air-sea rescue could not find them and the crew of five were lost. Croxton had flown as a novice second pilot with Brian on 1 June on the Essen raid just after he arrived in the squadron.

Two days later, on 27 June, Brian was part of a smaller raid on Bremen involving 144 aircraft, of which fourteen came from Marham. They carried a mix of GP and incendiary bombs, and again Brian recorded:

CLOUD and FLAK!!!

The results, however, were considered successful and it was a cheerful crew that landed, not only due to avoiding Bremen's air defences. They had taken off at 2359 hours and once they had circled up and were heading east, the clock ticked over to 28 June and the intercom hissed as the crew sang Happy Birthday. It was Ken Swann's 21st. Soon after landing back at home the mood of high spirits did not last long. All the squadron made it back but the Wellington flown by Brian's flight commander, Flight Lieutenant Sandes, was attacked and shot up by a night fighter on their way out. His tail gunner, Sergeant Billy McCann of the RCAF, was decapitated when cannon fire blew off the top of his rear turret, and three other crew – namely the navigator, wireless operator and front gunner – were wounded. Ben Sandes was unhurt and single-handedly got the aircraft home and crash-landed safely at 0323 hours. As dawn broke the medical staff at Marham would be busy and later that morning the Station Signals Officer Flight Lieutenant Keenan, went on board the Wellington to recover the signals codes and remarked that it was a shambles inside with blood everywhere – a gruesome job for the ground crew to sort out. The realities of the war were brought home to Marham that morning.

Terence Lindsay Sandes, known by all as Ben, was born in England but within a few months went to South Africa with his Anglo-Irish father and South African mother. His father was an outstanding surgeon and had been awarded the OBE for treating the severely disabled of the First World War.

Sandes went to the University of Cambridge in 1937, joined the University Air Squadron, learned to fly and at the outbreak of war volunteered to join the RAF. In the same year, he married and after the war he and his wife Diana went to South Africa, where they farmed until 1961 when, as an activist in the anti-apartheid movement, he was forced out. They moved to Ireland, where they settled in Co. Waterford. He died aged 89.

Sandes was rested for a few days but was back on ops by 11 July with a new crew and was promoted to squadron leader by the end of the month. He was later to be awarded the DFC for his actions that night on his way back from Bremen.

Two days later, another trip to Bremen on 29 June involved thirteen from 115 Squadron. Some crews saw no bomb bursts but others reported fires and it was fires that destroyed some important industrial targets, including the Focke-Wulf factory and the A.G. Weser U-boat construction yard. Pilot Officer Stanford's aircraft developed engine trouble and he had to turn back, eventually ditching in the Channel. Tragically, his front gunner, Flight Sergeant William Linwood, drowned. Linwood, a 20-year-old Canadian from Saskatchewan, had arrived at the squadron that day – it was his first operation. The rest of the crew got safely into the aircraft dinghy.

By 0525 hours the last of the squadron landed at Marham but, on hearing that Stanford had ditched, eight of the crews, including Brian, after refuelling themselves and the aircraft, took off again over the North Sea to sweep his last-known position. The Bremen raid logged just over five hours and the search for their missing aircraft took more than seven hours. They must have been exhausted but their efforts most likely saved that crew. The dinghy was spotted, its position sent to the air-sea rescue services and the crew were picked up. In the air, the spirit and morale of a crew was all important, within a squadron it was actions like this that bound crews together.

Later in July, the New Zealander Stanford would be hit by flak over Duisburg, forcing all to bale out. All but one of the crew survived and ended up in Stalag Luft III. The front gunner, Sergeant Maurice Colclough, was killed. Like Linwood, it was his first operation.

Brian had spent more than twelve hours of the last twenty flying and fortunately wasn't required that night. He and the crew had a good night's sleep, and they were going to need it.

Chapter 11

Bremen

On 2 July there was a further raid on Bremen, involving 325 aircraft. It was Bomber Comand's fourth in a week, and Brian's fifth, and as it happens last, visit to the north German city. It was also his tenth consecutive operation in X3662. Crews became attached to certain aircraft, superstition perhaps but this Wimpy was good to them. Brian and his crew were now very close to completing their tour of operations. It would be Sam Lowry's thirtieth. The others had exceeded this longed-for total and as they heaved themselves into the front hatch of their favourite aircraft in the darkness of a distant dispersal at Marham they, the most experienced crew in the squadron, knew there was this and one more to go.

The runway controller saw fourteen aircraft take off from Marham, six from 'A' Flight and eight from 'B' Flight, between 2316 and 2344 hours, every two minutes, and Brian took off at precisely 2320 hours. All bar one of the squadron aircraft were loaded with small bomb containers with either 4 or 30lb incendiaries. The weather over the target was hazy with occasional breaks and all aircraft bombed from between 12,000 and 16,400ft. Later, they reported that the dock area and a bridge appeared to be alight and fires were seen along the railway line. It was a reasonable success but of the 325 aircraft taking part, eleven aircraft did not return and X3662 was very nearly a twelfth.

Navigator Ken Dodwell, having finished in the bomb aimer's position, was back in his seat behind the armoured bulkhead that separated him from the wireless operator, John Burbidge, who sat immediately behind Brian, the three of them in line on the port side. As Brian lost some height and picked up speed in the unburdened Wellington, Ken gave Brian the new heading for home. Ken Swann was in the front and Sam Lowry in the rear turret both peering through Perspex for the entire raid. As was often the case, not one round of their .303 ammunition had been fired.

The flight time on the Bremen raids was between four and three quarter and five and a quarter hours. Their return route, as usual, took them back across Holland and with an empty bomb bay they flew at about 10,000ft, quite a bit lower than their bomb run altitude; they were cruising at about 150mph. The weather over the target had been clear but there was patchy cloud en route as Brian recorded four hours of the trip on instruments. As they flew over the Dutch coast, they had less than an hour of flying to get back to Marham. This wasn't a time to relax but the worst was over, a steady return with a bit of cloud, ideal.

Soon after crossing the Dutch coast, about 15 miles according to Brian's log, their peace was shattered as they came under intense fire from two unseen flak ships. In seconds the fuselage, port wing and engine had been raked with flak. Hydraulics on a Wellington III are a dual system but both pumps are run by the port engine. Without pressure a lot goes wrong. The undercarriage dropped half way, the bomb bay doors fell open and the wing flaps drooped. Those three problems alone increased the drag on the aircraft, slowing it down immediately, but the loss of the flaps reduced Brian's ability to achieve lift.

No one had seen a night fighter so they would have guessed pretty quickly what had happened and Sam or Ken may well have seen the flak tracer arcing up towards them from the boats. As they scrambled to fully assess the damage, and as if they weren't in enough trouble, they were attacked by a Ju 88. Taking on a night fighter was the nearest bomber crews would get to fixing bayonets. In their dark world of long distances and great altitudes, this was close combat. A simple duel, a dogfight with the odds against them even in a fully functioning aircraft. If Sam, in the rear turret, had wanted to return fire, he couldn't as the loss of pressure had rendered the hydraulically controlled rear turret incapable of the speed of movement required to track a night fighter. That first attack from the twin-engine attacker rattled more cannon shells into the centre and port side of the fuselage, which started a fire near the main wing spar behind the navigator's compartment, but that wasn't all. The elevators were also now u/s. The push-pull control rods connecting the elevator to the pilot's control column that ran down the port side had been damaged. The elevators are the control surfaces on the tail that enable the pilot to increase or decrease the pitch of the aircraft and control its altitude. With both wing flaps and elevators gone, gaining height was now impossible.

Then the port engine failed completely.

As soon as the night fighter attacked, Brian instantly started evasive manoeuvres but 'corkscrewing' with no elevators, no flaps and one engine was not easy. Every foot he dived he would not regain. As John tried to put out the fire with hand-held extinguishers, in a pitching and rolling aircraft, Ken Dodwell scrambled from his navigator's seat and through the fire to the astrodome to look out for the next night fighter attack. John hadn't put out the fire but knew that without the rear turret they were sitting ducks. He left the fire and moved back past Ken to man the single-beam .303 machine gun, which was fired out of the small diamond-shaped openings in the fuselage, to at least try and put off the next attack. The Ju 88 had guns and cannon mounted in the nose, so the pilot needed to point his aircraft directly at them as he attacked. Sam, in the rear turret, completely exposed and unable to fire back, now watched the attacking fighter heading straight for him. Ken, watching from the astrodome, had to judge when the Ju 88 was pointed directly at them and ready to fire and, as John returned fire, screamed 'move now' for Brian to turn and dive again. The night fighter attacked them three times, the last two being watched by Ken, with John returning fire and Brian throwing it around as best he could with one engine, no flaps and no elevators. On its third attack, as it flashed past, Ken Swann in the front turret managed to get off a long burst, which Ken Dodwell was convinced had struck the Junkers and Ken Swann claimed it as a kill. The Wellington had been hit again, causing more damage, but miraculously, none of them were injured. With less power, undercarriage and bomb doors dragging and repeated diving, Brian had now lost a lot of altitude with no hope of climbing.

Now, a bit of luck. Brian managed to get into some low cloud and, whether it was that or Ken's last burst, the night fighter didn't reappear, but they were still on fire. John and Ken continued to fight the fire with more hand-held extinguishers and eventually managed to put it out. Although the Wellington was seen as friendly and forgiving, it had one flaw. It didn't like flying on one engine. The newer, more powerful engines in the Mk III were better but if the surviving engine was run at full power to try and gain height it would overheat and have to be throttled back. Without flaps and elevators it was impossible. Typically on one engine a Wellington lost 100ft a minute. It needed care and judgement to fly any distance on one engine. They were now some way from the Norfolk coast with Brian battling to keep the aircraft from losing more height. The fire now out, John returned to his radio to report their plight, only to find it had been damaged in the attack. They knew that getting to Marham was unlikely and without alerting a closer airfield to light up a runway, they would be trying to find it and land, literally in the dark. Amazingly, John affected a repair and sent a Morse fix to Marham at 0345 hours just in case. He was able to keep in touch with base as they headed back towards the Norfolk coast. There was now need for some cool heads. Ken was hurriedly plotting their route home and by heading directly for Norwich they would be on track for the closest airfield at Horsham St Faith. That route also avoided any cliffs, which was handy as they crossed the coast and flew the last 30 miles at no more than 100ft. John, having repaired the radio, was able to warn Horsham St Faith to clear the airfield and at 0405 hours, with his crew braced for disaster, Brian belly landed without mishap.

I can only imagine how they felt. Luck, some fine individual skills and above all a crew working together under intense pressure had recovered from a situation that would claim many hundreds of aircraft. A less experienced crew would not have survived.

Within days Brian was awarded the Distinguished Flying Cross. The official citation for his award reads:

> This officer has completed many attacks on most important targets. On the night of 2 July 1942, he captained an aircraft detailed to attack Bremen. Having successfully accomplished his mission, he had just crossed the Dutch coast when his aircraft was heavily subjected to fire from two armed ships. The hydraulic system was rendered unserviceable, undercarriage, bomb doors, and flaps falling down; the rear turret and the elevators were also damaged. Almost immediately an attack was made by a Ju 88. Further damage was sustained, and a fire of alarming proportions broke out near the main spar, and was only extinguished after considerable difficulty by two other members of the crew. The aircraft was now only 200 feet above the sea, and the position seemed hopeless, but P/O Slade was determined to fly on as far as possible towards his country. Displaying superb skill, he succeeded in reaching an airfield, where he successfully crash landed his damaged aircraft. Though young in years, this officer has shouldered the responsibilities of operational captain in the manner of a veteran.

Brian wasn't the only member of the crew that night whose actions were recognised. The wireless operator, Pilot Officer John Burbidge, was also awarded the DFC and his citation reads:

On the night of July 2 1942, P/O Burbidge was the wireless operator of a Wellington detailed to attack Bremen. On the return flight shortly after crossing the Dutch coast, his aircraft was subjected to intense fire from two armed ships and severe damage was sustained. Immediately afterwards it was attacked by a Ju.88. P/O Burbidge, manning one of the beam guns, was able to engage the attacker. After the first attack he observed that a serious fire had developed near the main spar. He at once attempted to extinguish it. At first he was not successful, but, after the enemy aircraft had made three further attacks causing damage, he succeeded in extinguishing the fire. Returning to his post he effected some minor repairs to his damaged wireless set, and, from then on, kept in constant communication with base. In harassing circumstances, P/O Burbidge displayed skill and coolness which was of material assistance to his captain.

Brian's logbook entry was typically understated:

Operations as ordered Bremen – 15 miles off Dutch Coast on return met Flak ship – Hydraulics shot away – undercarriage, flaps and bomb doors hanging – 3 attacks from Ju88. Fuselage ablaze – Elevators U/S – Port engine lost Power – ASI – U/S. Belly landed at Horsham St. Faith.

I've recreated the events of that night from Brian's logbook entry, the two citations above, Ken Dodwell's first-hand account written more than sixty years after the war and Ken Swann's account written in 2011, all of which differ slightly over some of the detail. It was, by all accounts, quite a night and having landed they were taken to the Mess at Horsham St Faith and given a double brandy. I can't help feeling that they all deserved a medal.

Brian was wearing his DFC ribbon within days. It was announced in *The London Gazette* on 12 September and John's on 22 September 1942. Brian's citation describes him as 'young in years' as they thought he was 19 years and 11 months old. He was in fact 17 years and 11 months old when he completed this his thirty-fourth operation, officially still too young to start aircrew training.

Descriptions of the events that supported requests for awards were normally written by the squadron adjutants or commanding officers having had the opportunity to read the post-operation and intelligence reports and where possible spoken to the crew. Brian's commanding officer was Wing Commander Frank Dixon-Wright DFC, a popular, married 31-year-old who flew regularly with his crews.

No laurels, no resting and they were in the air again on the 5th, 7th and 8th for training and then their last operational sortie together on 9 July with two other squadron aircraft. Not a case of 'getting back on the horse' but an operational necessity. It was another gardening op with fifty-eight other aircraft, one of which was lost. Having consigned X3662 to a long period of repair, they were allocated an older Mk II, Z1607. They carried two mines and dropped them spot on target from 1,500ft. Business as usual but how much they must have wanted that one over.

The 'Q' for Queenie' crew were finished but the squadron continued work. July 1942 ended up being a terrible month for 115 Squadron. They had operations on 12 days with 13 targets and 131 sorties. They lost eleven aircraft that month, eleven aircrew became POWs and forty-six members of the squadron were killed, including Dixon-Wright. He was on his second tour of operations and leading fourteen Wellingtons of his squadron on another operation to Hamburg. In order to fly that night he stood down Squadron Leader Alan Cousens and captained his aircraft and veteran crew himself. On their way back they were attacked by a Messerschmitt Bf 110 night fighter. Night fighters had no respect for rank. He and his adopted crew, many of whom were also second tour veterans, and three other squadron aircraft and crews were lost that night.

The squadron lost more than half its aircraft and nearly half its aircrew in one single month.

The fliers wouldn't have known it at the time but over this period of the war typically only twenty-seven out of 100 aircrew in Bomber Command survived to complete their thirty operations and fewer than half of crews came through their first tour unscathed. The Slade crew were one of the few in 115 Squadron to see out their tour that year. The subject of the length of operational tours, and the survivability of aircrews on their first and second tours, was discussed at length within the Air Ministry. Within a few months a prediction presented to the Air Ministry suggested that only one crew in forty would survive a second tour. It was to prove chillingly accurate.

Other than the overriding desire to survive the next operation, it was how many more operations they had to fly before the end of their tour that preoccupied most aircrew. So for most counting down the numbers became obsessive.

But how did they know what constituted a tour? At the outbreak of war, and indeed up to the time Brian arrived at Marham at the end of 1941, there was no fixed policy of how many operations constituted a tour, only Air Ministry guidance that suggested thirty completed operations constituted a first tour. It was up to the judgment of flight and squadron commanders, possibly with advice from station medical officers when an individual or crew needed a break. This became more formalised at the start of 1943, and in addition a second tour of twenty and a single tour of forty-five for Pathfinders was adopted. There remained, however, considerable discretion even after the informal figures were adopted.

There were many reasons why an operation may not appear to have been completed and there was clearly some interesting interpretation of the operations Brian completed as recorded in both his logbook and the squadron ORBs. For instance, Brian was briefed and bombed up, took off and returned from operations thirty-five times, but in his logbook on three occasions he writes 'DNCO' (duty not carried out). By the end of his flying career he was judged to have done thirty-four in 115 Squadron, which suggests that someone interpreted two of those three DNCOs as completed operations. We can therefore make some calculated assumptions.

The first DNCO was the second trip he flew as second pilot to Jim Holder, the second was to Hamburg on 8 April 1942, and the third was the first Bremen raid on 25 June when they experienced a complete hang-up.

So how was it decided? It must have been hard to sit in front of tired, frightened faces and tell them that the last five hours they had spent over occupied Europe being shot at and avoiding night fighters was not going to be counted as an operation and they would have to do it all again.

Bearing this in mind, I have no doubt that the second and third DNCOs were treated as legitimate operations and it was therefore the trip to Emden with Jim Holder that didn't count.

The situation is even more confusing for a crew. It was deemed that Brian's crew had completed their first tour of thirty operations after their last gardening job. At that time each of them had, as far as I can see, completed a different number of ops. Brian had completed thirty-five; Ken Dodwell thirty-three; John Burbidge thirty-two; Ken Swann thirty-two (seven with 99 Squadron) and Sam Lowry thirty-one.

I can quite see the dilemma of a crew whose individuals may have carried out a different number of ops not being broken up but presumably someone, the squadron commander or perhaps his adjutant, had to exercise delicate discretion as to when the crew as a whole had completed their tour. I think Brian's crew did, comfortably.

Within days of that last trip they left Marham for leave to await their next posting. Goodbyes were often brief, job was done, no time to dwell on the past six months, and with their next postings unknown they would part company. They all went on their 'rest' tours to various OTUs and we will catch up with them all in a later chapter. Of the 125,000 volunteer aircrew in Bomber Command over the entirety of the war, only 7,000 would start a second tour. Brian would be the only one of his Marham crew to do so.

Chapter 12

Training 2 – Screened

No Rest for the Experienced
23 July 1942 – March 1943

Pershore

Having completed a tour of operations, Bomber Command considered that aircrew needed to be rested, not just a week's leave but a long spell without the pressure of operations. Although not qualified instructors, these resting aircrew could provide trainee pilots and aircrew with a real understanding of operational flying. They were therefore sent back to the Operational Training Units to pass on their valuable knowledge, albeit 'screened', the term given to resting crews who were not to carry out operations.

After his leave Brian was posted to 23 OTU at RAF Pershore in Worcestershire on 23 July. Two days later he celebrated his birthday. Even at his 'official' age of 20 he was a very young pilot, although a veteran of thirty-plus operations. His true age of 18 now made him officially old enough to start his aircrew training and as such he was younger than most of the trainees in his charge.

The duration of a spell at Pershore varied but most screened aircrew spent between six and twelve months at an OTU, with some staying for eighteen months. As well as using them to pass on their operational experience to new crews, it was the OTU's role to keep both the pupils and the experienced screened aircrew up to date with the constant advancements in aircraft, radar systems and tactics.

Brian flew thirty-six times in his first month. A great variety of training was carried out: cross-country navigation, practise bombing, aerial photography, infra-red photography, dive-bombing, circuits and landings, engine feathering practise and air-to-air firing to name but a few. The trainee aircrew benefitted hugely from the real and extensive operational experience of their mentors.

In that month Brian had no fewer than forty different trainee pilots and crew and flew in seventeen different Wellingtons. On two occasions he had to abandon the training flight due to engine problems. Many of the aircraft that the OTUs used for training were 'high mileage' and consequently less reliable. As he experienced with 12 OTU, only too often there were accidents and crews lost.

On 9 August he had routine training flight with a full crew, which included Sergeant Hornseth and Flight Sergeant Stewart, both Canadians. They flew to Marham and back on a cross-country exercise that took just over three hours. Two days later Hornseth and Stewart, while trying to land after some night training and trying to go round again, stalled and crashed, killing them both.

Brian had another week's leave at the end of August, a welcome break from the dangers of OTU flying. During the war 7,847 men were killed on training exercises, 3,000 from the OTUs and not just trainee pilots but the experienced instructors with them. There may not have been the dangers of operations but any lapses in concentration, any shortcuts, any errors by trainees, any major issues with the aircraft could end fatally. There was, however, no avoiding the relentless requirement for replacement crews.

It was not only the attrition of crews that needed correction. Vickers, at their peak in 1942, were producing about 300 replacement Wellingtons a month from their three factories.

The one that they flew most was X3662, 'P' for Peter, in which they flew twelve consecutive operations, the last of which Brian had to belly land after the eventful Bremen raid. She had arrived as a brand new aircraft from Vickers' Blackpool factory on 10 February 1942 and had a lot of operations under her belt before she became Brian's regular aircraft. She had been damaged on an earlier trip and was returned to the Brooklands factory at Weybridge for some repairs but was back at Marham after ten days. Bremen was X3662's thirty-ninth and last operational flight. After the crash landing she was designated as Cat. B, namely repairable at a maintenance unit but not at Marham. She was taken in parts to Vickers' shadow factory at Castle Bromwich for extensive repairs and then to 48 Maintenance Unit at Tatton Park. If judged beyond repair she would have been stripped for parts but X3662 was fixed and after some time in storage, by September 1943 ended up in 20 OTU at Lossiemouth, where many more aircrews trained in her. Sadly, after 329 flying hours, on a cold October night in 1943, while on a routine navigation training flight, she crashed into the sea off Dunvegan Head on the north-west side of Skye, killing all five of her crew. After a search, only her empty dinghy was found. The bodies of two of her crew eventually washed ashore, one in Orkney and one as far away as Norway.

X3662 became a bit of a celebrity more than anything due to an official photograph that showed her painted up with thirty-six bomb logos to signify the number of operations she had completed at that time. That photograph became an inspiration for at least two artists and indeed a painting that became the box design for a well-known plastic model kit that included its 115 Squadron decals.

Out of the twelve different Wellingtons Brian flew with 115 Squadron over those eight months, only one seems to have survived the war. Four were lost with 115 Squadron, three were lost with other squadrons and five went to OTUs but were also destroyed. At that time the life expectancy of an operational Wellington was about eleven operations.

On 3 September he went to No. 3 Flying Instructors School at RAF Hullavington in Wiltshire. It was standard procedure to train rested aircrew further in order to help prepare them for the instructional element of his tour at 23 OTU. He may also have been viewed as a potential instructor in the long term but I doubt he volunteered.

The results of Brian's instructors' course gave him an 'average' as a pilot and a 'below average' as a flying instructor. Perhaps he was tired, or perhaps he started to get thoughts about returning to an operational squadron. Either way, I suspect that his 'below average' flying instructor grade didn't worry him and on 3 October he was back at Pershore with the OTU to help more novice pilots.

On his return he learned that a further two Wellingtons had been lost on training flights. Over the next five months, Brian did numerous training sorties, the vast majority as first pilot with young trainee second pilots and crews. He had more than fifty different second pilots over that time and used a similar number of different aircraft as during his first month. These were well-used machines and training accidents remained numerous; the operational squadrons were first in the queue for the best and the newest. Not unreasonably, it was also the squadrons rather than the OTUs that had the best ground crews and the first call on parts. On three occasions mechanical failure caused Brian not to complete a training sortie and on one occasion forced him to land at a different airfield.

The inexorable training regime continued, as did the inevitable accidents. On 8 November, for example, Brian flew four training sorties in four different Wellingtons with at least three different crews. One of his second pilots was

Sergeant Bachelor, who later that same day would survive crashing another Wellington a mile west of the airfield. Sergeant Bellew and his crew of six flew with Brian on 4 December and two weeks later, while he and his crew were on a night bombing exercise to the Lake District, they went off track and crashed, killing all of them. On 28 December another crew was lost when their aircraft, flying in daylight but awful weather, hit a tree and crashed near Banbury.

In the seventh volume of W.R. Chorley's monumental reference works on Bomber Command losses (from which I quote extensively in this chapter) he describes each of these mishaps, some in great detail. It may be a generalisation but most of these crashes were simple human error at the hands of inexperienced trainee pilots and only occasionally the mechanical failure of heavily used aircraft. On 15 January the unit lost two aircraft and crews to the latter. On the same day two Wellingtons took off from Pershore on a morning navigation exercise and collided in scattered cloud at 2,000ft, killing all ten crew members.

Over the time he was on duty at Pershore, some 123 days, Brian flew 150 times and clocked up a further 171 flying hours. The exercises were much as before but with more Gee flights and many more practise bombing runs. In March there were a further two accidents, one seeing another aircraft and crew written off.

They may not have been on operations but this was hardly relaxing. Brian would have watched the novice crew arrive and over the months saw countless crews join their squadrons and, had he bothered, he would have seen their names on the casualty lists published every week by the Air Ministry. By then he well understood their prospects.

Brian had a good long period of leave over Christmas 1942 but for good reason he also had a few days off earlier in December. On Tuesday, 8th, Brian's parents, Bernard and Emily, went to London to meet up with their son, who was presented with his Distinguished Flying Cross by King George VI at Buckingham Palace. They must have hoped that he would now stay in training. Surely he had done enough? Their pride in witnessing his investiture must have been tempered by Brian's news. He had decided to return to operations.

Towards the end of his time at Pershore, Brian had a chat with his old navigator, Ken Dodwell. He expressed to his old friend a sentiment that must have affected many screened aircrew who found themselves frustrated with the unrewarding risk of an OTU. He told him that he had to get out of training 'before they kill me'. Once the decision was made he did have one very important job to do while at Pershore. He was to be posted to 83 Squadron, part of No. 8 Pathfinder Group, and would be flying Lancasters, the new four-engine heavy bomber. He was mixing with many experienced crewmen who like him were ready to volunteer for another operational tour. So Brian had a great opportunity to select and put together his next crew without going through the well-proven, but nonetheless random, crewing up process.

Chapter 13

Lancasters

O nly loyal Stirling and Halifax crews could question which was the best British heavy bomber in the Second World War. They could squabble over second position but there would be little dispute that the best was the Avro Lancaster. Brian's first bomber, the Wellington, was the product of a peacetime Air Ministry specification in 1932, whereas the requirement for the Lancaster was driven by an essential wartime need for a four-engine, long-range bomber capable of delivering a significantly greater bomb load. The Wellington went through a long design phase, a number of redesigns and improvements both before and after the first production versions were made. From that original specification in 1932, it wasn't until 1936 that the first production Wellington was produced and it did not enter service with the Royal Air Force until 1938, six years later.

The Lancaster's demand-led development was, in comparison, rapid. Its origin was the Avro Manchester, produced in 1939 following Air Ministry specification P.13/36 for a twin-engine medium bomber raised in 1935. The project was headed by Avro's Chief Designer Roy Chadwick and development progressed slowly, with prototype testing being carried out through 1938 and 1939. The Manchester had serious problems, particularly the reliability of its Rolls-Royce Vulture engines. It was not ready for production or service but remarkably the Air Ministry confirmed orders to a maximum of 1,200. It suggested the confidence that the Air Ministry had in Avro but in reality it demonstrated how desperate Bomber Command was to find a new heavy bomber, quickly. Over the winter of 1939–40 testing continued both at Avro and at RAF Boscombe Down with constant modifications being made until November 1940, when the first five Manchesters were collected by their crews from 207 Squadron at RAF Waddington.

August 1940. A smiling Brian at the recruiting centre in Blackpool a month after his sixteenth birthday.

No. 4 Initial Training Wing Paignton. How many times did they look at that face and question his age?

Above: Inset: Brian's father, Bernard Slade, in the 17th Lancers in 1917. Main photograph: as a Private in the RASC at the wheel of his 4-litre Vauxhall '25' bhp D Type staff car. The start of his love for big flashy cars.

Left: No. 16 Elementary Flying Training School Derby. Brian with one of his instructors.

All: Brian in his one piece Sidcot Suit invented by the remarkable Australian Sidney Cotton, aerial photographer pioneer, businessman, adventurer, gun runner and part time spy.

Above: No. 16 Course, 12 Operational Training Unit, Chipping Warden. Brian, middle row second on the left. Back row third from right is Sergeant Bibby who Brian flew with and who crashed on a night flying exercise killing his screened instructor Sergeant Leighton.

Below: RAF Marham, Spring 1942 'My Crew'. *Back Row:* Jack Reynolds, Ken Swann and John Burbidge. *Front Row:* Sam Lowry, Brian Slade and Ken Dodwell,

Above: RAF Marham. 'The two gunners' Sam Lowry left and Ken Swann right.

Below: RAF Marham. Brian with John Burbidge left and Jack Reynolds right.

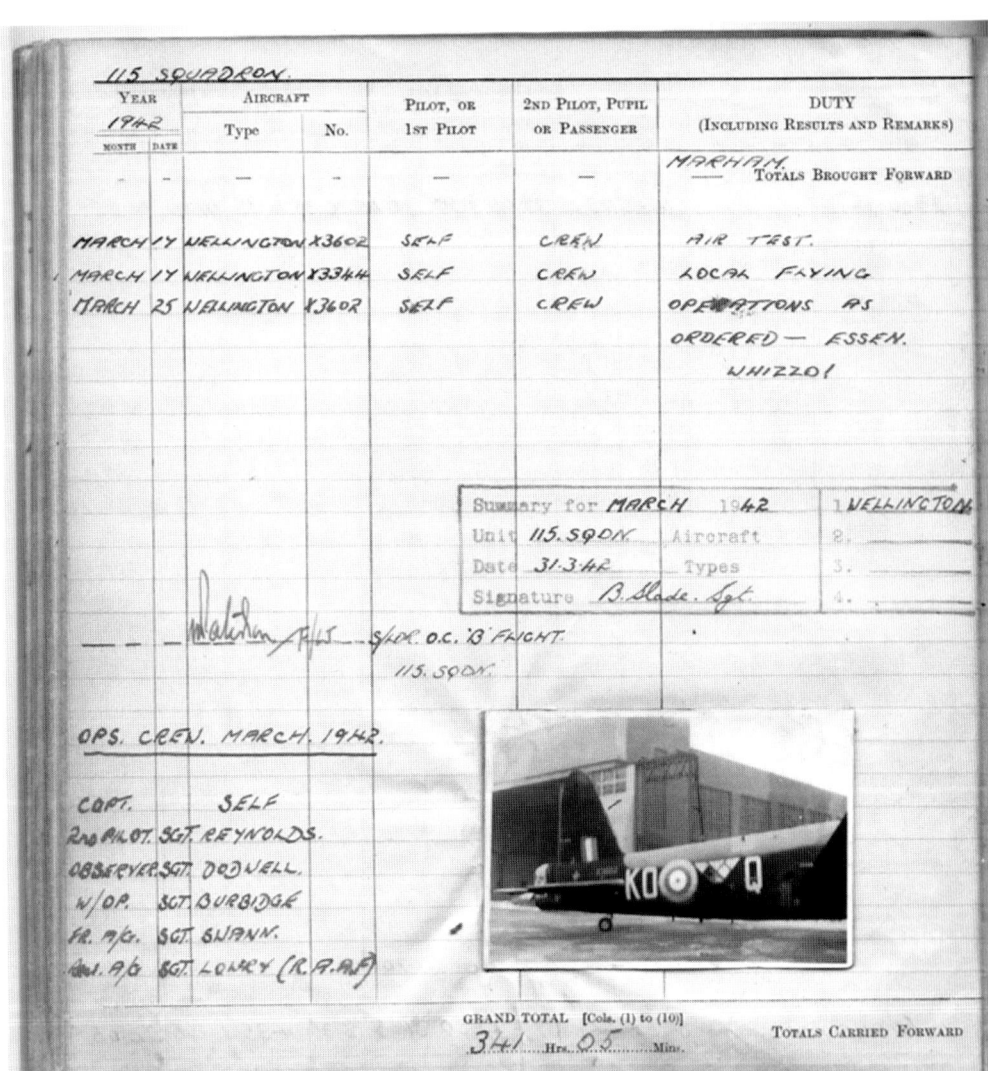

115 SQUADRON.

YEAR 1942		AIRCRAFT		PILOT, OR	2ND PILOT, PUPIL	DUTY
MONTH	DATE	Type	No.	1ST PILOT	OR PASSENGER	(INCLUDING RESULTS AND REMARKS)
—	—	—	—	—	—	MARKHAM.
						—— TOTALS BROUGHT FORWARD
MARCH	14	WELLINGTON	X3602	SELF	CREW	AIR TEST.
MARCH	14	WELLINGTON	X3344	SELF	CREW	LOCAL FLYING
MARCH	25	WELLINGTON	X3602	SELF	CREW	OPERATIONS AS
						ORDERED — ESSEN.
						WHIZZO!

Summary for MARCH 1942   1 WELLINGTON
Unit 115.SQDN   Aircraft   2.
Date 31·3·42   Types   3.
Signature B.Slade. Sgt.   4.

———— F/LT S/LDR. O.C. 'B' FLIGHT.
115. SQDN.

OPS. CREW. MARCH. 1942.

CAPT.   SELF
2nd PILOT. SGT. REYNOLDS.
OBSERVER. SGT. ORDWELL.
W/OP. SGT. BURBIDGE
FR. m/c. SGT. SWANN.
Rear. A/G SGT. LOWRY (R.A.A.F)

GRAND TOTAL [Cols. (1) to (10)]
341 Hrs. 05 Mins.

TOTALS CARRIED FORWARD

Extract from Brian's logbook with photograph of Wellington X3602 'Q' for Queenie – one of their regulars. He seems to have enjoyed that trip to Essen.

YEAR 1942		AIRCRAFT		PILOT, OR 1ST PILOT	2ND PILOT, PUPIL OR PASSENGER	DUTY (INCLUDING RESULTS AND REMARKS)
MONTH	DATE	Type	No.			
–	–	—	–	—	—	MARHAM. TOTALS BROUGHT FORWARD
APRIL	2	WELLINGTON	X3602	SELF	CREW	AIR TEST
APRIL	2	WELLINGTON	X3602	SELF	CREW	OPERATIONS AS ORDERED- POISSY (PARIS) - MATFORD LORRY & CAR WORKS - 3 DIRECT HITS!
APRIL	5	WELLINGTON	X3601	SELF	CREW	LOCAL FLYING.
APRIL	5	WELLINGTON	X3602	SELF	CREW	OPERATIONS AS ORDERED- COLOGNE - HEAVY, INTENSE, ACCURATE PREDICTED FLAK- VERY SHAKY DO!!!
APRIL	6	WELLINGTON	X3392	SELF	CREW	OPERATIONS AS ORDERED- ESSEN - VERY, NICE HECTIC WELCOME !!!
APRIL	8	WELLINGTON	X3602	SELF	CREW.	AIR TEST.
APRIL	8	WELLINGTON	X3602	SELF	CREW	OPERATIONS - HAMBURG. D.N.C.O. SEVERE ICING o STATIC - RETURNED TO BASE.
APRIL	10	WELLINGTON	X3602	SELF	CREW	OPERATIONS AS ORDERED- ESSEN - USUAL REPORT- BAGS OF EVERYTHING.
APRIL	12	WELLINGTON	X3602	SELF	CREW	OPERATIONS AS ORDERED - ESSEN USUAL SHOW.

GRAND TOTAL [Cols. (1) to (10)]

372 Hrs. 35 Mins.

TOTALS CARRIED FORWARD

115. SQUADRON.

An extract from Brian's logbook showing a busy ten days in April 1942. Up to that point, April 1942 was to be the busiest month of the war for Bomber Command with over 3,750 sorties.

Above left: 'Me at the controls'. A boy in the pilots seat of a Wellington.

Above right: Taken soon after his promotion to Pilot Officer on 1 May 1942.

Below: Brian and John Burbidge in the garden of RAF Marham's officers' mess, summer 1942.

Above: Brian with his little sister. It was this photograph of Brian and my mother that reduced 'Punch' Thompson to tears.

Below: A press taken photograph after the '1000' raid to Cologne on 30 May 1942 of the Slade and Stanford crews taken in front of Wellington X3662. Extreme left is Ken Dodwell, 2nd left Brian Slade, 3rd left Ken Swann, 5th left John Burbidge, and extreme right is Sam Lowry.

Left: One of the post Cologne press photographs. Brian joking with the WAAF driver. In the truck, Ken Swann on the right, Sam Lowry next to him.

Below: The RAF Marham Ops. Room Board for 2/3 July 1942, the Bremen trip. Note second crew down, Remarks column, 'belly landed Horsham Crew OK'. Photo courtesy of RAF Marham Aviation Heritage Centre.

Right: July 1942 at RAF Marham, after Bremen. Smoking was strictly forbidden near aircraft.

Below: A happy Brian on his Wellington also taken after the Bremen raid. He is wearing his DFC ribbon.

Vickers' Wellington Mk III X3445 'S for Sugar'. Served 115 Squadron well between April 1942 and February 1943.

Above: Vickers' Wellington Mk III X3662 'P' for Peter on dispersal at Marham getting some TLC. The Slade crews favourite for twelve consecutive operations.

Left: A rare Wellington to have completed forty operations.

Three images of X3662. Top: The 'official' photograph courtesy of RAF Marham Aviation Heritage Centre. Bottom: The plastic kit box version.

No. 83 Squadron: 'A Tight Crew'. Top Left: Brian. Top Right: Vernie Lewis (photograph courtesy of Paul Lewis). Bottom Left: Clifford Robinson. Bottom Right: Ron Turner. Centre: Bill Baker (photograph courtesy of Ken Baker). I have no photographs of Niven MacPherson or Harold Allen.

6.   Marking Technique.

(a) 8 OBOE Mosquitoes were to drop red T.I's at 52°50'N. 06°52'E (10 miles N. of track) and green T.I's at 52°35'N. 07°02'E (10 miles S. of track) to mark the rou[t] These markers were to be maintained throughout the passage of the main force.

(b) 8 blind-markers were to drop route markers (red spot fires) at 52°17'E, 12°32'E (8 miles S. of Brandenburg). These were to be maintained by 13 backers-up and 2 recentrers.

(c) Blind-markers were to drop red T.I's on the aiming point if certain of their position.

(d) Backers-up were to aim green T.I's to overshoot estimated centre of red T.I's by 2 seconds or of green T.I's by 3 seconds.

(e) Recentrers were to drop green T.I's using H2S if serviceable; otherwise revert to backers-up.

(f) Main force aircraft were to aim at the estimated centre of all green T.[I] or as directed by the Master Bomber.

(g) Release-point flares were to be dropped by all Y-type aircraft if neces[sa]

7.   Timing of Attack. Zero hour - 2345 hours. Period of Attack 2343-0027 hrs.

Pathfinder Force.

29 blind-markers at (Z - 2)
22 recentrers from (Z + 10) - (Z + 40) - 2 aircraft every 3 minutes.
7 backers-up at (Z + 1)
3   " " " (Z + 2)
27   " " from (Z + 3) - (Z + 39) 1 minute except at times for recentrers
8 OBOE Mosquitoes to drop route markers from 2210-2245 hrs. (one every 5 min.

Main Force.

90 Lancasters - (Z + 2) - (Z + 8)
113 Halifaxes - (Z + 8) - (Z + 15)
127 Stirlings - (Z + 15) - (Z + 23)
107 Lancasters - (Z + 23) - (Z + 29)
113 Halifaxes - (Z + 29) - (Z + 36)
88 Lancasters - (Z + 36) - (Z + 42)
10 Mosquitoes (Support attack) - (Z + 16)

8.   Markers to be Carried.

OBOE Mosquitoes: 2 T.I. red LB + 2 T.I. green LB.

Blind-markers: 29 Lancasters) 2 T.I. red LB + 2 T.I. green LB
                  9 Halifaxes) + 2 T.I. green.

Backers-up:)   29 Lancasters) 2 T.I. green LB + 2 T.I. green
Recentrers:)   15 Halifaxes)

                 15 Halifaxes: 2 T.I. green LB + 2 T.I. green + 1 red
                                  spot fire.

Master bomber: 1 Lancasters: 4 T.I. green.

Bomber Command Night Raid Report: Berlin 23/24 August 1943. One page from an eleven page report showing the complexity of a typical large Pathfinder led operation.

Above: Lancaster Mk III R5626 with other 83 Squadron Lancasters at RAF Wyton. Brian flew in this aircrafts 'sister 'aircraft R 5625 on his first operational sortie with the squadron. Photo courtesy of Corinne Mitchell.

Right: The front page from Ron Turner's Stalag Luft III diary.

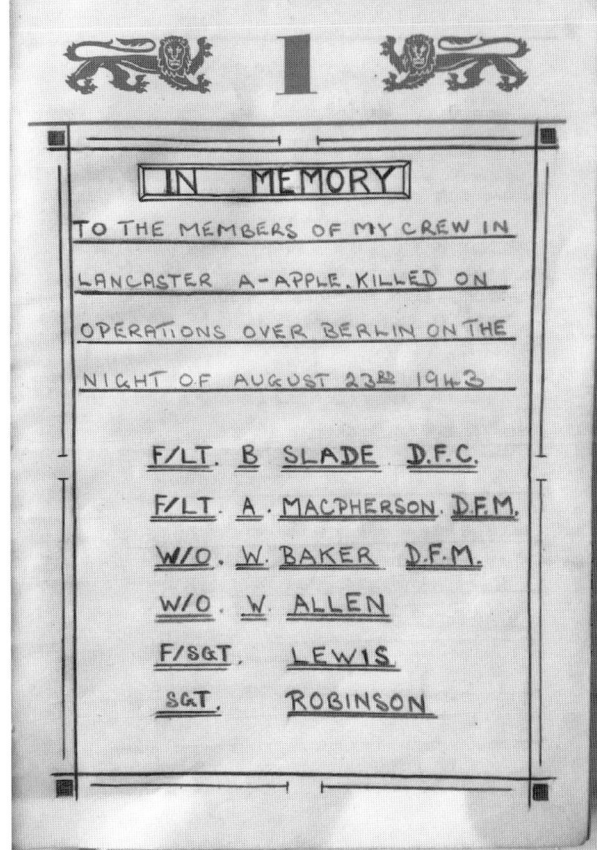

1

IN MEMORY

TO THE MEMBERS OF MY CREW IN LANCASTER A-APPLE, KILLED ON OPERATIONS OVER BERLIN ON THE NIGHT OF AUGUST 23ᴿᴰ 1943

F/LT. B SLADE D.F.C.
F/LT. A. MACPHERSON. D.F.M.
W/O. W. BAKER D.F.M.
W/O. W. ALLEN
F/SGT. LEWIS
SGT. ROBINSON

Above: Sketch of ED984 from Ron Turner's Stalag Luft III diary.

Below: The last page of Ron Turner's logbook with his retrospective entry.

WYTON		**83 SQD.** **P.F.F.**		AUGUST. 1943.	Time carried forward :—	217·34	218·23
Date	Hour	Aircraft Type and No.	Pilot	Duty	Remarks (including results of bombing, gunnery, exercises, etc.)	Day	Night
2·8·43	11·30	LANCASTER. F/LT. SLADE. D.F.C	REAR GUNNER.	N.F.T.		·30	
2·8·43.	23·15	LANCASTER F/LT SLADE. D.F.C	REAR GUNNER.	OPERATIONS = HAMBURG BOMBED:- CUXHAVEN. (ICING AND STORM)			5·25
10·8·43.	17·00	LANCASTER. F/LT. SLADE. D.F.C.	REAR GUNNER.	N.F.T.		·20	
10·8·43.	21·50	LANCASTER F/LT SLADE. D.F.C	REAR GUNNER.	OPERATIONS— NUREMBURG. D.C.O. RETURNED ON TWO ENGINES.			7·50
12·8·43	14·30	LANCASTER F/LT. SLADE. D.F.C.	REAR GUNNER.	N.F.T.		·35	
12·8·43.	21·30	LANCASTER F/LT SLADE. D.F.C	REAR GUNNER.	OPERATIONS — MILAN. DUTY-CARRIED-OUT.			4·45
15·8·43.	20·26	LANCASTER F/LT SLADE. D.F.C.	REAR GUNNER.	OPERATIONS — MILAN DUTY - CARRIED - OUT.			7·30
17·8·43.	20·55	LANCASTER F/LT SLADE. D.F.C.	REAR GUNNER.	OPERATIONS:- PEENEMUNDE RADIO LOCATION EXPERIMENTAL STATION. D.C.O			7·25
23·8·43	20·30	LANCASTER F/LT SLADE. D.F.C.	REAR GUNNER.	OPERATIONS — BERLIN SHOT DOWN BY NIGHT FIGHTER OVER TARGET *Ron was the only one to get out! & a running air craft.*			3·30
					TOTAL TIME ...	218·59	217·48

Of the initial order, only 200 were built and the crews hated them. John Bushby, in his book *Gunners Moon*, describes his feelings when 83 Squadron, then in No. 5 Group, were converting:

> F ... Manchesters! ... All in all, after barely two months experience with our Manchesters to say we had a lack of confidence in them is something of an understatement ... the whole machine was underpowered ... the Manchester crews of No. 5 Group were well aware before the first months of 1942 were out that they had a stinker.

Avro must have realised that the Manchester was, as one pilot described it, 'a turkey'. As early as 1939 the diligent and hard-working Chadwick was planning an improved four-engine version and wanted to use the Merlin engine. The Rolls-Royce Merlin was already proven and in July 1940 the Air Ministry agreed that Chadwick could develop the 'new Manchester' and use the engine. Chadwick modified the good Manchester airframe, which had a large bomb bay capable of carrying an excellent bomb load, and by January 1941 the first four-engine, 102ft wingspan prototype took to the air. The second improved prototype flew in May and tweaked the higher-output Merlin XX engine until it was finally approved, with the first production aircraft flying at the end of October. The original Manchester order was transferred to the renamed Lancaster and the first were delivered to 44 Squadron on Christmas Eve 1941. A gestation period of under eighteen months and, as aviation author Jim Winchester wrote: 'One of the few warplanes in history to be "right" from the start.'

Chadwick's modifications of the Manchester combined with the use of four Merlin engines produced a bomber that would become the workhorse of Bomber Command from the end of 1942 to the conclusion of the war. Eleven Victoria Crosses were won by Lancaster crew members, more than any other aircraft in the Second World War.

In terms of fuselage measurements, it wasn't that much bigger than the Wellington. It was only 5ft longer and 3ft taller. However, in order to hold four rather than two engines, its wings were significantly longer than the Wellington by 16ft at 102ft 6in, but with four engines its top speed was 25mph faster and it could now carry 14,000lb of bombs (against the Wellington Mk III's 4,000lb) and had a longer range of 2,530 miles. The Wellington, fully laden weighed 14 tons, the Lancaster more than 25 tons.

In total 7,377 were made by a variety of manufacturers and in a number of locations, including 3,673 by Avro (A.V. Roe) in their three factories, 1,080 by Metropolitan Vickers in their Trafford Park, Manchester factory, 535 by Vickers Armstrong and 430 by Victory Aircraft in Canada. By the autumn of 1943, about 160 Lancasters were being produced every month, more than five a day.

Once large-scale production was established it took only about ten weeks to build a Lancaster each one taking about 70,000 man hours. Early in the war a nationwide campaign to donate aluminum cooking utensils succeeded in involving every home in the country in aircraft production. Initially successful, it soon became clear that this would never provide enough. It was estimated that it would take 11 million saucepans to build a Lancaster.

Of the 7,377 made, nearly 60 per cent were destroyed during the war and only seventeen examples survive, with just two still flying; one in the UK with the Battle of Britain Memorial Flight and one with the Canadian Warplane Heritage Museum in Hamilton, Ontario.

The attraction for Harris and those who planned his operations was the Lancaster's ability to deliver a significantly heavier bomb load from a higher and supposedly safer altitude. The Stirling, although having a longer fuselage to the Lancaster, had shorter, thicker wings, which meant when laden it could not operate over 16,000ft, increasing its vulnerability. The Halifax carried a good bomb load but when fully bombed up had limited range and also struggled with higher altitudes. The Lancaster could operate comfortably over 20,000ft with 14,000lb of bombs and to a range of over 2,500 miles. It also had a bomb bay that was easily adaptable to a range of ordnance. Harris believed it was 'immensely superior' to the others and published statistics to show that for every 100 tons of bombs delivered it cost the lives of nine Lancaster aircrew, but the Halifax and the Wellington were more than twice as expensive. Looked at a different way, every Wellington lost delivered only 21 tons of bombs, while each Lancaster lost delivered more than 68 tons. In other words, it was more than three times more efficient. These are examples of the inhuman and calculating statistics required of the bombing strategist, but based on them it was no wonder that Harris wanted more and more of Chadwick's creation.

The secret of the large bomb load capacity was the unobstructed 33ft bomb bay (23ft for the Wellington) which could hold various combinations of the variety of bombs that were becoming available. The bomb bay extended so far forward that the front two rows of bombs were directly under the crew compartment. High-explosive bombs of 250 and 500lb were the mainstay of Bomber Command for the first two years of the war but as Harris's tactics developed the requirement for incendiaries increased both for target marking and their destructive capacity. In addition, the early bombs had a low 'weight of explosive/weight of casing' ratio and so bombs with a higher proportion of explosive were produced. Bombs no longer needed to be aerodynamic and the larger HE bombs became simple barrel-shaped containers of explosive. Fuzes also became more sophisticated and more varied. The ability to delay the explosion rather than explode on impact enabled bombs to penetrate before exploding.

The small bomb container, which was often part of Brian's Wellington load, was also available on the Lancaster. It was larger but again a preloaded, open-bottomed container, with 4lb incendiaries, released electrically by the bomb aimer.

Specific 'menus' of bomb loads became standardised and often given code names. For instance, a load for incendiary area bombing, subtly code-named 'Arson', was fourteen SBCs containing no fewer than 3,304 × 4lb incendiaries. A Wellington's maximum incendiary load was 486. A load code-named 'Usual' for combination blast and incendiary bombing contained one 4,000lb HC ('cookie') bomb with an impact fuze and twelve SBCs with 2,832 incendiaries. This load was favoured by the Pathfinders, where the cookie was often replaced by a coloured variant, the 'Pink Pansie' or 'Red Spot Fire', which Brian and 115 Squadron tested at Marham.

Later in 1943 and in 1944, modifications to the bomb bay doors were made in order to hold the very large 'Blockbuster' bombs that were being produced. Bombs weighing 8,000, 12,000, and 22,000lb were all used and delivered by Lancasters before the end of the war.

Brian would have been aware of the evolution of the Lancaster. When he started flying training in 1941 the Lancaster was being developed and tested. I imagine that there was much discussion in the crew rooms and messes about this new aircraft. There may have been some scepticism at first that it was being based on the Manchester, an aircraft with a poor record for reliability and not hugely popular with the crews. When Brian started his first operations in late 1941 he was flying his Wellington alongside Manchesters, indeed the Essen raid on 25 March 1942 included twenty Manchesters, five of which were lost. Those statistics may not have given much confidence in the new Lancaster but as it went out to the squadrons the good news travelled fast. On 8 April over Hamburg and 10 April over Essen, Brian, in his Wellington, flew with the new Lancasters on the same operation for the first time. On those two operations, one Manchester was lost each night, but no Lancasters.

The engines that powered the Lancaster are themselves stars of the automotive world. The V12 27-litre Merlin engine developed by the Rolls-Royce company first appeared in 1932 in the ill-fated Fairey Battle and was continually improved, resulting in 1935 in an uprated version called the Merlin XX. This powered the Hurricane and the Spitfire at the outbreak of war and throughout the Battle of Britain. The early production engines generated 1,030hp but the XX version produced 1,480hp. Not surprisingly, the four-engine Lancaster used more Merlin XX engines than any other aircraft, with the Mosquito twin-engine bomber next, and it was also used in the previously underpowered P-51 Mustang fighter by the USAAF. Nearly 170,000 were made, including 55,000 in the US under licence by Packard. The Lancaster that Brian was to fly most was ED984, a Mk III powered by four Merlin 28s, which were Packard-built.

The engine's inception was at the hands of Sir Henry Royce, one of the founders of Rolls-Royce, who had been asked in the late 1920s to collaborate with the British aircraft manufacturer Supermarine and develop an engine to help it win the Schneider Trophy, at that time the premier international competition for fast, single-engine seaplanes. R.J. (Reg) Mitchell, Supermarine's chief designer, wanted to replace the currently used Napier engines, even though Britain had won the 1927 race with an aircraft powered by a Napier Lion engine. Sir Henry proposed a supercharged V-12 and the Supermarine S6s powered by this new engine piloted by Flight Lieutenant Richard Waghorn won the race in 1929 at a speed of 328.63mph. That engine, initially named the 'R' type, went on to become the Merlin. At that point, following the stock market crash, the Air Ministry, directed by the Labour government, withdrew support funding for the Schneider Trophy, the gap filled with the private money of Lady Lucy Houston, who ironically was an extreme right-winger and would become an admirer of Hitler. It has been said that ten years of research and development was crammed into two years because of the desire to win the trophy, which Great Britain and Supermarine did in the last three runnings of the race in 1927, 1929 and 1931.

By 1932, as a direct result of this research, the first Merlin engine was produced. Reg Mitchell went on to design the Spitfire fighter and, of course, chose the Merlin as its power plant. By the mid-1930s, Rolls-Royce was aware it had a winner and established production lines in a number of factories. Initially its facilities in Derby and Crewe met the demand but by the outbreak of war, new 'shadow' factories were built in Glasgow and by the Ford Motor Company in Manchester, in production by 1941 and 1943 respectively. By using a novel lightweight alloy and the new supercharging technology, Rolls-Royce had produced a remarkably powerful and light engine that was fitted to five of the most successful aircraft of the war – Spitfire, Hurricane, Lancaster, Mosquito and P-51 – and various versions of it also powered a number of marques of the Fairey Battle, and the Bristol Beaufighter, Armstrong Whitworth Whitley, Boulton Paul Defiant, some Wellington Mk IIs and, of course, the other stalwart four-engine bomber, the Halifax and many more.

Predictably, by 1943 demand was huge. At its maximum production, Glasgow was making 400 engines a month and Manchester a staggering 200 per week.

Throughout the Lancaster's development the news that it was powered by the Merlin, that it had the new Nash and Thompson turrets and the newest navigation devices, and more critically that it had a huge bomb load, all indicated that this aircraft was something special. It did not take long for the Lancaster's reputation to grow and it became *the* aircraft that bomber pilots wanted to fly.

The crew entered a Lancaster through a door towards the rear of the fuselage on the starboard side by a metal ladder pulled up and stored inside. At this point there is almost enough space to stand up as you are behind the back of the bomb bay and the mid-upper turret but in front of the tailplane spars that cross the fuselage. Just inside the door to the left the rear gunner would hang his parachute. He had the same issue as the Wellington rear gunner in that there was no room for his parachute in the turret and if needed he had to reach out to get it. His advantage was that in the event of needing to bale out he was close to the rear door, the best exit to jump from. He had the same as the uprated Wellington rear turret with 4 × Browning .303 machine guns but with storage for 2,500 belted rounds per gun and stored in long tracks that extended up the fuselage on both sides. This spread the weight of the heavy 'ball' ammunition across the aircraft's centre of gravity rather than have it all near the tail.

As the crew turned right, the tail gunner turned left. For once a left turn in an aircraft that none of us would have liked to take. He would sit on and then swing his legs over the tail spar, then slide down the raised platform that covered the spar until his legs could fall into the base of the turret and he dropped onto the small padded seat. He could then slide the two doors together behind him, which when secured prevented him from falling out when the turret was rotated. It is a brutally cramped workspace sitting among a web of metalwork in a freezing Perspex bubble distant from the rest of his crew and with a parachute on the other side of the door. Once he had plugged in his heated suit and put on his leather helmet and oxygen mask, other than the intercom he was alone for up to seven or eight hours. This desire for clear all-round vision led to an obsessive cleaning of the Perspex to remove distracting specs, condensation or ice. As we know, some removed the centre Perspex section entirely. The intercom could be their lifeline and many skippers returned if that became unserviceable.

As with all sentries, staying awake was fundamental and few skippers would tolerate a 'sleeper' on their crew. Many found the levels of concentration easy – a blend of instinct, self-preservation and aggression; some were terrified from start to finish and some needed help to stay awake using caffeine or wakey-wakey pills. Smoking was not allowed but tolerated by some skippers. For rear gunners it was dangerous – cupped gloved hands shielding the red glow from the unseen night fighter pilot's eagle eyes. It was a long lonely, cold and frightening shift.

From the door and looking to the right you see the obstacle course the rest of the crew would have to negotiate to get to their positions. Immediately inside the door towards the front are two important gadgets. On the port side is the flare chute, which not only dropped flares but also window and pamphlets when required. Opposite is the gyroscopic distant reading compass situated here to avoid the influence of four large lumps of iron on the wings and connected to a display in front of the pilot on top of his cockpit displays.

The fuselage is covered in alclad, a light aluminium alloy sheet, which is riveted to the framework. The alclad skin, while thicker than the linen skin of the Wellington, is only just over 1.5mm thick, and provided little protection from the elements or for its fragile crew in the face of machine gun, cannon and flak shrapnel. It was, though, a significantly more sophisticated aircraft. For instance, unlike the Wellington, the Lancaster had independent hydraulic systems, which meant if one system was damaged much of the other systems kept operating.

The stressed-skin monocoque construction had fifty-one frames or formers, with many apertures providing conduits for the multitude of wires, cables and control rods; the working sinews of this great beast. Within a few steps you reach the back of the bomb bay, in which is a small door and two circular windows through which you see the inside of the bomb bay.

As with the Wellington someone, usually the wireless operator, would shine a torch through the small windows to ensure that all the bombs had released successfully and in extremis, though a number of small inspection panels in the bomb bay roof could encourage them to drop. The roof of the bomb bay then provides a platform, at the front edge of which is the first lateral wing spar, but before you get there you must negotiate the mid-upper gunners turret. The workings of the turret including the gunner's seat and the bags for collecting the spent .303 cases hang down into this part of the fuselage, which makes access even harder.

In Chadwick's original design there was a ventral turret, underneath the fuselage and behind the bomb bay, which was scrapped in order to increase the payload. This omission made the aircraft defenceless from attack underneath, a weakness that would be exploited ruthlessly by the German night fighters. Having avoided the mid-upper gunner and scrambled onto the roof of the bomb bay, you then have two obstacles, firstly the flap jack and then the first lateral wing spar, before arriving in the centre section. This had a rest bed in early Lancasters but housed radar equipment in later marks. The next hurdle was a bulkhead over the front and largest wing spar through which you could swing your legs to reach the navigator's and radio operators' area. On one side of this gap above the wing spar is the main hydraulic reservoir, which restricted the opening even further.

The wireless operator, having dropped off the boxed pigeon in its fitted rack, would head to his padded bench seat, which faced forward with his back against the forward edge of the wing spar. He had a small window on the port side that looked out at the leading edge of the wing and directly at the exhausts of the port inner engine – but at least it was a window. On the desk in front of him was his Morse key and above were the range of radios and equipment, including the R.115 radio receiver, the T.1154 radio transmitter, the fishpond indicator screen (for detecting night fighters), amplifiers for the intercom and crew radio. Above him was the astrodome for taking sextant shots and behind him was a hole through which he could fire a very pistol if signalling was required.

In front of his position a wooden bulkhead separated him from the navigator's map desk, also on the port side. There was a pull-out seat for the navigator but when sitting he restricted access for anyone, frequently the flight engineer, to get to the rear of the aircraft. Above his map table was a range of instruments including the air position indicator, the Gee direction-finder unit and receiver unit, the H2S radar (of which much more later) indicator unit and receiver/controller unit, air and ground position indicators, various power units and an instrument panel with many of the pilot's controls duplicated including altitude and air speed indicators. The large and distinctive bulge on the underside of the fuselage housed the H2S radar itself. On the starboard side behind his seat was the drift recorder and above him was the back of the large Perspex-panelled cockpit, which provided plenty of daytime light but required him to draw a curtain between himself and the pilot before he used a small flexible lamp on his desk. In front of him was the pilot.

The single pilot's seat is high, with a screen of armour plate behind his back and head, surrounded by the large Perspex panelled cockpit which provides excellent vision when airborne. To the port side (his left) he can see the entire upper surface of the wing, its control surfaces and both engines. The port inner engine exhausts are only about 10ft to his left and the tips of the 13ft-diameter propellers are within 5ft of his side-opening window. That window was important as the main windscreen had no wipers and in bad weather the pilot would often have to lean out for taxiing, with that propeller a few feet away. To the starboard side his vision was less good but he could still see the control surfaces and engines of the starboard wing. Taxiing though, could be tricky. With his head up the pilot could not see straight ahead and many pilots would 'weave' the aircraft by revving starboard and then port engines, enabling both the pilot and the flight engineer to look forward out of their side windows. The trickiest taxiing was manoeuvring around the peri tracks from dispersal to the main runway in a queue of other aircraft in the dark. A wheel on the soft grass with minutes to go to your take-off time and with a dozen Lancasters behind you was not recommended.

In front of the pilot was the typical array of blind flying instruments including air speed indicator, artificial horizon, rate of climb indicator, altimeter and altitude limit switch. On the top left of his control column was the intercom button to enable the pilot to speak to the crew. The direction finder indicator (principally a landing aid) and the compass were set high on the instrument panel. Most of the engine controls were situated centrally or to the pilot's right so as also to be accessible to the flight engineer. The additional engine controls and general sophistication of the Lancaster over the Wellington required the extra pair of hands and expertise of a flight engineer. Like the Wellington, the control surfaces were controlled directly by the pilot; the ailerons by cables, chains and tie-rods to the pilot's control yoke and, the elevator and rudder by metal control rods from the pilot's rudder pedals, all of which ran down the port side of the aircraft. At rest and at normal speeds the control surfaces responded surprisingly easily to the controls but at speed, particularly at take-off and when corkscrewing, more strength was needed to move these control surfaces, with the rudder and elevators more than 50ft from the pilot's pedals.

It was, though, an aircraft that responded to a light touch and this ease of control and responsiveness was the main reason why pilots loved the Lancaster. The Air Transport Auxiliary pilots, many of whom were women, could deliver an unladen Lancaster single-handedly.

The flight engineer had the most uncomfortable ride of all the crew. His folding dicky seat and its flimsy backrest, when he was seated, blocked access forward or back through the aircraft. In front of him were the engine controls such as the four throttles, which were controlled by the pilot but often with his help, particularly at take-off. There were a number of other controls such as four propeller speed controls, starter buttons, and master engine cocks, as well as fuel gauges, that were under the sole control of the flight engineer.

In front of the flight engineer's station was the small starboard side opening, through which the bomb aimer would drop down into his place of work. He would half kneel, half crouch, resting his chest on a padded seat in front of the huge domed window and centrally positioned Mk XIV bombsight with its stabilisation gyro. To the left of the sight itself was the computer cabinet. Sophisticated for its time, the computer was a simple mechanical analogue calculator that had dials for setting wind direction, wind speed, target altitude and the terminal velocity of the bombs, as well as dials giving airspeed and direction. Most of these inputs were pre-set by the bomb aimer before take-off but the wind speed and direction would be calculated and reset just before the bombing run. Air speed and height above target were fed in automatically from the aircraft's instruments. This ability to 'pre-programme' the majority of the settings enabled the bomb aimer to concentrate on locating the target and directing the aircraft on the final bomb run. Having applied the final settings, he would give the minor adjustments to the pilot and release the bombs when the aiming point on the ground was in the right place as seen through the sight.

Below the starboard window was an array of instruments, namely the sixteen bomb selector switches, the stick bombing timing device, which controlled the time between each bomb being released, the bomb dropping selector box, which controlled the order of bomb release so as to retain trim of the aircraft during the bomb run, and the camera switch and photo flare switches. The camera was situated almost underneath the bomb aimer just in front of the bomb bay. It must have been an exhilarating ride for this most forward crew member, travelling at 250mph with a thin piece of Perspex between him and his target and having to concentrate on those final few minutes when outside all hell was being let lose.

Photographs or films of a bomb aimer's view give no idea of the reality. For a start, you're a long way from your target, up to 4 miles. When you next fly, try this little experiment. An average modern-day passenger aircraft climbs at about 2,000ft per minute, it can climb faster but that is a practical rate for passenger comfort. On a clear day try and time the flight from the take-off for about eight minutes. You will then be at about 16,000ft or 3 miles, the average bombing altitude. What can you see out of the window? Can you pick out that factory, that bridge? Bear in mind you will be looking for an aiming point about a mile or two in front of you and … it will be dark and someone's trying to shoot you down.

Later, the H2S navigation radar system was linked to the bombsight, enabling the final bomb release to be made by watching the aiming point on a screen rather than on the ground.

On a Lancaster in nearly all cases the bomb aimer doubled up as the front gunner and so he would have to stand up, step up into the turret and then swing the collapsible gunner's seat into position underneath him. Either side of the seat were the two ammunition boxes containing the 1,000 rounds of .303 ammunition for the two front turret machine guns. This, of course, remained a cold place and again he was issued with the usual gloves, boot liners and the electrically heated suit, the latter of which was not universally popular. It was unreliable and often burnt one part of your body while the rest froze. The main crew compartment was heated by hot air vented directly from the engine exhaust of the port inner engine, which entered the crew compartment by the wireless operator's desk and it was he who controlled the flow of hot air. Complaints about being too cold were always directed at him and most of the time, in an attempt to keep the rest of the crew warm, he sat and roasted in the direct flow of hot air.

There is only one way to find out about a Lancaster and that's to get close to one.

Its vital statistics were greater than the Wellington but the first impressions as you approach a Lancaster are that of a significantly larger and altogether more impressive aircraft. From a distance it seems to sit back on its small tailwheel, its head raised, nose in the air looking ahead to a distant sky. Its back is girder straight, the vast wide wings effortlessly holding up those four huge engines. When you get closer you are soon looking up at its sinister black camouflage paint on the underside, which casts a dark shadow. It's a magnificent hulking beast of a machine. It's undoubted beauty comes when charged with energy from its four Merlins and, as all large aircraft do, it seems to defy gravity in dragging its vast bulk into the air. Having tucked its undercarriage away, it flies flat, looks forward and becomes the most awesome and beautiful flying machine.

From the inside it is very different. A Lancaster has a harsh and utilitarian interior. It's also surprisingly cramped. A large aircraft it may be but internally it is similar to a small private jet, having 5 to 6ft internal headroom and, although 5 to 6ft wide, restricted by a mass of protruding hardware. Whereas a small jet's cabin is about 20ft long, the Lancaster's is 45ft from rear door to pilot's seat, and more than 60ft from bomb aimer to tail gunner. If your executive jet was tipped up you could fall from the cockpit door to the galley without injury. You would slide and glide gently over carpet and smooth seating, risking only a bruise or two. Not so in this functional military vehicle. Its interior is a narrow, dark obstructed tunnel with very little that is not sharp, jagged and hard. Even level and stationary and in daylight it is tough to make your way from entry door to the bomb aimer's space without banging an elbow, knee or head. The young agile crew dressed in flying helmet and flying gear would make it with ease, although having done it myself I was reminded of the ghastliness of potholing. In a dark, spinning, g-force-affected plunging aircraft you would crash and bounce from one metal obstruction to another before finding an exit, if you were lucky. Great to fly but sheer hell to get out of.

There were statistics produced about the survivability of crew in bale-outs and while the Lancaster's loss percentage was good in comparison to the other 'heavies', when it was shot up and being evacuated the Lancaster crews had the lowest survival rate. The statistics vary according to source and which period of the war but the survival rate for Lancaster crews was about 13 per cent, Wellingtons at 17 per cent, Halifax crews a little better at about 22 per cent and Stirling crews even better at about 24 per cent.

The amount of time a crew had to bale out would vary according to the damage but a 20-ton plus bomber with no or reduced power, possibly damaged flying surfaces and on fire, however hard a pilot may try to stay straight and level, loses height very quickly. The bomb aimer had to bale out of the hatch under his station but it was small and bigger men often could not fit with their parachute on. There were reports produced recommending this was enlarged but despite Harris's protestations bombers could not be taken off operations due to aircraft shortages and the retooling required on Lancaster production lines would halt production. If the aircraft was diving it was not unknown for those baling out of the small front hatch to hit the fixed tailwheel.

The navigator, wireless operator and the mid-upper and tail gunners would use the rear hatch but all would need to collect and put on their parachutes before launching themselves on their first parachute jump into the freezing black unknown. Again, it was possible, particularly if the aircraft was not level and steady, that those using that rear hatch would hit the tailplane after their exit. The tail gunner also had the option of having put on his parachute inside the rear turret and with the doors open he could rotate it to one side, lean back and fall out. The flight engineer and the pilot would be last but so often the aircraft was too low or simply disintegrating before they had a chance. Their last-minute scrambles down to the front hatch or through the fuselage and over the wing spars in the dark in a plunging twisting aircraft, often in flames, must have been terrifying.

There were also three push-out emergency panels, one above the pilot and two more further down the fuselage, but only for use after a crash landing or ditching. A type J dinghy was situated on the starboard side of the fuselage and released from both inside or out. Crews practised their dinghy drills regularly, as you will read.

Despite how difficult it was to get out of, crews liked its overall survivability; they felt safer in a Lancaster than any other aircraft. During testing, Avro's test pilot, Sam Brown (whose son, Alan, flew Wellingtons with 214 Squadron) on landing reported excitably to Chadwick: 'It was marvellous – easy to handle and light on the controls.' Roy Dobson, an Avro director, is also supposed to have commented: 'Oh! Boy Oh! Boy, what an aeroplane, what a piece of work.' It is difficult to imagine such a huge and heavy machine being 'light on the controls' but pilots loved it. The Royal Navy pilot Captain Eric 'Winkle' Brown, who was one of the most accomplished wartime test pilots, described the Lancaster as being 'vice-less'.

I have been lucky enough to clamber all over the inside of a Lancaster and sat in every crewman's seat. Cramp and dark, full of obstacles and hazards to head and limbs give one a flavour of what a workplace it was. But I have also stood behind the pilot's seat, listened to the roar of four Merlins start up and been utterly thrilled by the power and the noise as the great beast comes alive, and as so many pilots testified – this incredible machine had life and a soul.

By the start of 1943 its operational reputation was established and I imagine that Brian couldn't wait to get his hands on one. He was now about to fly one of the war's most advanced and sophisticated aircraft and in a role he'd had a taste of with 115 Squadron.

Chapter 14

Pathfinders

The difficulties of navigation, particularly in bad weather or at night, and the consequent challenges to achieve accurate bombing hampered all air forces and most experimented throughout the inter-war years including the RAF, who developed improved navigation techniques, night bombing and target marking when in the Middle East. The concept of elite crews, bombing accurately with highly visible incendiaries or flares before the main force, who would then bomb at or by reference to those marked areas, evolved fast through the 1930s.

The Luftwaffe learned a great deal from its own Condor Legion's bombing operations in the Spanish Civil War in 1937. It continued to experiment in Poland in 1939, again with slightly more accuracy over Rotterdam in May 1940 and devastatingly on Coventry in November 1940. The Coventry attack saw the Luftwaffe use its radio navigation device, which guided thirteen Heinkels to drop marker flares accurately. The main body of about 500 bombers was then able to concentrate its efforts using those flares as aiming points.

The development of radio navigation technology, which became known as the Battle of the Beams, started operationally with the German twin-beam *Knickerbein*, which was a development of the pre-war and commercially available Lorenz blind landing system to assist pilots in landing in poor visibility conditions and used by Bomber Command. This was improved into the more sophisticated *X-Verfahren* system (*X-Gerät* was the on-board apparatus), which guided their elite target-marking aircraft and was used so effectively on the Coventry raid. Both systems were eventually successfully jammed, as was their third iteration, Y-Gerät, in another chapter of the continual technological advancements required to negate those of the enemy.

As you have read, Bomber Command practised daylight, low-level bombing at the start of the war and very soon moved to higher-altitude bombing at night, the poor results of which were well known. Finding and seeing the target was hard enough, hitting it, particularly a small target, was almost impossible. Britain's own beam technology was soon to help Bomber Command.

Brian's first squadron was one of the first to trial and develop the Gee system from August 1941 and was tasked regularly to develop the early target-finding and marking tactics. These early experiments gathered pace and effectiveness, and soon the idea of having a dedicated force to carry out this role was promoted. Harris had experimented with target marking in Iraq with his own squadron and supported the concept but resisted a separate elite force, which he felt would be divisive and have a negative effect on Bomber Command as a whole. This was countered by Sir Henry Tizard, a scientist and advisor to the War Ministry, who said rather loftily: 'I do not think that the formation of a 1st XV at rugby union makes little boys play any less enthusiastically.'

Harris also felt strongly that an elite force would drain talent from the other groups, which risked losing a significant proportion of talented crews. He suggested that each group should have their own Pathfinders but despite his many vociferous and blunt objections he was overruled and the PFF (Pathfinder Force) was created in August 1942. Harris did, though, insist on its new commander, a technically brilliant young Australian officer called Don Bennett. This 33-year-old had a very non-standard background. As a young fighter pilot he transferred from the RAAF to flying boats at RAF Calshot and later to 210 Squadron, where Harris was his squadron commander. The ambitious, resourceful and technically proficient young flier impressed Harris and Bennett described Harris as 'full of fire and dash ... remarkably intelligent and a real man'. While flying long-range flying boats, Bennett, who was often pilot and navigator, championed the need for precision in basic navigation and developed advanced navigation techniques, eventually writing a seminal handbook on the subject. He then left the service and worked as a commercial pilot, clocking up thousands of flying hours, particularly on a number of record-breaking, long-haul flights. In 1940 that expertise was employed as a ferry pilot bringing aircraft from the US and the following year he rejoined the RAFVR, was promoted to wing commander and given command of 77 Squadron, a bomber squadron then with Whitleys, and then 10 Squadron with Halifaxes. He insisted on flying operations himself and on one operation, having been shot down over Norway, evaded capture and returned home via Sweden.

His was a meteoric rise and his appointment to lead the PFF a controversial decision, as Bennett was not only young but an outsider known for being difficult and distant. His crews had the utmost respect for him but little affection. He was opinionated, outspoken, direct and unswervingly confident in his methods, and it was no wonder he fell out regularly with other group commanders (most notably Cochrane of No. 5 Group), who were nearly all twenty years his senior; he though, had more flying hours, more operational experience and more technical knowledge than any of them. He had been an advocate of marking the aiming point for some time but his early pleas also fell on deaf ears. He didn't suffer fools and had a typical colonial's impatient disregard for British bureaucracy. In his autobiography written about ten years after the war ended he declared: 'Personally I think the British Treasury still is one of our greatest enemies.'

The initial Pathfinder Force was made up of five squadrons, one from each of the groups to be based at adjacent airfields within No. 3 Group's area with its headquarters at RAF Wyton. From No. 5 Group came 83 Squadron, where Brian would next be posted. The PFF's creation potentially complicated the chain of command by adding another layer. In practice it worked well with the initial orders from High Wycombe also going to PFF HQ and their subsequent detailed target-marking plans then going direct to the groups and on to stations in time for the individual squadron briefings.

The first few operations of the newly constituted force were unconvincing. Although the founding squadrons carried out intensive training, the early operations were anything but successful. The first saw only about 50 aircraft out of 159 hit the city of Nuremburg, with some bombing Erlangen, 10 miles away. Soon after, on an operation to Saarbrucken, 231 aircraft bombed the town of Saarlautern some 13 miles away, which had been marked in error by the Pathfinder aircraft. An ideal opportunity for its supporters to blame Harris and its detractors to crow. Things had to improve, and slowly but surely they did.

To solve these problems, certain new tactics were developed and refined by necessity, on the job. For instance, on some early operations the Pathfinder force was split into three, with the first group dropping white flares to mark the route in. The second group would then drop coloured markers on the targets and, if accurate, the third group would drop incendiaries onto those markers, the resulting fires lasting long enough for the main force to have a clearly marked target to aim for. While Brian was at 12 OTU, this technique was used on a raid on Bremen on 4 September 1942 and it was a judged a great success, causing considerable damage. At the same time a variation on the 4,000lb cookie was produced with a significant content of red illuminator, which the crews nicknamed the 'Pink Pansy'.

On 10 September both the spilt force and the new cookie techniques were used on Düsseldorf again, to devastating effect. There were continual improvements to the marking hardware and by early 1943 a new target indicator was produced that became the standard until the end of the war. It was a standard 250lb bomb casing but filled with coloured flares, which by barometric fuze could be ejected at various heights or on point detonation. Those on the ground described the airburst version as 'Christmas trees'.

With the increasing success of these operations, PFF soon expanded and in January 1943 was officially named No. 8 Group (PFF). Bennett was able to demand more aircraft and received two more squadrons in March 1943 and a further two, this time Mosquito squadrons, in June. The de Havilland Mosquito was a small, wooden-framed, twin Merlin engine light bomber capable of 375mph, crewed by two, well suited to make both high- and low-altitude bombing runs and able to outrun the Luftwaffe night fighters. The conundrum of balancing altitude against accuracy was being addressed by using lower-level, faster and less vulnerable aircraft doing the initial marking with the higher-altitude main force using improved navigation aids and bombsights to improve accuracy.

In spring 1943 the next generation of radar navigation systems including Oboe and H2S were being introduced and soon the Oboe-equipped Mosquitos would advance the accuracy of initial marking significantly. Another crucial initiative was the concept of the master bomber. Up to that point the crews executed the given plan with little room for initiative to adapt to conditions or events over the target. Unobserved errors were so often compounded by the main force's inability to deviate from the plan. The arrival of the 'master of ceremonies', as they were first known, was a command and control improvement that put a senior pilot, often a squadron leader with considerable operational experience, in charge of the operation from the air above the target. He directed the marking, re-marking and the waves of the main force to the aiming point by reference to those early indicators. All these improvements were making the new No. 8 Group's reputation spread far and wide. It became clear to Bennett and his squadron leaders that a critical part in the effectiveness of their Pathfinders was the quality of their crews. The best crews were being plucked out of their squadrons and the talent spotting extended to the OTUs where the best were being tempted to join the new elite for a second tour.

Chapter 15

Why a Second Tour?

A ir Ministry directives about second tours changed on a number of occasions and were increasingly flexibly interpreted according to the prevailing operational demands. After their rest tour at an OTU, assuming physical and mental fitness, aircrew would be posted but not always back to an operational squadron. Some would stay in the training system like John Burbidge, some posted to the many staff jobs at group level, Ken Dodwell did both, and some back to stations but on non-operational duties. Non-pilot aircrew often retrained in a different trade, including a large number who went on to pilot training like Ken Swann and Sam Lowry. The shortage of crews, however, meant that many had no choice and were posted back to operational squadrons. The exception were those who went to No. 8 Group, the Pathfinder Force, as they were volunteers. When Brian joined in March 1943 the length of second tours in non-Pathfinder squadrons also varied but generally they were a further twenty operational sorties. Pathfinder tours were normally a single continuous tour of forty-five sorties for new aircrew to No. 8 Group but some on their second tour volunteered for what became known as a 'double Pathfinder', or a total of sixty operations, which often then rewarded them with the chance to be permanently screened from future operations. A few volunteered for a third tour. Whatever rules were current, they were treated flexibly, and what squadron or group commander wouldn't in order to keep good experienced crews?

No. 8 Group had an ace recruiter in the extravert Group Captain Hamish Mahaddie, a double tour veteran who with great charm poached countless crews from squadrons and OTUs. He was known as Don Bennett's 'Horse Thief'. I don't know whether Brian was approached by one of the No. 8 Group talent spotters like Mahaddie but he had to volunteer to join what was considered to be the elite of Bomber Command. Why having completed his allotted operations, having experienced the danger, the fear and the exhaustion and with an acceptable reason to move to a training unit, would he volunteer for another thirty and with a unit where the risks appeared higher than other bomber squadrons. What could have influenced him?

The progress of the war perhaps, and there had been a number of significant events in the previous months. In November 1942, General Bernard Montgomery's Eighth Army defeated General Erwin Rommel's Afrika Korps at the second Battle of El Alamein in Egypt. Soon after, the first (of many) joint landings of US and British forces took place in Morocco and Algeria. The Afrika Korps would soon be squeezed from the east and west.

As the Russian winter took hold at the end of 1942, Hitler's push into Russia on the Eastern Front faltered, which gave time for Stalin's armies to regroup and enlarge. The siege of Stalingrad became pivotal and in early 1943 the reinforced defenders of that city pushed out and encircled the German 6th Army, which eventually surrendered. This signalled a reversal of fortunes for the Wehrmacht as Russian forces began to push them back across the Eastern Front.

In the Pacific, US forces battled to retake Guadalcanal, a brutal hurdle to jump as they pushed steadily into the Japanese-held islands of the Western Pacific.

In January 1943 Churchill met Roosevelt in Casablanca and, buoyed by recent successes, agreed three key initiatives. Firstly, there was to be an invasion of Sicily and Italy, secondly a future invasion of mainland Europe and thirdly that the only end to the European war would be an unconditional surrender of Germany. Spring 1943 also saw an increase in the numbers of daylight missions flown by the USAAF from an increasing number of English bases. At that stage the USAAF and Bomber Command operations were led separately but synchronised in terms of targeting. The combination of his night operations and the American's daylight missions reinforced Harris's increasing conviction that strategic bombing could end the war. That optimism filtered down to the groups and the crews.

After El Alamein, in Churchill's 'end of the beginning' speech at the Lord Mayor's Luncheon he also said of Germany:

> Henceforth they will have to face in many theatres of war that superiority in the air which they have so often used without mercy against other(s).

Superiority of the air over continental Europe over the next twelve months would be brutally fought over.

The crews of Bomber Command would have listened with interest to Churchill's cautiously optimistic remarks and the positive messages filtering down from High Wycombe. Did they see that now was the time to press home a slim advantage? I suspect that they were told so and reminded that they remained the only force damaging the German war effort on mainland Europe. In so doing they continued to distract significant Luftwaffe resources both on the ground and in the air, which otherwise would have been redeployed both to the Eastern Front and the south.

There were, for Brian, more personal reasons to get back to operations. As he told Ken Dodwell, he wanted to get out of training. He loved flying but training was unnecessarily dangerous. There will have been other reasons. Brian knew he was a good pilot – he had survived so far, was very experienced, had been decorated and I'm sure he enjoyed the respect and blandishments that came with that reputation. If he was to be sent back on operations he might as well do it with the elite of Bomber Command where lay promotion and better pay. He enjoyed the camaraderie of an operational squadron and wanted to get back to it, to work closely with a new crew and new friends in a squadron and in a mess. Overall I believe that he enjoyed his job. He loved flying, he was good at it, he enjoyed the social life and, regardless of the dangers, he wanted to get back to it.

Having volunteered for a second tour with No. 8 Group, Brian now needed another crew and, having met many at Pershore, he selected five men from 23 OTU.

His navigator was to be Niven Macpherson. Born on the last day of May 1919 in the high-rise tenements of St Leonard's Hill on the southern edge of the Old Town of Edinburgh, Alexander Niven Macpherson was a clerk in Civvy Street and perhaps looking for a more exciting life.

Like so many, he was almost certainly influenced by the situation in Europe, and so volunteered for the RAFVR in February 1939 as a 19-year-old. Seven months later, a day after Poland was invaded, he was mobilised to the Glasgow Training Centre, after which his training started with a posting to RAF Penrhos on the Welsh coast, home to No. 9 Bombing and Gunnery School. It was clear that he wanted to become a pilot but after four further months' training including a course at No. 2 Flying Training School it was decided that this bright Scot's future was in navigation. Combined with his bomb aimer training, he not unreasonably became a navigator/bomb aimer and joined IX Squadron, then flying Wellingtons out of RAF Honington, Suffolk.

Due to the whim of an early First World War commanding officer, his first squadron was generally described with Roman numerals rather than Arabic. IX Squadron was one of the oldest dedicated bomber squadrons and claims to have dropped the first bombs of the war on 4 September 1939. Niven Macpherson completed a tour of operations with IX Squadron and on the night of 28 September 1940, when 109 aircraft flew to various targets in Germany and the Channel ports, his Wellington was returning from Hanau (a German town that was to be virtually destroyed by British bombing in March 1945) when it crashed coming in to land. It's not known whether the aircraft was damaged or simply ran out of fuel but both the pilot, Flight Lieutenant Tony Cox, and his second pilot, Michael Nicholls, were killed, one of the air gunners and Niven Macpherson were injured and for his part in the incident he was awarded the Distinguished Flying Medal. His citation describes, as well as good work on his previous twenty-seven operations, that:

> On one occasion Sergeant MacPherson was involved in a night flying accident and, although himself injured, he showed great courage and presence of mind in helping the surviving members of his crew escape from the burning aircraft. He has displayed coolness and courage in all circumstances.

After another six trips his screened tour started at an air navigation school for three months and then to No. 20 OTU at Lossiemouth, now not so far to see his parents in Glasgow but a long journey to London to receive his DFM from the king on 26 September 1941. For whatever reason, he then did a second tour of five months with No. 23 OTU, where he arrived as a newly commissioned pilot officer and became a bomber leader instructor. It's curious that he did a second OTU tour, and maybe he hadn't fully recovered from his Wellington crash, but it is interesting to note how his transition from bombing and gunnery school through the joint role of navigator/bomb aimer in Wellingtons to solely as navigator reflected the separation of those trades in the four-engine bombers. He was now a highly qualified and experienced navigator with thirty-three operations completed, although he was ring rusty having had more than two years away from an operational squadron. He was 24 when he went to Wyton.

Clifford Robinson was the bomb aimer and the operational virgin of the crew, serving at 23 OTU as a trainee rather than as screened veteran. What was it that impressed Brian and his experienced crew about Clifford? This bright young Canadian was brought up in Michel, a mining town in

British Columbia, by his Canadian father and Scottish mother and educated in Fernie where he did well, earning a place at the University of British Columbia in Vancouver. He was a good sportsman, excelling in athletics and skiing, and joined the OTC as soon as he arrived at university. Like so many young Canadians who joined up, he had a back-country outdoor upbringing that produced so many tough, resourceful young men. Halfway through his second year in March 1942 he joined the flood of Canadians and enlisted in the RCAF. Early on in his training he was identified as a potential pilot and officer, but after his basic training he went to No. 2 Bombing and Gunnery School and then No. 1 Air Observers School in Nova Scotia. As did many thousands of Canadians, Clifford then had the uncomfortable prospect of joining an Atlantic convoy, which sailed from New York in November 1942. After a week at sea, he went to 23 OTU to complete his training as a bomb aimer/air gunner. The 23 OTU was traditionally popular with the Canadian squadrons of No. 6 Group and I suspect Clifford was destined to join one of them but for some reason he was approached by Brian and the rest of the crew and persuaded that his future lay with the Pathfinder Force.

Clifford's father, Peter, like Brian's father, had served in the First World War, but had an altogether more arduous time. Having enlisted in August 1914, only days after war was declared, and after very little training he sailed with the Canadian Expeditionary Force in October and found himself in Ypres with the 2nd Canadian Division in April 1915. On 24 April he took part in what became known as the Battle of St Julien, part of the Second Battle of Ypres, where the Germans first used chlorine gas to support their advance. Robinson senior was injured in the foot, captured and spent the next three and a half years as a prisoner of war in various camps. He was released on Christmas Day 1918 and returned to Canada in March 1919, being discharged a month later. Although his foot healed, his breathing suffered for the rest of his life from the after-effects of the gas. Perhaps another son looking for an alternative to their father's army experiences, Clifford was posted to 83 Squadron the day after his 22nd birthday.

Ronald Frank Weston Turner, known to all as Ron, was born in Leytonstone, east London, in June 1920 and was educated at Leyton Technical College. His father was a milliner and it was thought that Ron would follow his father's footsteps but in June 1939, just a few weeks after his 19th birthday, he volunteered to join the RAF. As was often the case, he spent as much time at home waiting to be called forward as he did on basic training as the pre-war recruiting and training system had no need for urgency. By September 1940 he had completed his basic training and a double dose of trade training at both electrical and wireless school and bombing and gunnery school. His operational training was at Bassingbourn with 11 OTU, from where he was posted in November 1940 to 214 Squadron at Stradishall flying Wellingtons. He completed thirty-one operations as a Wellington tail gunner and then a relatively long spell of nineteen months at 23 OTU, the second half of which he was a gunnery instructor and where he was promoted to pilot officer. After a month at the RAF Cosford Officers' School in September 1942 he was promoted again to flying officer, then returned to 23 OTU, where he met and eventually crewed up with Brian. He would become the squadron gunnery leader in 83 Squadron.

The youngest member of this new crew, other than Brian, was William 'Bill' Charles Baker. When Bill joined the RAF in May 1939 he wasn't quite 17 years and 6 months, and was the eldest of seven children, the youngest being 2-year-old twins. Bill's father, although born in 1900, did get to serve in the last few months of the First World War with the Royal Warwickshire Regiment, after which he followed in his father's footsteps and became a scale maker and brought up his large family in the Lozells area of Birmingham. Still six months short of his 18th birthday, Bill should not have been able to officially start his aircrew training but the RAF seemed to bend the rules and sent him to start his trade training at the Electrical and Wireless School at RAF Digby until the end of the year, when he turned 18 and went on to Bombing and Gunnery School at RAF Jurby on the north-west tip of the Isle of Man. After six weeks he was posted to 13 OTU but until a place on the next course was available he spent a week in Blackpool, writing to his parents: 'We are having a fine time here, almost a holiday in fact. Pity it is only a week.' The delay in starting was almost certainly due to 13 OTU having only formed a few weeks before at RAF Bicester specifically to train crews for Bristol Blenheims. Bill's joint trade training fitted him nicely into the wireless operator's seat, which had the joint role of manning the dorsal gun turret.

Not surprisingly, Bill was posted to 15 Squadron flying Blenheims, which at that time was at RAF Wyton. In June 1940, when Bill joined the squadron, they had not long returned from France, where they had been one of the ill-fated Fairey Battle squadrons of the AASF. At Wyton the squadron was mainly occupied with cross-Channel raids by day and night to disrupt the assembly of invasion barges. On 18 July various Blenheim sorties involving about forty aircraft from different squadrons were tasked to targets in Belgium, Holland and Germany. One, skippered by Flying Officer Mahler with Bill as his wireless operator/air gunner, was to bomb, in daylight, the synthetic oil refinery at Sterkrade Halter, just north of Duisburg. Within 10 miles of crossing the Norfolk coast on the way out the Blenheim was attacked by three Messerschmitt Bf 110s. Mahler turned for home and fought off the fighters but during one attack the inner fuel tanks were set on fire. Mahler dived the aircraft and crash-landed on the beach. Incredibly, the three crew managed to escape unhurt just before the aircraft exploded. Mahler received the DFC and Baker and the navigator, Robert Pavely, received the DFM. Baker also claimed the downing of one of the Bf 110s.

In June 1941, after twenty-five operations with 15 Squadron, Baker was posted to 23 OTU, where he spent more than twenty months, a relatively long OTU tour. He did, though, have a six-week temporary posting at RAF Shipdham in Norfolk in November 1942, just after the USAAF arrived in the UK in the form of the B-24s of 44 Bombardment Group. As a wireless operator instructor at the OTU he would have been training the American aircrew on RAF radio procedures, a requirement should they need to communicate with RAF airfields in an emergency.

One great advantage of his long tour at Pershore was it was only 30 miles south of his home in Birmingham, which enabled him to get home regularly to see his girlfriend, Betty Purslow, who lived in the same street in Lozells. On 5 September 1942 at St Paul's Church, Lozells, 20-year-old Bill and Betty were married. Perhaps he liked Wyton and was happy to return, but at some stage Brian tempted him to get back to operations and join him as his wireless operator. He was 21 years and 3 months old when he was posted from Pershore.

Harold Edward Allen was another very experienced crew member, having completed thirty-four operations on his first tour. His parents were married in Oswestry and would eventually settle there. Then they lived for a while in Crewe, where Harold's father worked on the railways before moving to Birkenhead to work in the world-famous shipyards, which were the dominant local employer. Harold, an only child, was born and brought up in Birkenhead and at the outbreak of war was an apprentice in the shipyards with his father, testing electric meters. He joined up in July 1940, aged 18, and spent the first twelve months being shunted around various recruiting and training centres, including his trade training at a bombing and gunnery school. He ended up at 20 OTU at Lossiemouth, finishing as a wireless operator/air gunner. In August 1941 he was posted to 7 Squadron at RAF Oakington, part of No. 3 Group, just north of Cambridge. No. 7 Squadron flew Stirlings at the time and would become a Pathfinder squadron after Allen left, eventually converting to Lancasters. Having completed his thirty-four Stirling trips as a flight sergeant, he went on his screened tour to 23 OTU, where he met Brian and eventually become his mid-upper gunner. He was 21 years and 7 months old when he joined 83 Squadron and received the expected promotion to warrant officer.

The last member of the Slade crew was already at 83 Squadron. Vernon 'Vernie' Charles Lewis was born and raised in Pembrokeshire, South Wales, by his father Hubert and mother Edith. His father, known as 'Stokey', was a bit of a local celebrity, being the winner of a Victoria Cross in the First World War and presumably, just in case his son forgot his father's celebrity status, he thought that christening him Vernon Charles would act as a permanent reminder.

Stokey served during the First World War as a private with the 11th (Service) Battalion, Welch Regiment. On 22–23 October 1916 at Macukovo on the Salonika Front, Greece, Stokey was part of a raiding party, and as they advanced up a steep, rocky slope they were fired upon and Stokey was twice wounded before reaching the enemy trenches, but refused to be attended to. While clearing the enemy dug-outs, he came across three German soldiers, immediately attacked them single-handed and with butt and bayonet captured all three. Later, during the raiding party's withdrawal, he noticed a wounded comrade and carried him for two hours under shell and rifle fire, bringing him to safety, after which he collapsed. 'Private Lewis showed throughout, a brilliant example of courage, endurance and devotion to duty.' For this he was awarded the Victoria Cross and having received it from King George V at Buckingham Palace, he was sent back to the front, where he could have received a second award by saving the life of his company commander. Despite being gassed, he survived the war and returned to his home town of Milford Haven.

Vernie joined the RAF aged 15 in September 1936, embarking on a four-year course as an apprentice ground flight mechanic at RAF Halton. During that four years he was sent on a number of 'work experience' periods to a variety of stations. He had many short temporary postings to 54 Squadron at Hornchurch, the first just as they received their Spitfires in early 1939 and again in 1941 and early 1942, that squadron by then having taken part in the Battle of Britain. When he volunteered for aircrew training, with that background he was destined to be a flight engineer and his intimate knowledge of Merlin engines led him to a Lancaster squadron. By April 1942 there was a specialist trade course to cater for the new trade of flight engineer but Vernie's technical knowledge from his four-year apprenticeship was significantly greater than a trainee fight engineer would have gained from the six weeks of training. These new flight engineers were also expected to able to stand in as air gunners and accordingly also did that trade course. Very soon that second trade course was scrapped as it was realised that the job of flight engineer on a Lancaster was a full-time and indispensable job. By the spring of 1942, and following a spell at Air Gunnery School, Vernie went to 1654 Conversion Unit at RAF Wigsley, instead of an OTU, then directly to 83 Squadron by late August.

Vernie's regular first tour skipper was Squadron Leader John Hurry DFC, an experienced pilot, and he flew with him on his last operation to Berlin on 27 March. Hurry, having completed his operational tour of sixty-two operations, was awarded the Distinguished Service Order soon afterwards, his citation concluding 'his courage and determination have been most outstanding and praiseworthy'. He retired as a group captain in 1975 and died in June 2015, having lived up to his personal mantra of 'press on regardless'.

Vernie had completed twenty-six operations with 83 Squadron in the Hurry crew and after some leave was put into Brian's crew. He was lucky to get this well thought of flight engineer who knew every nut and bolt of a Lancaster, had so many trips in his logbook and knew Wyton like the back of his hand. Over the next six months Vernie would do much the same as his father and, as you will read, would also be decorated.

Towards the end of March, and after some leave, this very experienced crew were all posted to Wyton, where they met up with Vernie Lewis. Between them they had completed 184 operations, won a DFC and two DFMs and their average age was 21 years and 6 months.

135

Chapter 16

A War of Two Caps

It was a Jekyll and Hyde existence really, and it was funny to just ride around your bike among the fields, and think, well, it's not many hours since we were in another, completely different world. And probably thinking maybe just once or twice about friends who hadn't come back. It was a schizophrenic life really. You had to have two caps, one to enjoy yourself and one to get serious.

Roy MacDonald (as quoted on BBC History site)

Bomber crews had a unique position within the three services, enjoying and enduring an exhausting and demanding cycle of highs and lows. An unpredictable sequence of the pressure and stresses of operations alternating with the safety of days on home soil, whether that be socialising with comrades or on leave with their families. While many fighting men of other services expressed envy and anger at the crew's ability to enjoy regular spells of home normality, few had the emotional extremes of the bomber crews. Half the crews lost did not complete ten operations. It was said that the worst operations were between the fifth and the fifteenth. For the first five you knew little of what was to come, the ignorance of the unknown, and after the fifteenth you were getting to be good, better at keeping out of trouble, perhaps getting luckier but importantly also developing strategies to cope with the stress. But not all could.

In the First World War, symptoms of combat stress, often named 'shell shock', were recognised and victims taken out of combat and treated, albeit basically and often experimentally. Severe shell shock was debilitating and rendered victims unfit for duty, requiring their evacuation and treatment. Although some senior officers suggested that sufferers were malingering, generally there was no official assumption that sufferers were cowards, although a few were treated and punished as such.

In the same conflict the Royal Flying Corps understood and were generally sympathetic of airmen's stress, quoting conditions such as flying stress, aviator's neurasthenia and aeroneurosis. Between the wars the medical community developed their understanding and treatment of stress and associated mental conditions but the RAF did not. Suggestions were made that officers were less susceptible and that their social background and education produced a more robust temperament. Absurdly, this influenced recruiting policy throughout the 1930s. By the start of the Second World War the belief that combat stress was more due to a flaw in character rather than the stress of operations remained but the numbers of medical cases grew steadily in the first years of the war.

The issue for Bomber Command was that an increasing number of aircrew were either refusing to fly or being taken off operational duties at a squadron and station level due to legitimate stress and anxiety. The efficiency of both the crew and the squadron was affected by sufferers and the absences their treatment created. By early 1940 there were an increasing number of these psychiatric casualties and up to that point an airman identified with one of these conditions could be removed from flying duties, treated and in extremis discharged.

Faced with a shortage of crews and an impending invasion, terrified senior RAF officers decided to impose penalties on aircrew who showed signs of stress. It was feared that many would seek a psychiatric assessment as an honourable way out, thus depleting squadrons of desperately needed aircrew. They also thought anxiety was contagious.

As early as the spring of 1940, the term 'lack of moral fibre' (LMF) was used in a set of rules circulated to all commands providing guidance about how to deal with airmen who refused to fly. It was revised on a number of occasions and with loose, non-medical definitions it was interpreted very differently by recipients and ignored by many. This resulted in aircrew's treatment varying wildly between operational stations, complicated by the range of conditions displayed. Some airmen's refusal to fly was simply a defiance of orders but others were genuinely suffering from stress-related disorders. Those making initial decisions about these 'waverers' were often entirely unqualified to do so and when that decision was deferred to medical officers they were in the main dealt with sympathetically and sent away for assessments and treatment. Many medical officers (MOs) refused to use the LMF label.

LMF was not a medical condition but a concoction from senior RAF officers as a way of preventing aircrew finding a way out of operations. Being labelled as LMF often led to loss of rank and privileges, posting to another unit often doing basic menial tasks and eventual discharge in disgrace with no pension.

In 1942, a report entitled 'The Influence of Psychological Disorders in Operational Flying' claimed that the 'harshness' of the policy was keeping those with genuine neurosis on operations, which clearly led to accidents, early returns and excessive sick reporting. It reported: 'The employment of air crew suffering from psychological disorders may conceivably be the cause of much operational inefficiency.' The report was ignored.

Amazingly, the existence of the LMF label was seen as a positive deterrent to aircrew who otherwise would have sought treatment for stress. It was supported by Harris, and one senior and highly decorated officer after the war described it as 'justified in a desperate situation'.

Very rarely were the victims publicly humiliated, and it was certainly not official policy, but the rumours spread and the deterrent nature of LMF became effective. Individuals would rather expose themselves to the dangers of operations than be branded LMF. They learned to live with their fears and hid them as best they could. This must have put aircraft skippers in difficult positions. They could not risk a key member of their crew endangering the aircraft by not being able to do his job but it was a ghastly prospect for any skipper to report a crew mate and often a close friend, causing them to seek help that could result in an assessment, disgrace and discharge ignominy. The answer within crews was to 'keep their spirits up', often through the actions of the skipper and other senior crew members. High morale within squadrons was seen as the way to minimise the stress that crews suffered and many units achieved a low number of assessments. A post-war medical report stated:

> The morale of a squadron was almost always a direct proportion to the quality of leadership shown by the squadron commanders, and the fluctuations in this respect were most remarkable.

The officer who described LMF as 'justified' was Leonard Cheshire VC, 617 Squadron commander, who was highly decorated in wartime and lauded (and lorded) post-war for his charity work. His wartime and post-war reputation has never been tarnished. He was an excellent leader, aided by his perceptive man management, but ruthless over LMF. If a crew member was having problems, he took them under his wing, placing them in his crew until their confidence returned. Affected pilots, however, were posted out immediately. He said: 'There was a worry that one really frightened man could affect others around him.' His approach was not uncommon and those who showed such signs of stress and being unable to fly were simply posted out to non-flying jobs without the disgrace of being branded LMF. Good leadership started with the skipper and early recognition and a sympathetic approach by squadron and station commanders and medical officers kept many cases away from an LMF label. Later in the war the obliquely named 'refresher courses' were established to give stressed aircrew a break.

Because of the range of symptoms and the varied interpretations, statistics about how many suffered from combat stress and became operationally incapable or were branded LMF vary and quite frankly do little to enable us understand the issues for crews. From a contemporary perspective it seems obvious that some crew members will have suffered combat stress but very few, in percentage terms, probably between 0.3 per cent and 1 per cent, were labelled LMF. Post-war research typically looked at the RAF as a whole and included the commands other than Bomber Command and even ground crew, resulting in the bomber aircrew figures being diluted. It is clear that many more non-commissioned officers than officers were sent for assessments. Perhaps this was because station medical officers were commissioned themselves and knew the afflicted more personally, or because officers were expected to have stiffer upper lips, different from their non-commissioned crew mates.

While the crews would have heard of the LMF gossip, for the vast majority I doubt it was a day-to day obsession. John Searby, Brian's future squadron commander, in his book *The Bomber Battle for Berlin* writes: 'Many endured terrible ordeals but in my experience morale was never a problem in Bomber Command and cases of LMF were exceedingly rare.' He goes on to write, '... once in the swim the crew as an entity took care of itself.'

Perhaps an overly optimistic view, but Searby was not only a skilled pilot but also a fastidious squadron commander and most who served with him credit the excellent morale of his squadron directly to his leadership. At Wyton, Searby's approach was supported by Squadron Leader John 'Doc' Macgown, who was No. 8 Group's medical officer in 1943 over the time that Brian's crew were at Wyton. He was a fascinating and inspirational man who, at twice the age of many aircrew, flew operations himself and always had his crew's best interests at heart, dealing with issues including

LMF humanely and sensitively. Importantly, his approach was supported by Bennett, which must have filtered down through the group's chain of command. This resulted in cases of aircrew stress being identified and treated early, which, albeit anecdotally, seems to have led to Pathfinder squadrons having comparatively low numbers of LMF cases.

The debilitating effects of low morale were more extreme in the American crews of the USAAF, due partly to their high loss rate but also the visual impact of seeing in broad daylight other aircraft that they could identify and whose crews they knew being attacked and exploding or spiralling earthwards in slow motion. For Bomber Command, although there may have been empty seats at breakfast, at least at night those explosions were unidentifiable and impersonal.

The full story of LMF is a complex tale of human frailties and misguided and fearful leadership. Its invention is a blot on Bomber Command's reputation and it clearly identified that senior officers knew full well that their aircrews were operating under extreme pressure but were terrified of the consequences and clueless to cope with them. Whether the treatment of the day would have helped is debatable but many were affected for the rest of their lives, as you will read in the last chapter. The only distant reward that crews had to reach for was that they could complete their tours unscathed, so they developed an extraordinary accepted fatalism; there was no way out, they had to fight.

> If you live on the brink of death yourself, it is as if those who have gone have merely caught an earlier train to the same destination, and whatever that destination is, you will certainly be sharing it soon, since you will almost certainly be catching the next one.
>
> F/Lt Denis Hornsey, 76 Squadron, 1943

Miles Trip, a pilot, said:

> So far as I could see, we should go on flying until we were all killed and there wasn't any point in teasing oneself with the prospect of ultimate safety. Having accepted the worst, it was easy to live for the best and for the moment.

This acceptance of the risks and the apparent inevitability of death was often expressed through black humour. Bill Baker, Brian's wireless operator in 83 Squadron, jointly with three others of the same trade wrote a poem that makes light of the injuries and death of one of their number. An extract reads:

> … And then to his wondering comrades
> These brave parting words he did say
> 'Take the morse key out of my larynx
> and the aerial out of my neck
> Remove from my kidneys the tetrode
> There's a lot of good parts in this wreck.
> Take the phone jacks out of my stomach
> And the 'A' coils out of my brain
> Extract from my liver the tone wheels
> And assemble the old set again.
> I'll be riding a cloud in the morning
> With no blasted morse code to cuss'…
>
> Here's health to a dead Wop already
> And to hell with the next one to die.

Some felt they were indestructible. Rear gunner John Wainright said: 'This vague, hard-to-explain feeling of immortality, the confident belief that, whatever was happening to other people, you and your crew mates would survive.'

Maurice Chick, who was a pilot in 83 Squadron and a great friend of Brian's, wrote after the war:

> When the flight crews arrived in the Mess you got an idea from their general behaviour and attitude how long they would last. We would bet among ourselves – 'Oh, he'll make it' or 'He won't make it'. Sitting in a corner writing home was not the sort of thing the average chap did. There were too many things to do to worry about your mother. The young marrieds were the ones who suffered most. We just enjoyed ourselves in our free time. We loved flying. There were sadder times, if a crew didn't return. One night we lost three aeroplanes, 21 people. There was the ritual of moving their kit from the room. Not 24 hours later, or even less, a truck would come through the gates with the new crews to replace those lost.

They would come into the Mess where those who had been on the squadron for a month or two were considered old hands.

I don't think we worried about it at the time. We had a job to do. Our role was flying aeroplanes to do whatever we could for the war effort. Of course, one never got to know people for any length of time. On the Squadron we knew that it was short-lived, that we would move on if we survived to the end of our tour. We sorted out our friends. The loners, the ones who sat writing letters home, these were the ones that didn't seem to last. The ones who enjoyed life, who seemed a bit juvenile at times, survived. My best friend on the Squadron survived with me. There were others that I knew very well who were killed. That was Mess life. Squadron life. It was an odd feeling – I could look back and think I was very hard, that people were hard, but they weren't really. It was a matter of accepting it. This is what happened in war.

Richard Overy,
Bomber Command 1939–1945

This and comments in the ORBs suggest to me that, in 83 Squadron at least, the constant loss of life or the threat of LMF did not have as much effect on aircrew morale as you might imagine. They seemed to be more affected by unsuccessful operations and even more so the lack of operations, particularly when the weather was bad, as will you read. They responded to the influence of good leadership and their spirits were raised by witnessing good results and hearing from their manipulative superiors that their sacrifices were important and appreciated. That would change over the next two years but in the summer of 1943, morale in the majority of Bomber Command squadrons seemed remarkably high. I like Miles Trip's comment 'live for the moment'. The greatest dent to the morale of a squadron when on the ground would more likely have been the mess running out of beer.

Chapter 17

83 Squadron

'Strike to Defend'

24 March 1943 – 24 August 1943

Brian arrived at RAF Wyton on 24 March after a week's leave. Wyton was a small community and its close neighbours Houghton and the larger St Ives were the airfield's nearest villages. The nearby River Ouse meanders across the flat featureless landscape and, usefully, is visible from the air. Wyton is about 21 miles north-west of Cambridge, where Brian and his crew often let off steam. As with Marham, in 1916 there was a circular grass aerodrome for the Royal Flying Corps, which was closed in 1919 and then upgraded in 1935. Having acquired more land, it opened a year later with a longer, hard-surface runway, now with its trademark 'hump' in the middle, four large hangars and the usual ancillary brick buildings including accommodation and administration blocks. In 1942 yet more land was acquired, both to extend the runway on the arrival of the heavies but also to provide more dispersal areas as it had two squadrons from late 1942 as well as being No. 8 Group Headquarters. As with many airfields in the flat lands of the east, in the winter when the cold easterlies blew it could be a chilling, bleak place to work, as those dispersed ground crews would testify.

Like the majority of RFC squadrons, 83 Squadron disbanded in 1919 and reformed in 1936 at RAF Turnhouse in Scotland. In March 1938 it moved to RAF Scampton, initially equipped with Hampdens, and on 3 September 1939, only hours after the declaration of war, it carried out its first operation.

In January 1942 it was one of the first squadrons to be re-equipped with Manchesters, which led to an influx of trainees and an outflow of experienced crews to the few remaining Hampden squadrons. As we know, the Manchester experiment was short-lived and in April the first Lancasters arrived and crews started to convert throughout the month, culminating in the partly converted squadron putting out thirteen Lancasters and six Manchesters in the first thousand-bomber raid to Cologne on 30 May. On 11 August, the squadron took part in a raid on the historic city of Mainz and the following day, at a squadron meeting, they were told of the creation of the Pathfinder Force. Although it was intended to be a voluntary group, 83 Squadron was being asked to volunteer en bloc, which it all did bar a handful of aircrew nearing the end of their tours. Events moved quickly and two days later they had one hell of a party to stay goodbye to Scampton.

The following morning the squadron flew, with hangovers and aircraft packed with their personal kit, in formation to their new station with the ground crews in convoy below, to be part of the newly formed Pathfinder Force, No. 8 Group. RAF Wyton was to become the beating heart of Pathfinder operations.

Brian's arrival at Wyton seven months later was slightly unusual. Typically, pilots and crews attended a course at one of the Heavy Conversion Units to convert from medium bombers such as Wellingtons to heavy bombers like Lancasters. Those courses were flexible in length but aircrew typically completed between ten and forty hours' flying. Harris wanted as many of the new Lancasters to become operational rather than go to the HCUs. He therefore decided that his crews would do their heavy conversion training on Halifaxes and later if they were to go to a Lancaster squadron they would briefly attend a Lancaster Finishing School. Not for those aircrew posted over the winter of 1942–43, however. They were to do their conversion training with their new units and dodged the HCU Halifax experience entirely. Within the first two weeks of his time with 83 Squadron, Brian did twenty hours of training sorties as first pilot with his new crew, five at night and two operations as second pilot/engineer before his first trip as skipper. Only two of his crew had experience with heavies, the rest having come from Wellingtons or Blenheims. They may have been a very experienced crew but as far as flying the most sophisticated aircraft in Bomber Command on some of the most technically difficult operations, this was a very challenging form of learning on the job. The experience of Vernie Lewis's twenty-six Lancaster operations must have been invaluable.

A great surprise to many newcomers to Wyton was the standard of accommodation. There was a large brick-built, ivy-clad officers' mess and most officers had their own rooms. Quite often they could change into their flying gear in their rooms and be taken by bus outside the mess to their dispersal. The sergeants' mess was similar and other ranks all reported that their accommodation was a step up from some of the smaller stations with unheated Nissen huts.

Brian's arrival in March 1943 coincided with what was to become known as the Battle of the Ruhr, the period of Bomber Command's operations between then and the end of July. Although Harris saw Berlin as the ultimate target for his bomber fleet, the devastation of which he believed would break the German spirit and shorten the war, targeting Berlin (a seven-hour round trip) was not possible during the short nights of the spring and early summer. Equally, accuracy remained a problem as, even with the new Pathfinder tactics, navigation was not improving. Technology, however, was and experiments with Oboe were proving effective. Although its range was limited, it covered the industrial city targets of the Ruhr Valley and Cologne. The two issues that made these 'Happy Valley' operations particularly challenging was the regular appearance of industrial smog, which Oboe and target-marking techniques mitigated to a degree, but also, and of more concern to the crews, was the increasing effectiveness of their defences.

The *Kammhuber* line of *Himmelbett* night fighter defences was becoming thicker and more effective to the west of the Ruhr Valley. Better radar, improved command and control and increased numbers of night fighters made the approach to each target more and more perilous. By the middle of 1943 no fewer than 1,000 Krupps-made 88 mm anti-aircraft guns and 1,500 smaller-calibre guns were deployed to defend the valley's main targets. Coupled with the radar-controlled searchlight systems, the defence of this key industrial area was formidable. Luftwaffe night fighters were also becoming more effective.

Night fighters were feared by the crews as there was something more predictable about flak, but these silent brutally effective killers could arrive unseen at any time and any altitude. Their only limitation was the skill of their crews and the weather. Although their tactics would change dramatically over the next few months, as would the aircraft and the weapons they carried, at this stage it was the aircraft of the radar-directed *Himmelbett* boxes that ruled the approach to most targets. The two aircraft almost exclusively used were the Messerschmitt Bf 110 and Junkers Ju 88. Although there were countless marks, versions and variants, they were both light bombers, twin-engine and fast, crewed by two, three or sometimes four depending on their role. As night fighters they bristled with aerials needed to link them to their ground controllers but also to facilitate the *Lichtenstein* radar systems that enabled them to detect their targets. They also had a variety of armaments but mainly a combination of machine guns and cannon, which as you will read were used in a variety of ways. It was the cannon that the Lancaster crews feared most. Whereas a machine gun, like the .303s in the Lancaster turrets, fired a copper/nickel bullet, a cannon, usually of larger-calibre, typically 20mm (nearly three times the diameter), could have an explosive head that would detonate on impact. A bullet was bad enough but if hit centrally by a cannon shell a body simply exploded. On impact within an aircraft, it would shower the interior with shards of hot metal, damaging the working parts of the aircraft and the crew. A direct cannon shell hit on the wing tanks or in a full bomb bay quite often had catastrophic effects. Whereas a bullet tended not to set things on fire, an exploding cannon shell did, as Brian experienced on his way back from Bremen. The ability to get within range of a bomber without detection and the destructive effect of a burst of cannon shells made the night fighter a terrifying adversary.

Before we get back to 83 Squadron's part in the Battle of the Ruhr, it is worth dwelling on the increasingly complex tactics and the advances in equipment that the Pathfinder crews had to deal with. While Bomber Command would be looking to increase bombing accuracy, the crews would have viewed these improvements differently. They wanted to bomb more effectively but also to minimise their own vulnerability, ideally to get in quickly, avoid detection, drop the most effective payload as accurately and destructively as possible, then come home and hopefully not have to go back. Any tactics and 'kit' that would do that, they accepted willingly, however tedious the training.

These tactics were evolving constantly with tweaks and changes throughout the life of the Pathfinder Force from January 1943 to the end of the war. By the time Brian joined, those tactics had evolved into three approaches to target marking.

The first was visual ground marking, often given the code name Newhaven. Sometimes carried out by heavy bombers, it was more often the job of the fast Mosquitos at relatively low altitudes and needed a visual identification of the target and an accurate drop of target indicators (TIs). These could be white, red, yellow or green and were varied in order to stop decoy fires of the appropriate colour being lit on the ground away from the true target. The Mosquitos often had technical assistance in the form of Oboe and later H2S to get them close but they would identify visually and

146

so needed clear conditions both in terms of weather and smoke haze from the ground.

Where visibility was good but the target was not easily identified, the first aircraft over the target area could drop powerful white illumination flares that hung below parachutes and illuminated the target area for the visual markers to identify the aiming point.

As TIs had limited burn time (typically three minutes), they needed to be topped up throughout the bomber stream by further Pathfinder bombers known as backers up or visual centrers. When an operation was coordinated by a master bomber, a number of backers up could be kept circling ready to be deployed when the master bomber needed more TIs, repositioned TIs or even colour changes.

The second approach, code-named Parametta, also used ground marking but more often by aircraft equipped with Oboe or H2S, which not only guided them to the target but also identified it. This was, not surprisingly, known as blind marking and was normally planned when visibility over the target was predicted to be poor but it could be adapted easily if targets could be identified visually. Again both Mosquito or 'heavy' could do the initial marking but bomber crews initially disliked marking by Oboe or H2S as it required a steady run-in to the target, making them more vulnerable. Backing up was done in the same way as a Newhaven op.

The third technique was known as Wanganui, the code word for a sky marking operation, which is described later as Brian was involved in one of the first large-scale applications. These wonderful code words all came from members of Bennett's staff and were based on their home towns, a testament to the Commonwealth flavour of Bomber Command. Some wag also added to the lexicon of code words by naming a blind sky marking operation done by Oboe Mosquitos a musical Wanganui and it stuck.

On any operation, crews were allocated tasks and these all had their own names. First over the target area were the 'finders', often Mosquitos, equipped with TIs or white flares depending on their specific roles. These crews could also be tasked with marking the route into the target both with ground markers and flares. Finders went in early and, depending on conditions, were either Oboe- or H2S-equipped blind markers. The first, were primary blind markers or the visual markers if visibility was good. For some ops it was Pathfinder heavies that took both these roles. The most exacting role was that of the visual markers, which needed positive identification of a target and accurate, visually dropped TIs. The first in, once again, were known as primary visual markers.

147

The next in were those tasked to drop the coloured TIs on the accurately marked aiming points, which were then topped up by the backers up throughout the raid. Some raids had aircraft called re-centrers, which could re-mark the aiming points if the original flares had gone out, normally under control of a master bomber. 'Illuminators' dropped the flares, normally white, to either illuminate the target for visual marking to be carried out or to mark a target for a sky-marking operation.

These roles all required particular skills and were carried out by crews who had proven their abilities. Less-experienced Pathfinder crews would start as 'supporters' with a few ops as main force bombers listening in to any relevant radio transmissions and observing how the operation was managed. The next step up in responsibility were the backers up and then the markers. Visual and blind markers each had a different set of skills dependent on the navigator's abilities and crew's observational skills and, for blind markers, how well they used and interpreted the information from Oboe and HS2. When blind marking and bombing there was no need for an old-fashioned visual bomb aimer as the bombs were often released by the flight engineer or the navigator while watching his H2S screen. Senior squadron officers, in appointing aircraft to roles, took into account crew's experience and skills, and in reading the 83 Squadron ORBs you can see how crews worked their way up the hierarchy of Pathfinder responsibilities. A future squadron commander of 83 Squadron would describe these primary marker crews as 'the creme de la creme of the PFF'. They were also the crews who showed determination to 'press on', often through the early barrage of predicted flak. For them, the pride in a target well marked was the prize.

Churchill said: 'Plans are of little importance but planning is essential.' However competent the crews, a large part of the success of these increasingly complex Pathfinder operations was the detail of the planning, the clarity of the briefing and how well each crew knew precisely their role. However, much could go wrong.

Firstly, so much could change between briefing and the final bomb run. It was often the role of the first Mosquitos to get a message back to HQ if conditions had changed significantly. They may have been able to get messages to the aircraft and change some detail of the raid, and in some circumstances scrap it and recall all aircraft, although that was rare. For instance, as wind speed and direction were critical to bombing accuracy, if the Mosquitos detected changes from those predicted they could pass that on to the main force for the bomb aimers to change the settings on their bombsight computers.

148

Secondly, the enemy had a part to play. It's an old and often quoted military truism that 'No plan survives contact with the enemy', or as Mike Tyson put it more recently, 'Everyone has a plan 'til they get punched in the mouth.' This applied so often to these bombing operations. Thirdly, adverse weather conditions in an age of inaccurate meteorological forecasting added a natural uncertainty that was so often the cause of poor results. Even assuming favourable weather, an early error in marking could throw off the entire raid and an increasing amount of effort on the ground was put into decoying and distracting those first Pathfinder aircraft. Once the bombing run started, it was then down to the initiative of commanders at all levels to make the best of it, and too often the results were not good enough. And so it was a desire to add more command and control of an operation while in progress that led to the introduction of the master bomber, most often a senior pilot, who would circle the target making the appropriate changes to both the Pathfinders and the main force. Pilots would listen in to the Darky frequency on their T1154 radio ideal for the short ranges required around the target. Rapid decisions by alert commanders, or situational awareness as it was known, was a quality required of the best military leaders and particularly master bombers. Just as an artillery observer could adjust fire onto the target, a master bomber, by observing the first markers, could adjust subsequent marking onto the aiming point for the main force to bomb.

We will soon see the commanding officer of 83 Squadron acting as the master bomber on one of the iconic bombing raids of the war.

The bomb loads of each aircraft in 83 Squadron were clearly dictated by the role that aircraft was playing. A standard load for an aircraft bombing in the main force was $1 \times 4,000$lb high capacity cookie and a mix of 1,000 and 500lb medium capacity high-explosive bombs. Main force bombers could also carry LBCs with 4lb incendiaries when ordered. The markers would have TIs of the appropriate colour (white, yellow, red or green) and a cookie, often the coloured variety and possibly some 500 pounders. Those backing up, the same. Those sky marking would have flares and, if backing up as well, the normal mix of TIs and HE bombs. Early warning to the armourers with the role of each aircraft was essential as it took time to prepare and load two, three or even four different loads for one squadron operation.

A lot had changed but Brian would have been excited to be back on operations despite the apparent risks. Over the winter and into the spring of 1943 losses were now averaging 5 per cent a night. When a first tour aircrew flew their twentieth operation they were on borrowed time, and that they knew. They were not aware though, that by the end of 1943, the statistical risk predicted by the Air Ministry earlier that year would come true and that only one in forty crews would survive their second tour – and Brian's was now getting under way.

Bombing had come a long way from 'fly in, drop your bombs and fly home'. Strategic bombing was now highly sophisticated and complex to execute, but when all the variables aligned it was to become extraordinarily effective, to the delight of its planners and practitioners and the terror of its recipients.

Although familiar with Gee, the newer navigational aids like Oboe and particularly H2S would need some getting used to and a great deal of training would be needed by all crews. As all 83 Squadron Lancasters had been fitted with the SBA (standard beam approach), Brian's first three flights were back in his old friend, the Airspeed Oxford, to familiarise himself with the latest development of this landing navigation system, which had only been fitted to a few Wellingtons in 115 Squadron.

On 28 March, Brian climbed into a Lancaster for the first time and, as second pilot to Pilot Officer Cyril Calvert, went local flying, including practise bombing and air firing, and then a day later he completed a night flying test with Calvert again.

Pilot Officer Calvert, from Sussex, had just returned to the squadron with his navigator, Pilot Officer John Ridd, a 31-year-old married man from Essex, where his wife Lilian still lived. Having both volunteered for a second tour, a few days later this experienced double act and a crew of newcomers went on their second trip together to Essen, which saw the squadron suffer its heaviest loss on a single operation. Three crews did not return and Calvert, Ridd and their novice crew was one of them, having been shot down near Monchengladbach, reinforcing the fearsome reputation that Happy Valley's defences enjoyed.

Over the next week Brian took eleven training flights, nine on Lancasters, which included circuits and bumps, cross-country bombing, NFTs and general but intense familiarisation with this new aircraft, some with other pilots as their second pilot including his flight commander, Squadron Leader Hurry, and some as the skipper. On 8 April he flew as flight engineer on his first Lancaster operation with Flight Lieutenant Smith and his crew, to Duisberg. It wasn't a great start as thick cloud prevented them marking the target accurately and the bombing of the main force of 392 aircraft was scattered. Overall nineteen aircraft were lost, some 4.8 per cent, but all 83 Squadron returned safely.

On 10 April, again acting as flight engineer, he flew with Flight Sergeant Sammy Milton on operations to Frankfurt. This was another big raid involving 577 aircraft, 203 of them Lancasters, but it was another very poor result.

They had planned to use another of the new Pathfinder tactics mentioned previously called sky marking, but what did it entail?

In bad weather, specifically low cloud, even though the target may be marked accurately with ground-burst flares, when the main force arrived, sometimes at greater altitude, their view of the markers was often obscured. The Pathfinders developed a system where they would drop coloured flares, typically white, fitted with parachutes that would fall slowly and were very visible as they drifted through and illuminated the cloud, thereby giving an aiming mark for the bombers well above them. This was called sky marking. The application of accurate meteorological data was essential, particularly wind strength and direction. The sky-marking flares were dropped up wind to drift on top of the aiming point when the bulk of the main force was over the target. The early aircraft might bomb upwind of the target and the late aircraft may be downwind but generally the results were good.

When they arrived over Frankfurt, the cloud was thinner than predicted between 8,000 and 10,000ft, so instead of dropping sky markers the leading Pathfinder crews decided to drop ground markers, believing the main force would see them through the thin cloud. They couldn't and the bombing was scattered with no photographs of any targets hit.

All of Brian's training flights were now as captain but on 13 April he flew a Lancaster on operations for the first time as first pilot on one of his longest operational sorties, eight and a half hours to La Spezia in Italy, one of the homes of the Italian navy. This was also the first op with most of his newly created crew, namely Niven Macpherson, Baker, Robinson, Allen and Turner, and until Lewis joined them, Flight Sergeant Maxwell was their flight engineer for six ops. There had been reports that three Italian warships were in the harbour at La Spezia and the ten 83 Squadron aircraft carried 2,000lb armour-piercing bombs each as well as their normal markers. The route from Wyton to Italy took them south overland, avoiding London, then across the Channel towards Cherbourg. They crossed France to the east of Paris, gained altitude to cross the Alps and then descended to cross the broad Po Valley between Turin and Milan. Many crews commented that the moonlit Alps were spectacular. With the coast in sight at Genoa, they would follow it east to La Spezia, 50 miles beyond. That night most of them reported seeing glimpses of the target area but no ships as there was a great deal of smoke from fires in the town and around the docks, and therefore they resorted to bombing the aiming point. There were 211 aircraft involved, of which four were lost and a further three were so damaged and unable to make it back home that they headed south, landed on an Allied airfield in North Africa and after repairs, were later flown home. All 83 Squadron aircraft got back, although three nearly ran out of fuel and one had to land at the nearest airfield, which was Tangmere in Sussex. Although no ships were hit, the operation was deemed a success as considerable damage was caused to the docks. In fact, there were ships in harbour but the deliberate smokescreen and smoke from the early fires had done their job.

The following night Brian took charge of a different Lancaster, R5629, and joined 462 aircraft on an operation to Stuttgart. Although they had taken R5629 out for a daylight NFT in the morning and all seemed OK, an hour after taking off it suffered engine problems, with the port inner engine failing and the port outer engine overheating. Flying on three engines was possible but two on the same wing and having hardly got to the Dutch coast was not worth the risk. Having dropped his cookie and two 1,000-pounders in the Channel, Brian got home, as did all the squadron aircraft. Overall the operation was a reasonable success as the early markers were accurate but twenty-three aircraft were lost – 5 per cent of the force.

In W4955, which they took up for a NFT in the morning, they flew on an operation to Pilsen on 16 April. Pilsen, in Czechoslovakia (now in the western Czech Republic), was another long operation, taking just over eight hours. The specific target was the Skoda factory, which was one of the largest armament production complexes in Europe. Twelve aircraft took off from 83 Squadron and joined a force of 327 aircraft bombing under a full moon. The squadron crews all had target indicators and flares bar the three rookies, including Brian, who had a cookie and two 1,000-pounders. The first crew over was Squadron Leader Shaw, who reported that some of the main force had bombed early, creating fires and obscuring the target. The next crews marked as best they could but the main force did not find the target accurately, with only six aircraft returning with photographs taken within 3 miles of the target.

It was a very bad night for crews as of the 327 aircraft that took off, 36 did not return, 11 per cent of the force. These comprised eighteen Lancasters and eighteen Halifaxes, both with seven crew. A total of 252 aircrew were listed as missing.

Two aircraft from 83 Squadron were among the losses and another three had flak damage from various areas, both on the way out and back.

Pilot Officer McNichol of the Royal Canadian Air Force signalled base at 0411 hours that he had one casualty, only two engines and he was on his way home. He must have been losing height fast but managed to get his crew out, all of whom survived and were taken prisoner, but he was killed when eventually the Lancaster crashed north-east of Paris. Another captain getting his crew to safety but not himself. McNichol and his crew had started on Lancasters when 83 Squadron was at Scampton and after a spell away volunteered for PFF duties and returned to the squadron at Wyton. They were described as 'a most dependable, happy and popular crew ... very keen and well liked for their attitude to ops'.

You may remember that Brian got to know Flight Sergeant Sammy Milton and his crew when he flew with them as second pilot less than a week before, and soon after landing he heard that they also had failed to return. Their Lancaster had been damaged over the target and crashed at Dobrany, about 10 miles south-west of Pilsen. Milton was described as 'an outstanding NCO in the air and on the ground. He and his crews were exceptionally competent – mainly due to Milton's good and sound captaincy.' Milton's wireless operator was a Canadian, Sergeant Al Podolsky, who always wore his pyjamas under his uniform, which brought him luck on their forty-five previous operations. On that night he decided not to, just to see what happened.

The loss of these two popular crews hit the squadron hard, with eight dead and six out of the fight in POW camps.

There was another operation that night to Mannheim involving 271 crews where a further 18 aircraft were lost, making a record Bomber Command loss for one night of 54 aircraft and more than 370 men killed or POWs.

The following day was an ops stand down, with a lecture given to all crew from a submarine captain who had recently returned from duty in the Mediterranean, and in the evening, twenty-four hours after losing two of their most popular crews, they took the most appropriate medicine and threw a squadron party. Brian was back in an experienced operational squadron with like-minded souls who could handle the pressures and the tragedies in the best way possible.

Spezia was clearly bugging Bomber Command as they tasked 178 aircraft, including eight from 83 Squadron, to bomb the Italian port and again with limited success. One aircraft was lost but all the squadron crews got home safely. The next night another raid to Spezia was planned but scrubbed at the briefing. That was a relief as these Italian raids were exhausting and the routes out often took them over various flak hot spots and then attracted the alerted night fighters on the way back. Even with no problems fuel management was tricky but if an engine was damaged or failed the other engines would be asked to work harder and subsequently use more fuel. Equally if fuel was lost though damage to a wing tank they would struggle to get home.

Their next operation was much more successful, with reports suggesting that the Pathfinder aiming point marking was perfect. Their target was the Baltic port town of Stettin (now in Poland), another long flight taking seven hours and twenty minutes. On 20 April the weather was clear and as a coastal target the navigation and target finding was relatively straightforward. This led to some very accurate marking by the Mosquitos, with four 83 Squadron Lancasters following up with markers and GP bombs, concentrating on the dock area. The raid was seen as very successful with about 100 acres in the centre of the town devastated, 13 industrial premises and 380 houses destroyed. Some 586 people were killed.

It was also another tough night for the crews; 339 aircraft took part and 21 did not return, 6.2 per cent.

I have resisted the temptation to swerve too far off Brian's story but he worked with so many remarkable people that it is worth diverting to hear about one Canadian pilot and his crew.

One of the 83 Squadron crews who flew to Stettin that night had a rather longer operation than had been planned. Pilot Officer Charles McDonald's Lancaster was shot up by a Ju 88 night fighter just as it crossed the German border at about midnight. They had been hit by machine gun and cannon fire, which struck the fuselage and the port inner wing tank, causing a fire. The mid-upper gunner had been wounded when a cannon shell shattered his arm. Regardless, McDonald pressed on but, realising he would not reach Stettin, he bombed a secondary target. It soon became clear that their damaged aircraft would not get home but without the bomb load McDonald felt he might make Sweden and made the decision to turn north. Luckily the night was clear and the navigator guided McDonald visually towards Bulltofta Airfield near Malmo. He sent a message at 0114 hours that read 'baling out', as he was concerned the spreading fire would weaken the wing, and ordered the crew to jump. They refused, having confidence that McDonald could get them down but also wanting to avoid a dunking in the cold Baltic. Losing altitude all the time, they ditched just off the coast near Malmo. Later it was confirmed via a Stockholm radio broadcast that the aircraft had managed to ditch close to the shore at Klagshamn, just 10 miles short of Malmo airfield, and all survived as McDonald had skilfully put them down in 3ft of water. They all got out and Sergeant Chis Ford had his arm treated by two local farmers, who also informed the local military authorities. McDonald and the rest of the crew were taken to Klagshamn. They then went through a very gentle interrogation with officers from the Swedish air force and the Swedish army. This included being put into a local hotel and then being taken to a party, where the gentle questioning continued. They then met further members of the Swedish air force, who escorted them by train to Stockholm to meet two RAF officers, both members of the British Legation in Stockholm. The train journey gave the Swedes time for a little more gentle questioning. Having arrived, this rather bizarre episode continued and they were taken to a hotel, given civilian clothes and then met the two officers, namely Group Captain Haycock and Squadron Leader Fleet, and later visited Haycock's flat, where he continued the questioning. After this less than gruelling interrogation process, on 23 April they were escorted to an internment camp. All very civilised.

Their altogether gentlemanly treatment in Sweden was due to the liaison between the Swedish authorities and MI9, a section of the Directorate of Military Intelligence and a department of the War Office principally tasked with supporting the various networks of resistance across Europe and using them to help repatriate downed Allied aircrews.

At that time Germany occupied Denmark and Norway but Sweden maintained its neutrality. Although declaring itself a non-belligerent in the Finnish war against Russia, as many as 8,000 Swedes fought for Finland in that conflict. Sweden's neutrality in terms of their approach to both Allies and Axis was best described as pragmatic as they exercised realpolitik in their dealings with both. Sweden traded with Nazi Germany, particularly iron ore, and allowed German troops to travel through the country to Norway. Sweden did, though, become home for many refugees from Norway, was close with its neighbour Finland, which was co-belligerent with Germany in its mutual hatred of Russia, and by keeping the Allies out of its country, the Swedish government was able to deter Germany from invading it; a complex and fragile neutrality. An additional advantage to the Allies and now to Charles McDonald was their beneficial treatment of downed aircrews.

He and his crew were interned in the camp at Främby, near Fälun some 300km north of Malmo, where the regime was relaxed to say the least, with the aircrew able to come and go as they pleased, many making friends with the locals. Jöran Grandberg, a local resident, remembers well the crew visiting his family's summerhouse at nearby Rostberg and for many years he kept in touch with the crew and their families in Britain and Canada. Several American bomber crews also ended up there, where their pay was transferred and their full wallets made them popular short-term residents.

McDonald's crew stayed in Sweden for about four months and on 16 August they returned to Stockholm for their journey home. Amazingly, there were regular civilian flights throughout the war from Leuchars to Stockholm by BOAC (British Overseas Airways Corporation was created in 1939 and was the forerunner of today's British Airways). These flights were seen as an important gesture of support by the UK for neutral Sweden and were a clandestine conduit between Axis and Allies and often used by MI9. In all, between 1939 and 1945 about 6,000 passengers were moved between the two countries but they were not without danger. On 4 April 1943, just before McDonald's adventure, a Lockheed Lodestar operated by BOAC was shot down and crashed off Skagen, Denmark, killing all seven on board. A variety of aircraft were used but latterly faster Mosquito bombers painted in civilian livery. On 18 August McDonald and his crew were flown back overnight to Leuchars, arriving the following day and debriefed. On 27 September he was back on operations with 83 Squadron.

McDonald was a highly decorated pilot. In March 1943 he was awarded the DFM after thirty-one operations and was described as an inspiration to the squadron. You may recall that on 13 April Brian's first operation as a Lancaster captain was to Spezia and one crew nearly ran out of fuel and landed at Tangmere. That was McDonald, who even though he was running low on fuel, went on to bomb the target and then, using the most economical settings, nursed the aircraft back home. For that he was awarded his first DFC. On 14 November 1943 he was repatriated to Canada but he clearly wasn't ready to stop and so rejoined 83 Squadron in early 1944. The citation for his second DFC sums up this extraordinary man:

> Despite setbacks he has continued to show undiminished keenness to operate with coolness and courage in the air which are worthy of the highest praise. In April 1944 he was shot down into the sea but he rejoined his squadron and on his first sortie was forced to abandon his aircraft by parachute when he sustained a broken ankle. Again he rejoined his squadron in May 1944, when he participated in an attack on a target in France. Flight Lieutenant McDonald circled the target at a very low altitude in the face of persistent fighter opposition.

He displayed superb airmanship in controlling his aircraft
despite the intense blast effect of many exploding bombs.

He served until the end of the war and retired on 8 June 1945.

Following Stettin and the Italian job, on 26 April, Bomber Command
was back to Happy Valley and another mixed result. A total of 561 aircraft
took part and although the Pathfinders, which included fourteen Lancasters
from 83 Squadron, were sure they had marked the targets accurately, the
main force bombed the north-east of the city. It was thought that a large
part of the main force had bombed the areas where false fires had been lit;
an increasingly common tactic by city defences. All the squadron aircraft
were all through early, reported less searchlight activity than normal and
returned safely, although a couple came back with holes. In all, seventeen
aircraft and their crews were lost.

Sky marking was tried again on 30 April when three squadron Lancasters
joined 305 aircraft to bomb Essen. The Mosquitos, using Oboe, sky marked,
with the main force bombing on their white flares with reasonable success,
the Krupps factory being hit once again.

A similar problem with decoy fires arose a few days later on 4 May
when Dortmund was attacked. Fourteen Lancasters from 83 Squadron were
part of the 596 aircraft that formed the largest force assembled since the last
thousand-aircraft operation. The two flight commanders, Squadron Leader
'Wimpy' Wellington of 'B' Flight and Squadron Leader Norman Hildyard
of 'A' Flight, led the squadron's contingent, with eight of them acting
as backers up, loaded with red TIs – some of them the new 'long-burn'
variant, and six bombing with the main force. It seems the Oboe Mosquitos
marked accurately with greens and those were backed up accurately by the
83 Squadron aircraft with their reds. Despite decoy fires, about half the
main force bombed within 3 miles of the aiming point and considerable
damage was done, with 3,359 buildings destroyed or seriously damaged.
A number of crews reported large explosions, seeing the red glow of fires
from as far as the Dutch coast as they returned home. Several reported more
searchlights than usual but luckily not much flak.

The weather at home was grim, scattering aircraft far and wide looking
for a clear airfield to land. Brian lost an engine on the way back but
managed to land at Wyton without mishap and Sergeant Renton lost two
and just struggled back to Gravely. Two were diverted to Swanton Morley,
two to Marham and one to Downham Market. Can you imagine a five-
and-a-quarter-hour journey, dodging flak and night fighters, desperately

trying to stay steady and bomb accurately, only to return through clear continental skies to a foggy East Anglia to be told you cannot land at your home airfield and, exhausted, having to divert to another where you may never have landed before? Relying on basic navigation, steadily reducing altitude, groping through the mist to search for runway marking flares in the gloom and landing on an unknown runway. Then a few hours' sleep in a chair and then, when the fog lifts, flying back to Wyton to get ready for the next night's work.

Overall it was night of big losses, with thirty-one aircraft failing to return and a further seven crashing near their bases due to the fog. It was a sad night for the squadron. Their commanding officer, Wing Commander James Gillman, had joined Sergeant Leigh as second pilot but R5629 crashed over the target and all were lost.

Gillman, an Old Haileyburian, joined the RAF after school and after training at Cranwell was promoted pilot officer in 1934 and then to flight lieutenant in 1937. In December 1939 he went to France with 218 Squadron flying Fairey Battles to support the BEF, where the squadron suffered appalling casualties. He was promoted to wing commander in September 1941 and was posted to HQ Bomber Command at High Wycombe. He only commanded the squadron for three months but in the ORB it comments 'during his short stay created a good squadron spirit and at the same time helped both morally and numerically to build up the squadron'. His grave is in the Reichswald Forest War Cemetery with the inscription 'Sursam Corda' (Lift up your Hearts). He was 31 and left behind his young wife, Edith, and their baby.

The system worked quickly to find a replacement and within a few days, on 9 May, Acting Wing Commander John Searby from 106 Squadron was posted in as the new commanding officer. He had been interviewed by Don Bennett up at Castle Hill House, the Pathfinder headquarters in Huntingdon, in early May but there were no squadron commands available. Gillman's demise gave Searby his opportunity. Searby did not have a traditional pre-war RAF career. His father was killed at the Somme when Searby was aged 3. A grammar school boy, he became an apprentice at RAF Halton at the age of 16 and after that three-year course was marked down as potential pilot material. In 1935 he went for flying training and became a sergeant pilot with postings to 104 and 106 squadrons, and at the start of the war in 1939 was posted to 108 Squadron on non-operational duties. He then went to Canada on a specialist navigation course and on return requested an operational tour. He went to 9 Squadron, a Wellington unit at Honington. Later that month, he was posted yet again to another Wellington unit, 405 Squadron, at Pocklington and then after only a few operations he went first to No. 4 Group HQ and then No. 2 Group HQ as group navigation officer. In September 1942, in the light of increasing crew losses and despite little operational experience, he was sent to 106 Squadron as a flight commander, which at that time was commanded by the highly decorated and experienced Wing Commander Guy Gibson. He was a short-fused man who did not suffer fools gladly and could not have been hugely impressed by the arrival of a flight commander with such little operational experience. At that stage he had only flown two operations. Sending the inexperienced Searby to Gibson was a risk and came about because Searby had an interview with Air Vice Marshal Alec Coryton, who was then No. 5 Group commander and had Gibson's 106 Squadron under his command. Coryton saw the potential in Searby and hoped that Gibson could turn this inexperienced navigator staff officer into the steely operational squadron leader they needed. It was to make Searby and was a turning point in his career.

By March 1943 Searby had completed his operational tour, having become an experienced Lancaster skipper with a further thirty-five operations in his logbook and having learned a huge amount from Gibson about commanding an operational squadron in testing times. Gibson was away much of the time planning the creation of a specialist squadron to carry out a raid on a top secret target. Searby took over the squadron when Gibson left in early March. Searby not only learned from Gibson but also from Coryton, who he described as inspirational. He also picked up a great deal from the from the eccentric Syerston station commander, Group Captain Irving Bussell, an old school RAF officer with high standards and the ability to draw all the staff at Syerston into a happy, hardworking station. Before Gibson could persuade Searby to join him for his new adventure, Bennett at No. 8 Group grabbed him to replace Gillman.

On 12 May the squadron briefed and dispatched fourteen aircraft to Duisburg, and the rest of the squadron, including Brian, were stood down. It was a successful raid but thirty-four aircraft did not return and Flight Lieutenant Rickenson from 83 Squadron was one of them. Rickenson was new to the squadron but his crew had been there for some time, having seen Squadron Leader Cooke through his tour. Their Lancaster was attacked by a night fighter before their bomb run and they crashed with a 4,000lb cookie on board, but there was an explosion as the aircraft descended and the navigator, Flight Lieutenant Horace Ransome, was miraculously thrown clear of his position just behind the pilot. Badly injured and with no memory of his descent, he spent two months in hospital and ended the war in Stalag Luft III.

After the first disappointing raid on the Skoda factory in Pilsen, Bomber Command tried again on 13 May. Twelve aircraft from 83 Squadron took off for Czechoslovakia, two on marking duties and the remainder to join the main force with 156 aircraft. However, once again the target was hard to find and was not marked well. Although crews at debriefing were convinced they had seen, marked and bombed the factory complex, there were no direct hits and little damage was inflicted. Another seven-hour round trip and a long way to go for little result and the loss of nine aircraft, one of which was from the squadron. Sergeant Renshaw was attacked by a night fighter over Holland and crashed on the eastern shore of the IJsselmeer. Only wireless Operator Sergeant Gould survived and became a prisoner of war.

On 16 May 1943 one of the most famous operations of the war was undertaken by 617 Squadron, which was formed specifically for it. Searby would now understand why his previous commanding officer had been away so much. Wing Commander Guy Gibson, from 106 Squadron, took the nineteen Lancasters of his new squadron on their first operation to bomb the Ruhr dams with the remarkable bouncing bombs designed by Barnes Wallis.

Of the dams that provided electricity for the industrial Ruhr Valley, two were breached. Significant damage was done and many were drowned below the Möhne Dam. The effect on the Ruhr Valley in terms of restricting water supply or power for industry was short-lived, although considerable resources were diverted to effect repairs of the two damaged dams. However, in terms of the brilliant innovation required to develop such a unique bomb and the ability to deliver it with such precision, it was an exceptional feat and it provided a huge lift of morale at home and for all the crews who flew night after night. It remains a mystery, however, that if this was a target of strategic importance, it's rebuilding was not harassed continually by further traditional raids. Within months the dams were repaired and functional again.

Operation Chastise, the 'Dams Raid' was much vaunted, albeit eight aircraft were lost and 53 of the 133 participating aircrew were killed. The surviving aircrew were all decorated, their leader being awarded the Victoria Cross to add to his DFC and Bar and his DSO and Bar.

From 16 May for nearly a week the squadron and indeed most of Bomber Command was stood down other than a few minor ops and training, even though the weather was perfect. What to do with a couple of hundred young bloods wanting to do their own 'dam raid'? On Thursday, 20 May they were told that there was to be dinghy drill that afternoon. As described earlier, the Lancaster had a number of escape hatches and safety features including the Type 'J' dinghy for which regular training was encouraged. A technical manual (known collectively by the aircrews as Tee-Emms) of 1941 advised:

> All those, therefore, who are at any time likely to have to use a 'yellow donut' are advised to study the drills carefully and to find out everything about the dinghy and its equipment. 'Taking to the boats' is one of those things you may never have to do – but if you do have to do it, you want to do it pretty quick.

With that training in mind, three coaches were booked to take all aircrew to a local river, the Great Ouse. By a convenient coincidence, that river happened to run through the garden of a nearby pub called the Pike and Eel, a venue that was entirely suitable for some serious training but a good time was had by all with plenty of crews getting a soaking. They were joined by some crews from 35 Squadron, another Pathfinder squadron from nearby Gravely. A riotous inter-squadron dinghy race ended proceedings. The following day, although two crews had to do some training, the weather continued to be good and there was a cricket match between 'A' and 'B' flights. The next evening a coach took crews into Cambridge for more steam letting.

The crews' social life was normally conducted at quite a pace, as those who put their lives so regularly in danger are want to do. Brian became great friends with Walter 'Punch' Thompson, who you may remember had swerved a court martial and ended up flying Lancasters with 106 Squadron. He had the unnerving experience on the day of his arrival at Syerston of flying his first dicky seat operation to Stuttgart with the squadron commander, Guy Gibson. Flak put out one engine on the way out and a second on their return, resulting in a fairly bumpy landing. Gibson got a Bar to his DSO that night. An eventful welcome to operations for the 22-year-old Canadian. After eleven operations he was poached to be a Pathfinder with 83 Squadron, arriving in late April. He wrote in his book *Lancaster to Berlin* (1985):

> Brian was a good friend, a voluble Londoner ... always sang the loudest, drank the most and told the funniest jokes on the nights out. I think too that he was loved by most of the WAAFs for he was another who refused to obey the non fraternisation rule.

161

He also wrote of a night out with Brian in Cambridge when they came across:

> Clark Gable, a gunner with a nearby Fortress squadron, with his foot up on a brass rail of a Pub near King's Parade, his hat bent correctly at the peak and olive green trench coat turned up at the collar; we were impressed to find a movie star who actually flew on operations, he flew about 5 of them and of course was not alone.

Gable served with 351 Bomber Group USAF at RAF Polebrook, just 30 miles north of Cambridge. He trained as an aerial gunner but was specifically tasked with filming aerial combat and archived 50,000ft of footage, much of which was used in the film *Combat America*. He completed five operational missions.

The pub was almost certainly the Eagle in Bene't Street, just off King's Parade. It was a favourite haunt of bomber crews, both RAF and USAF, and in one of the back bars the airmen would mark the ceiling with candles or petrol lighters with graffiti of their squadron numbers. On one side is '83 SQDN'. That graffiti, after a campaign to preserve it, is still there.

Searby will have heard all about his old commanding officer's exploits leading 617 Squadron on the Dams raid and only had to wait a few days until 23 May to lead his first squadron operation in an 826-aircraft raid to Dortmund. Fourteen squadron aircraft, four with TIs, reported clear conditions, a bit of industrial haze but good concentration of fires across the target. It was judged a very successful raid with nearly 2,000 buildings destroyed, including the Hoesch steelworks put out of production. Some 599 people were killed and 1,275 injured. The well-defended Happy Valley claimed thirty-eight aircraft in all but none from the squadron and only two Pathfinder aircraft.

Squadron morale was high but they were frustrated by two layers of cloud on 25 May when 14 squadron aircraft joined a force of 759 aircraft to bomb Düsseldorf. The marking crews, including Brian, reported that the reds of the early Mosquito blind markers were difficult to see, which made their backing up difficult and, additionally distracted by the decoy fires, the main force bombing was scattered and ineffective. Twenty-seven aircraft were lost but the squadron returned intact.

On 26 May, RAF Wyton had some Royal visitors when King George VI and Queen Elizabeth II were shown the station and the aircraft by No. 8

Group's commander, Don Bennett. A few other squadrons' 'brass' flew in to be part of the visit.

The following night, fourteen aircraft were briefed and ready for an op to Cologne but the weather closed in and about an hour before take-off it was cancelled. The next night fourteen aircraft were briefed to visit Essen. Brian was one of five markers that were again cancelled at the last minute, although the others joined the main force. It seems that cloud appeared over the target and at the last minute it was decided to sky mark rather than use visual TIs on the ground. With the five marking aircraft already loaded with TIs and no time to rearm, they were stood down.

This unexpected time gave Brian the opportunity to remember his family back in Hemel Hempstead and so he sent his little sister a birthday card, as his next operation was on her birthday, 29 May. She was to be 14 years old.

That next op on 29 May saw a resounding success using the steadily improving tactics of Oboe-equipped Mosquitos. There have been several references to this navigation system but what was it all about? Oboe operated with two radio transmitting stations sending signals that the aircraft used to fix their position and receive guidance from the operators when to release their bombs. The two stations were Walmer, near Dover in Kent, and Cromer, on the Norfolk coast, both almost as far east as you could get. One station, known as the cat station, would transmit a signal that kept the aircraft flying along an arc from the cat station to the target. When it was flying along that curved course towards the target, the second station, the mouse, would warn the aircraft as it approached the target and then indicate the precise point when it was above it. This system was open to being jammed assuming the German radar stations knew the frequency, which they soon did. However, the Oboe system soon changed to a micro frequency but continued to transmit on the old frequency to confuse the German jamming efforts, which it did successfully until 1944 when Oboe III was introduced.

The Mosquito, the fast, twin-engine light bomber that was capable of flying at higher altitudes and faster than the larger bombers, was ideal to use the Oboe system.

That night 719 aircraft bombed Wuppertal and it was judged an outstanding success. Wing Commander Searby led fourteen aircraft, with six backing up the earlier Oboe-directed ground markers with green and yellow TIs, two with GP bombs and six, including Brian, with a 'cookie' and more than $1,000 \times 4lb$ incendiaries. Visibility was clear with only high-level cloud and some ground haze. Pathfinder marking and backing up

163

and main force bombing was accurate. Wuppertal had two built-up areas, Barmen and Elberfeld, and it was the former that received all the attention. The damage was extreme, mainly due to fires starting in the narrow streets of the old town that started what was to become known as a 'firestorm'. Apparently the fire services were ill equipped to deal with this raid as not only was it the first large-scale attack on the city but it was a Saturday night and many of the fire chiefs were out of town. The geography of the town also had an effect as many of the buildings were within fairly steep-sided valleys.

About 40 per cent, some 1,000 acres, of Barmen's built-up area was destroyed. Five factories, 211 other industrial buildings and 4,000 houses were destroyed. Approximately 3,400 people were killed in Wuppertal that night.

Back at Wyton the mood could not have been in greater contrast as all of 83 Squadron's crews returned enthusiastic about the result of the raid. Many reported a clear view of the early TIs through their bombsights and saw their own green TIs well concentrated and their incendiaries straddling those markers. They saw the built-up areas lit up in the glow of huge fires with a column of black smoke rising to 10,000ft. Searby, who signed off the crew's reports, was the only one to comment at the post-op debrief that there were no defences at the target, although in his monthly summary he noted that the flak on the run-in was heavy between Düsseldorf and Cologne and that combined with night fighter activity for the later aircraft was the reason for thirty-three aircraft losses overall.

Early June was beset by poor weather and it would be 11 June before the next working night. Even a concert in the airmen's canteen by Vera Lynn and a dance orchestra could not entirely cure the frustration felt by the lack of operations, which was made very clear in the ORB with these comments: 'All crews dying to get cracking as they know recent raids have been a very telling blow for the "Hun"', and when an op was cancelled there were 'Howls of dismay' and 'Disheartened is hardly the word, some crews were so keen they would have gone on their own.' For two of the squadron leaders the wait for another op was even worse. Squadron leaders Wellington and Blair had one more op to complete to end their tour and the wait was excruciating. The ORB comments: 'S/Ldr Blair, navigation bag between his legs, to stop his knees battering themselves to death.'

These two were great characters. Wimpy Wellington always flew in highly polished riding boots, having ridden a great deal in South America as a child. He also insisted his Lancaster had the motto 'Filha da Puta' painted on the nose. In Portuguese it means 'Son of a Bitch'. The ruddy-faced Tommy Blair, who was a prodigious consumer of beer, was also a highly skilled navigator who completed the rare feet of more than 100 operations. On at least fifty of those, and against all the rules, he was accompanied by Sammy, his cocker spaniel.

There was a further lift to morale when, on 9 June. Flight Lieutenant 'Joe' Ogilvie walked in the officers' mess and received a 'voracious welcome and congratulations' from the more senior members of the squadron as he had just returned from Spain, having evaded capture after his aircraft was shot down on 11 March. His aircraft, ED313, piloted by Flight Lieutenant Norman Mackie, was shot down by a night fighter on their way back from Stuttgart. Mackie was able to crash-land in France between Epernay and Saint Dizier but sadly two of his crew were killed and two were soon captured and made POWs. Mackie, Ogilvie and Sergeant Ralph Henderson avoided capture and Ogilvie made his way with the support of the French Resistance through occupied France and into Spain, where he was imprisoned. Our friends from MI9 got to work and he was repatriated to the UK in June, much to the delight of his friends at Wyton. We will meet Ralph Henderson again.

Great efforts were made by all the senior officers to keep crew busy when stood down from ops with lectures on a variety of subjects including stick bombing, pyrotechnics, tactics and aircraft recognition. There was more dinghy training, this time not in the pub garden, and a rain-interrupted inter-flight cricket match was won by 'A' Flight. There was also plenty of training, including flying training when the weather allowed, in particular for Brian and a few other crews to practise using a new radar.

Although this period of the area bombing campaign was concentrated on the Ruhr, other operations were carried out, including an unusual raid on Münster, which was a Pathfinder-only task and a large-scale test of the new H2S ground-mapping radar system. This system had been under development for some time and tested with various squadrons. If successful, it would allow more accurate bombing deeper into Germany, Berlin in particular, but why not Gee or Oboe?

Both of these and a similar system developed by the Luftwaffe needed ground stations to transmit radio signals that could be picked up by the aircraft. The range of such systems was limited as it needed an 'optical line of sight' between transmitter and aircraft, which was limited to under 400 miles, due to the natural curvature of the earth. With the Germans able to have their transmitter stations on the Dutch coast, they were able to operate over much of England. British-based transmitters were as far east as possible but that only took the range as far as the Ruhr Valley. Britain needed a system that would be effective much deeper into Europe, hence the development of a ground-mapping system operated from the aircraft without the need of a ground-based transmitter.

Throughout 1941 and 1942 government scientists worked to develop the concept. In March 1941 a test flight over Southampton and Salisbury was carried out with enough success to encourage the project to be improved and for security reasons moved to various sites around the country, ending up in Malvern, given its own premises (initially in Malvern College) and significant staff. In July 1942 Churchill, on hearing of a particular breakthrough in its development, called a meeting with his advisors and the senior scientists working on the project. Although a tragic accident had killed several senior project staff only a few weeks before, the progress they had made encouraged Churchill to insist that 200 sets were fitted and operational by the autumn, a deadline thought impossible by the scientists.

They were late but the H2S sets did arrive with the squadrons in early 1943 and after some operational testing it was concluded that they should become standard on Pathfinder Lancasters; by the summer they were in regular use. Initially the images were difficult to interpret by the crews but an improved screen arrived later fitted to the radio operator's desk. Essentially it gave a 'picture' of the ground, showing differences between water, different land types and buildings. Combined with the new bombsight, it started to have improved if inconsistent results. Some early examples were examined by German scientists from downed bombers and it wasn't long before they were able to jam and track those H2S-equipped aircraft. Initially the sets were very unreliable and typically as many as 50 per cent would not work on any given operation but the Pathfinder squadrons continued to install them and train crews with the intention that all Pathfinder heavies would have them. This was ground-breaking technology and it is interesting to note that a similar but upgraded version of H2S was installed on Vulcan bombers and used effectively as late as 1982 on the Black Buck bombing operations of the Falklands War.

While Bomber Command continued its relentless operations, the demand for improved technology and replacement aircraft kept British scientists and the military industrial establishment working around the clock.

On 28 May there was a new arrival at Wyton. From their Manchester factories AV Roe were churning out about twenty-five Lancasters a week and one in particular was finally assembled, checked, tested and flown by an

ATA ferry pilot from the AV Roe aerodrome at Woodford to Wyton. Having arrived, the new Lancaster Mk III, ED984, was checked out by the ground crew and various modifications made including the fitting of the H2S radar. On 5 June Brian took her up for the first time and then on a number of training and test flights over the next week; by the afternoon of the 11th, she was ready for her first operation. She was now his and he didn't fly another Lancaster on any future operations. He had flown new Wellingtons but a brand new shiny and dependable Lancaster Mk III powered by four Packard-made Merlin 28 engines and stuffed with the most current and sophisticated technology was now his. Flying these machines must have been daunting but an exciting professional challenge and he and his crew soon had confidence in ED984 with its new callsign, 'A' for Apple.

As the newer Lancaster IIIs arrived, the original BIs were transferred out and the previous 'A' for Apple, W4123, was sent up the road to the PFF navigation training unit. However, her operational days were not over. As new squadrons were created, these older aircraft were pressed back into service and W4123 joined the newly created 576 Squadron at Elsham Wolds in early December. She was lost with her crew on an operation to Frankfurt a few days later.

Although planned for 6 June, the Münster raid was postponed on three nights before eventually happening five days later. Brian was flying one of the only four 83 Squadron aircraft fitted with H2S (code-named 'Y'). Flying Officer Tilbury was first in as a blind marker, Brian second a minute later, and Flight Sergeant Britton third, both as visual markers, while the rest bombed with the main force. Tilbury's yellow markers dropped by H2S were visually confirmed as accurate by Brian and Britton. This was seen as an important test for the squadron, not only being first in but having producing two excellent photographs showing accurate marking. It was a success for the squadron and for the raid as a whole as considerable damage was done to railway installations and residential areas. Brian's log states:

P.F.F. only – 'Y' marking'. Photo. – 800 yds aiming point.

This is an interesting note as Brian's logbook entries for individual operations are rarely self-congratulatory and normally understated. Any photograph of an aiming point showed the accuracy of a crew's bombing and when the OBRs mention this in relation to a crew or an individual it is done as a significant plaudit, even at considerably greater distance than 800 yards. No wonder he was pleased.

As ever, though, it wasn't all good news. Squadron Leader James Swift was a second tour skipper and older than the average at 30. He took advantage of the poor weather and the cancelled op the day before by driving the two hours or so to see his young family. They were all looking forward to some leave he had coming up in a few days' time. He left them at 0700 hours the next morning and was back at Wyton by 1000 hours in time for prep and briefings. He was in the main force to Münster and on the way back was attacked and shot down by a Bf 110 night fighter and crashed in the sea. His body was washed up with one other of his crew and they are both buried in Holland. None of the others were found. Swift left his young wife, a son of 4 and daughter of 2.

On the same night six squadron aircraft joined a force of 783 to bomb Düsseldorf and had a testing time over Happy Valley with night fighters active and flak heavy, resulting in Pilot Officer Mason being coned, holed in the tailplane and at the back of the fuselage but he still got home.

That night was also good news for Squadron Leader 'Wimpy' Wellington and two of his crew, Squadron Leader Blair and Flight Lieutenant Harley, who could now breathe more easily having completed their tours. As they awaited their next posting both Blair and Harley were awarded DFCs.

The following night, 12 June, 'A' for Apple took part in an operation to Bochum with 503 others. On this operation Oboe Mosquitos marked accurately with red TIs and seven of the twelve squadron aircraft, including Brian, backed up with greens, the remainder joining the main bombing stream. Most reported the marking scattered and it seems that some of the main force bombed ground markers and some cascading TIs as a form of sky marker. In his logbook Brian confirmed all this with the comment, 'a bit scattered'.

Some 130 acres of the centre of Bochum were destroyed, which included 1,465 buildings either destroyed or severely damaged, and 312 people were killed. Searby, in his summary, commented that the flak was particularly heavy due to this being a 'heavies'-only raid. In fact, only Lancasters and Halifaxes took part, both of which could fly higher than the Stirlings. When Stirlings were mixed with the heavies the anti-aircraft guns would be constantly readjusting to fire at different altitudes, whereas with only Lancasters and Halifaxes, once their altitudes were established the fuze settings would be fixed.

That probably contributed to the loss of twenty-four aircraft, 4.8 per cent of the force, another high percentage. No. 83 Squadron lost one. Flying Officer Tilbury, who led the Münster raid with Brian the night before, was attacked by a night fighter on the way back and crashed into the IJsselmeer with no survivors.

The squadron was stood down for three days, the first a complete rest day the next two training but curtailed by poor weather. Then a rather strange sortie as Brian and three others flew aircraft loaded with TIs over to Scampton and then back to Wyton. Perhaps 57 Squadron had run out.

The refinement in the use of these new systems continued, with Brian's next raid on Cologne on 16 June. As with Bremen, this was his fifth and last trip to Cologne and he knew full well the strength of the defences around this city just south of the Ruhr Valley. Although within Oboe range, the Mosquitos stayed at home and it was sixteen Pathfinder heavies with H2S that carried out the marking. Using H2S, the plan was to sky mark both the route in and the target with flares and TIs. The target was cloud covered, many of the H2S sets malfunctioned and thus the sky marking was too spread, and so was the main force bombing, even though many could see the early ground target indicators. Of the fourteen squadron aircraft, two carried H2S with both flares and TIs and returned apparently happy with their work. The remainder bombed early in the main stream and many reported seeing the sky-marking flares in their bombsights. In fact, only the first 100 of the total of 202 aircraft bombed, the remainder could not see the target and took their bombs home. Notwithstanding all this, considerable damage was inflicted on the already heavily bombed city. Some 401 houses were destroyed and about 13,000 were damaged. Fourteen Lancasters were lost, one of which was ED907 from 83 Squadron piloted by Pilot Officer Murray, who was attacked by a night fighter, and although five of the crew ended up as prisoners of war, Murray and the tail gunner, Flying Officer Mckay, were killed. A number of squadron crews felt the full force of the Cologne defences, with three being damaged, and one receiving both a cannon shell in the starboard side in front of the rear turret and also being riddled with machine gun fire from a night fighter. Amazingly, no member of these three crews were injured.

These comparative statistics of crews lost and damage done were clearly important to both Bomber Command and the crews. Although we now have more accurate and verified statistics, to the general public, often through the mainstream press of the time, the positive statistics were exaggerated and the losses and poor results were under-reported. Those who had experienced the German bombing of British targets knew only too well that Bomber Command's relentless strategy of area bombing would result in huge civilian casualties. Public opinion remained in favour of this strategy but Bomber Command needed to justify the cost and were constantly doing do so to the War Cabinet. The crews, though, knew well the successes and failures of the strategy, and while they may not have known the details of the German casualties, they witnessed at first hand the conflagrations they were creating in these built-up areas and could imagine only too well what effect that was having on those below. What they did know precisely though were the aircraft and aircrew losses. They were watching aircraft blown up before their eyes, they saw the empty dispersals, the constant arrival of new aircraft, and new, green aircrew. There were new faces in their messes and bars before the lists of losses were posted on flight and squadron noticeboards recording that their friends had not returned. Bomber Command also knew it. Every operation order from High Wycombe was sent in the knowledge that 3 to 5 per cent of aircraft would not return.

The squadron was stood down on the 18th and bad weather restricted training, with the few aircraft that went off on a practise bombing exercise having to return due to low cloud. One of them piloted by the Australian Flight Sergeant Max Cummins, who was a new member of the squadron, came out of the cloud and hit a farm building at Swaton near Grantham before ploughing into a copse of trees. All nine on board were killed, which included two ground crew. The squadron's monthly summary reported 'it disintegrated and became unrecognisable as an aircraft'.

The following night another curious and slightly experimental operation was carried out which was only partly successful. For the squadron this was a new and special target. It was the Schneider armaments factory and the Breuil Steelworks in the French town of Le Creusot and the Montchanin transformer station 5 miles to the south-east, some 200 miles south-west of Paris. A six-hour round trip and out of Oboe range. The previous year a daylight raid was attempted and judged ineffective but now with H2S a night raid could be contemplated.

The plan, as the weather was good and visibility clear, was that the first H2S Pathfinder Lancasters would illuminate the Le Creusot area with flares and the main force of Stirlings and Halifaxes would identify and bomb their targets visually and then circle again to repeat the process. The H2S Lancasters would then fly on to Montchanin, illuminate for visual markers and then a small force of twenty-six Lancasters would bomb the transformer station.

The Le Creusot part of the raid started well, with the area illuminated and the early visual bombing accurate, but as the area became increasingly affected by smoke, the main force, so used to bombing to ground markers, struggled to identify the targets and bombing was scattered. Accuracy overall was reasonable as all bombs fell within 3 miles of the targets but it was a small target and only one in five hit the factories.

At Montchanin the illumination was carried out as planned and then Brian and the other two squadron aircraft did their bombing run. As expected, there would be no ground air defences, so each bomber would circle as many times as needed to identify and bomb the quite small target. Brian was the first squadron aircraft in and dropped his green TIs at 0156 hours, then circled and dropped $4 \times 1,000$ pounders four minutes later and then circled again to repeat. The lack of ack-ack encouraged him to fly lower and improve accuracy, so his first two runs were at 7,000ft but the last at 4,500ft. The other two ran through at the same time but at different altitudes. Now marked, the main force including the rest of the squadron's eight aircraft did the same, some circling five times until they were happy the target was identified, which became harder as smoke obscured the area. Most of the crews reported that all seemed to go well and they witnessed accurate bomb flashes. Brian also reported seeing many fires at Le Creusot as they flew over on their way home.

Wing Commander Searby, who commanded the main force at Montchanin, bombed on those markers and witnessed fires and flashes synonymous with hitting electrical targets. An aiming point photo seemed to confirm the operation's success. It was later found that a small factory had been mistaken for the target, which went unscathed. A complex plan, seemingly well executed and a long night but with little to show for it. Due to the almost non-existent defences, only three of the 212 aircraft didn't return.

Another experimental raid, known as Operation Bellicose, took place the next night but 83 Squadron was not involved. The target was the Zeppelin factory at Friedrichshafen on the shores of Lake Constance that was then manufacturing the Würzburg radar sets used by the night fighter boxes. The operation was different in a number of ways, not least that it was only the second master bomber-controlled operation, and instead of returning to the UK they confused the night fighters waiting for their home run by flying on to North Africa, refuelling and returning the following day, bombing La Spezia on their way home. It was also a raid where some of the main force were to bomb on markers and some on a 'time and distance' method being tested by No. 5 Group. No aircraft were lost, although one was written off on landing having been damaged by a hung-up red TI that exploded as they lost altitude. The master bomber had to hand over control to his deputy when his port inner engine, which powered the bombsight, caught fire. The initial marking and re-marking was chaotic, not helped by the deputy MB's watch being set an hour wrong. The main force, having been told to increase altitude at the last minute due to unexpectedly heavy flak, went into stronger winds, which affected their unadjusted bombsights. Amazingly, the bombing was a partial success but unbeknown to them the factory was not only producing radar sets but also V-2 rockets. Less than a month later a raid on the Germans' experimental rocket establishment would be made.

The fact that so many of their recent missions were slightly experimental says a lot for Bomber Command's desire to bomb more effectively. There was no time for comprehensive testing and practice or numerous training flights and rehearsals to perfect the new equipment and tactics. For the Pathfinders this was on the job training. It also indicates that while area bombing remained the strategy, occasionally important small targets were attacked and methods using the new technology to achieve more accuracy had to be rehearsed. They were also constantly monitoring and changing their own tactics to counter those advances made by the Luftwaffe.

This crew were now getting attached to ED984. They had used it for their last four operations and many, many training flights. Superstition or not, they liked this machine.

They climbed into 'A' for Apple again two nights after the Le Creusot job and ten of the fourteen squadron aircraft were briefed to back up ground markers for a large operation to the Ruhr Valley town of Krefeld, about 25 miles north-west of Düsseldorf, where factories produced steel and parachute fabric. Just over 700 aircraft were involved, one of the largest in recent months, with aircraft coming from all bomber groups. As usual with a trip to 'Happy Valley', they approached through the *Himmelbett* boxes and thirty aircraft were shot down by night fighters on a clear moonlit night. Flak claimed a further eight aircraft, although there was little flak over Krefeld itself. They did, though, experience heavy flak on the way out over Eindhoven, Rotterdam, Amsterdam, Utrecht and Leyden as well as a flak-boat off the Dutch coast: what a journey. As was often the case, the ground defences struggled to cope with such high numbers of aircraft and on this occasion the main force, nearly 600 aircraft, which was through the target in about forty-five minutes, experienced little or no flak. The first Pathfinder 'heavies', however, did attract some on their first runs.

The raid started with ten Oboe Mosquitos accurately establishing the main aiming point with red target indicators. Then the Pathfinder Lancasters, including the ten from 83 Squadron, did the backing up role at various intervals, further marking the targets with a variety of green and yellow TIs, a cookie and 6 × 1,000-pounders. These were accurate and provided excellent aiming points for the main force. In all the main force dropped 2,306 tons of bombs over a relatively small area, starting extensive fires that burnt for several hours as they could not be controlled. The whole centre of the town was destroyed, some 40 per cent of the built-up area. There were 11 factories and 12 other industrial buildings that were destroyed, as were 5,517 residential properties. Some 1,056 people were killed and 4,550 injured, while 72,000 people lost their homes. Crews could see the fires from the Dutch coast as they made their way back to Wyton.

Forty-four aircraft were lost, including two Lancasters from 83 Squadron. These were flown by Flight Sergeant Fletcher, a leading 'Y' captain, whose crew had not been together that long, and Flying Officer Mappins, whose aircraft crashed into the sea off the Frisian Islands. Later three bodies were washed ashore and are buried near Terschelling.

The following night Brian's crew were stood down but nine 83 Squadron Lancasters joined 557 aircraft on another highly successful operation to Mülheim. However, thirty-six aircraft were lost including one, Sergeant Rust, from 83 Squadron. Nearly 14,000 houses were destroyed or damaged. Flight Lieutenant Wilmott had an interesting night, being coned for six minutes over the target, and then a Lancaster from 156 Squadron hit his starboard wing, breaking off 6 square feet and smashing the rear turret Perspex. It's amazing that in a pitch black night or cloud more mid-air collisions did not take place. As we know, crews were encouraged to keep close through the target. Some weaved, some didn't, mostly they avoided each other but not always.

On 23 June the crews were stood down. Wing Commander Searby, Brian and his crew attended the funeral of Flight Sergeant Cummins, who crashed near Grantham the week before. Cummins and his Canadian rear gunner are buried in Grantham Cemetery. Later that day two coaches took air and ground crew into Cambridge.

The Battle of the Ruhr continued, with another large raid on Wuppertal on 24 June. This was the second of the two large raids on this Ruhr Valley town. Brian had participated in the first on 29 May that destroyed the Barmen half of the town. He and two others took off with the yellow TI/GP mix; four others had the same mix with greens and one had just incendiaries. This raid was aimed at the other major conurbation, Elberfeld. A total of 630 aircraft were involved, and once again the evolving tactics of the Pathfinders enabled them through accurate Oboe Mosquito marking and backing up to mark the targets exactly. Although the main force bombing was not as accurate, 94 per cent of Elberfeld was destroyed, 224 industrial premises were destroyed or seriously damaged and 5,500 houses similarly affected. About 1,800 people were killed and 2,400 injured. In two raids Wuppertal had been devastated. Once again the fires were seen as the aircraft crossed the Dutch coast 100 miles away. None of the other crews mention too much about flak and Brian records nothing in his logbook but in debrief he mentioned that they had been hit by ground fire, which put the rear turret's hydraulics and R/T out of action and put a few holes in the wing and the fuselage of his much-loved ED984. Many others weren't so lucky; thirty-four aircraft were lost, 5.4 per cent of the total.

For the next few days the squadron was stood down from ops but the normal range of training continued. The 'erks' (who rather liked their unofficial motto of *Ubendum, Wemendum*) once again worked their magic and had ED984 repaired and ready, as on 26 June Brian took the Lancaster on what was known as fighter affiliation, which was regular occurrence for all crews. One of the local fighter squadrons would provide a few aircraft and conduct mock attacks for the bomber crews to practise their drills, like observation, reporting accurately and promptly to the pilot over the intercom and evasive flying like corkscrewing. The gunners also practised engaging moving targets. Gunners in the 83 Squadron Lancasters continued to have occasional clay pigeon training to practise swinging through and leading moving targets. On 27 June Brian had an exam. Having now flown ten Pathfinder operations, he and Flying Officer Maurice Chick sat their PFF board and passed. With effect from 7 July they received the much coveted Pathfinder badge.

On 28 June, eight aircraft were readied for a raid to Cologne in a force of 653. The gremlins were out for the squadron that night, with one aircraft not taking off due to engine problems and two more returning early. The rest completed their job but with 10/10 cloud masking what was happening below, no one came home happy. It was, however, a lethally effective raid with more than 6,400 buildings destroyed and 15,000 others damaged. A total of 4,377 people were killed, approximately 10,000 injured and 230,000 were forced to leave their damaged homes. A reminder, if one was needed, of the extensive damage bombing inflicted on large urban targets.

For the first two days of July they were stood down yet again and poor weather prevented any flying, which prompted the comment in the ORB, 'weather holding up our war'. Maintaining crews' enthusiasm for flying operations never seems to be an issue in this squadron and periods of no work were clearly frustrating, as the ORB describes. What prompted this next comment is unknown but something had happened; 'Lecture by Station Commander to all aircrew without exception. Severe ticking off administered, Flight Commanders lectured crews on same subject afterwards regarding "Lax Discipline".' It's worth noting that the bollocking was delivered by the station commander of Wyton rather than their squadron commander, who probably had other things on his mind.

On Saturday, 3 July after a brief training flight, Brian and his crew went on leave and as they all scuttled out of the gates I'm sure the last thing on their mind was the station commander's tongue lashing. As they went, nine crews were being briefed for another trip to Cologne. This city was becoming the new favourite and the ORB, which was quite full for this raid, noted that crews saw a mass of fires, with one crew of the opinion that it was better than a '1,000 raid'. More than 2,000 houses were destroyed, 1,588 people killed or wounded and 72,000 people bombed out. The crews also noted that the defences were above average and the night fighters were out in force with 'aircraft dropping out of the sky left and right on the way in'. This explained the fact that 30 of the 653 aircraft were lost, although everyone from 83 got home.

The author of the monthly summary clearly had a sense of humour, an essential I would imagine when having to keep such a diary. Pilot Officer Alec Shipway reported at the post-op debrief that he had to return early as his navigator was sick. Apparently it was then discovered that he was actually having stomach problems and the ORB author described: 'P/O Shipway returned early, his navigator paying more attention to the "Elsan" than the "box". A case of inserting the "digit" for better results.'

Alec Shipway was a Bristolian, grammar school educated, and he broke away from the family seafaring tradition to join the RAF. After school he worked for the large Bristol employer Fyffes and returned to them after the war.

This, the second of the Cologne raids, introduced a sinister new night fighter tactic from a specialist unit, *Jagdgeschwader* 300. It seemed that single-engine German fighters that were more normally used in daylight now patrolled above the bombers while over the target area using the light from the ground, namely searchlights, flares and ground fires, to silhouette the bombers. This tactic was code-named *Wilde Sau* (Wild Boar) and after this success other specialist units were established and two aircraft in particular specially adapted for these ops, namely the Focke-Wulf Fw 190-A and the

Messerschmitt Bf 109-G. *Wilde Sau* required the anti-aircraft batteries to set their fuzes to a certain altitude, above which the night fighters could operate safely. On that operation British crews reported that other bombers were firing on them as none had experienced night fighters in the flak zone over the target area before. This new unit claimed twelve downed bombers using their new tactic. It was to become yet another hazard for the bomber crews. The Luftwaffe night fighter pilots liked the freedom this tactic provided rather than being restricted by the 'box' system and within a month it was being adopted widely across the night fighter network.

Weaving remained a tactic for pilots and to many an effective way to make their aircraft as hard a target as possible. It also gave them a feeling of being a little more in control of their fate; at least they could do something to make life harder for the searchlights and the night fighters. This tactic was endorsed by Searby and used by all squadron pilots. It remained controversial, however, and on occasions bitter disputes arose between pilots and their seniors. After Brian's time in 83 Squadron, a new squadron commander, Wing Commander Abercromby, banned the practice as cowardly and wanted his crews to fly straight and level, believing the air gunners and bomb aimers could be more accurate. An argument developed in the mess between Abercromby and several senior pilots, with Flying Officer Maurice Chick bluntly telling his squadron commander that if he persisted in flying straight and level he would be dead within a month. Many experienced pilots ignored the diktat on the basis that it had kept them alive so far and Chick went on to complete his tour of forty-eight operations. Abercromby, though, served as their commanding officer for less than a month as he was shot down by a night fighter on a raid to Berlin.

A third Cologne raid on 8 July signalled the end of the Battle of the Ruhr. Seven squadron aircraft were briefed for this musical Wanganui but two were stood down before take-off and two more returned early. The remaining three were part of the 282 that conducted another successful raid on this devastated city. A further 2,400 buildings were destroyed. In total over the three raids about 5,500 people were killed and a further 350,000 had to be rehoused. In total sixty-two aircraft were lost.

It is clear that this campaign severely disrupted German production, with steel manufacture reduced significantly, and that created a real shortage of numerous components. German aircraft production ceased over this period and remained critically low until early 1944. The damage to the industrial process was severe and a vast number of residential properties were destroyed, causing a mass displacement of people and a housing crisis, with the enormous casualties diminishing the local workforce. All of this had a real effect but did not crush the morale of the German people.

It was also a considerable drain on Luftwaffe resources. By July 1943 the Ruhr's defences totalled 1,000 large flak guns and 1,500 small-calibre guns, which represented a third of all anti-aircraft guns in Germany. In total, more than 600,000 Luftwaffe personal were directly involved in the air defences of Germany at a time when the need for these resources for other fronts was becoming desperate. Although Bomber Command was distracting extensive Luftwaffe resources, the cost in their aircrew was high. Five thousand members of Bomber Command aircrew were killed during the five months of the Battle of the Ruhr. Although there were more raids on the Ruhr Valley before the end of the war, Harris was soon to shift his focus to another city target.

Just as it is a criticism that Harris didn't harass the rebuilding of the dams, it remains a question why he didn't continue to punish the Ruhr. If he didn't know the effect these raids were having, it is an indictment on the effectiveness of his post-op intelligence gathering. There was real evidence that not only were they diverting extensive resources to defend the Ruhr but also having a real effect on Germany's military industries. At this stage of the war planning for an invasion of mainland Europe was well advanced and a precursor for success was to weaken the Luftwaffe to the extent where the Allies had clear air superiority. The daily bombing raids by day and night were stretching Germany's ability to replace aircraft and crews, as much by direct attrition as by damaging the Reich's ability to manufacture replacements. By June the following year when Operation Overlord was launched, that air superiority had been achieved, but it could well have been sooner if pressure on the Ruhr had continued.

While Brian was on leave there were a good few days of warm weather and back in Hemel he bumped into his old schoolfriend Tony Horton:

> The first time I was on leave I came to Hemel Baths for a swim and lying on the grass was Brian in his swimming trunks. He must have been all of 19. Anyway, I went off and had a swim and then went into the changing room. He and I were both getting changed at the same time. In those days you wore you uniform all the time. I was getting into my Ordinary Seaman's uniform and Brian, a year older than me, was getting into his Flight Lieutenant's uniform and he had got a Distinguished Flying Cross (DFC). He said, 'You didn't join

that lot did you? Why didn't you join the RAF?' I wasn't that brave or that foolish.

His comment about not 'that foolish' reflected everyone's increasing awareness of the growing Bomber Command casualties and the real dangers of their work.

While Brian was on leave, the squadron stayed busy with a lecture from Flight Lieutenant Neal about escape and evasion techniques should any of them end up on the ground in occupied Europe. This was of real interest to crews, having heard from Joe Ogilvy of his long walk to Spain when he returned in early June. Neal was one of the more engaging speakers from RAF intelligence and had a happy knack of enlightening and absorbing the attention of all present.

Filthy weather on 11 July led to the op for fourteen aircraft to be scrubbed after briefings but the following night the same number made the long journey to Turin, which meant taking off in daylight and only crossing the French coast as the light went. They crossed the cloud-covered Alps but it was clear on the Italian side as they approached the target. The squadron provided one visual marker, four blind markers, three backers up and the rest in the main force, and by all accounts it went well. Some 295 aircraft went to Italy and thirteen did not return. Group Captain Graham, on his first squadron trip, was attacked and shot up by a Ju 88 but made it home, and another crew suffered damage from flak ships. Maurice Chick's crew spotted two U-boats off Saint-Nazaire and machine gunned them in passing, then having reported the sighting, a Beaufighter was tasked later that day, found and sunk one of them. All 83 Squadron aircrew returned by 8.30 and after the normal post op procedures, slept. As the ORB put it the next day: 'Hardly a soul stirred before 16.30.'

The next day they had another lecture on escape and evasion, and the presence of someone who had done it must have added some relevance to proceedings. Sergeant Henderson, who went down with Joe Ogilvy, also returned to the squadron with a new crew. With only training sorties the next day, it was another good excuse for a celebration that night.

Chapter 18

From Happy Valley to Gomorrah

B rian and his crew were now back from leave and keen to get started again but it was another day with no ops, so more training for the 'Y' crews and one 'Bullseye' exercise for Squadron Leader Manton. Bullseyes were training exercises when a bomber would be tasked, as if for a legitimate operation, to approach and attack a local town or city for them to test its searchlights and air defence systems. It was seen as a good rehearsal for new crews to work together and get used to the routines of an operation. It was also an opportunity for pilots to practise their response to searchlights and, although an exercise practised at some OTUs, for some squadron crews it was one of the few opportunities to try corkscrewing.

There followed two more days stood down but at least there was a coach to Cambridge to relieve the boredom. At last, on the 19th, twelve crews were briefed but soon cancelled. The crews were becoming very dejected with all these stand downs. They were briefed the next day but it was scrubbed due to bad weather yet again. At least the essential 'Y' training was going well and the squadron now had thirteen fully trained crews. They were stood down early the next day and even the gunnery training and fighter affiliation flights were scrubbed due to the bad weather. With so much intensive training, they were given the afternoon off but had to attend a lecture on 'Nazi Socialism'. For balance, a bus was laid on for Cambridge that evening. For the third time in a week, fourteen crews were detailed and attended briefing at 1800 hours only to sit impatiently for forty-five minutes until they were told the trip was scrubbed. As the ORB noted: 'An air of gloom spread rapidly, it's so long since we went to war.'

Security, particularly information about impending targets, was always a concern for Bomber Command. The ORB states: 'We were given alternative targets to be decided upon at briefing – dace or salmon. If salmon we should not be required.' One of these city objectives was also named later in that day's report but it was clearly redacted in the final copy signed off by Searby. The demand for security needed no explanation; as for the code words for the targets, that story goes to the top of Bomber Command.

Sir Arthur Harris' deputy was Air Vice Marshal Sir Robert Saundby. He had known Harris for many years, having worked with him in Iraq in the 1920s and as one of Harris' flight commanders when he commanded 58 Squadron. Saundby went to Bomber Command in High Wycombe in November 1940 and was made deputy commander-in-chief by Harris in February 1943. The two men were very different but complemented each other and worked well together. Saundby was a large stocky man, cultured, amusing and a good man manager. He would happily spend time socialising with junior staff and became a good two-way link between Harris and his subordinates, who viewed Harris as distant and unapproachable. As deputy commander-in-chief, Saundby was responsible for day-to-day operational matters and as such had become very concerned that information on targets was leaking out and getting back to the German cities' air defences. I'm not sure how legitimate his concerns were but security paranoia has always been the territory of senior commanders. To counter potential targets being named too early in warning orders and briefings, he produced a list of the ninety-four top targets and allocated them all code names. He was a very keen fly fisher (he found time to be the president of the eminent fly fishing club the Piscatorial Society between 1932 and 1950) and, happy with his own company, would retire to a chalk stream to escape the High Wycombe hothouse. Not unnaturally, the code words he chose were all fish, Bremen being salmon, Berlin was whitebait, Hamburg was dace and Cologne was trout (his favourite quarry), for example. The two targets mentioned were therefore Bremen or Hamburg. These code words went into common usage in official communications in 1942 and the secret list became known as the 'fish list'.

For the fourth time in as many days, fifteen crews were warned off for either dace (Hamburg) or jack (Mönchengladbach), briefed and aircraft prepared, only for the op to be scrubbed. It seemed that the only thing to do was have a party and, although they never needed one, they found a reason; a farewell to 109 Squadron and a welcome to 139 Squadron. The two Mosquito squadrons were doing a swap to and from RAF Marham.

No. 139 (Jamaica) Squadron had a tough start to the war, having lost virtually all its aircraft in France to the advancing German army as it swept into France. Equipped with Hudsons, it had a general reconnaissance role and bombed fringe targets in Europe. In early 1942 it re-equipped with Mosquitos, making low-level, often daylight, precision raids before joining the Pathfinders at Wyton in July 1943. It received its 'Jamaica' title in 1941 after a Jamaican newspaper, *The Daily Gleaner*, started a fund to raise money as part of the Bombers for Britain fund and, having raised enough for twelve Blenheims, had its name permanently attached to the squadron.

The frustration and irritation of the weeks following the Ruhr campaign now came to an end and the Battle of Hamburg, code-named Operation Gomorrah, was about to start. This north German port city (the largest port in Europe) had a population of 1.75 million people, a large industrial area, shipyards, U-boat pens and oil refineries. It was out of Oboe range but was seen as being a good H2S target with easily identifiable physical features, being situated on the wide River Elbe some 45 miles from the Baltic. Being easy to find and having many important targets, it was very well defended, second only to Berlin.

Well before the end of the Ruhr campaign, Harris set his sights on Hamburg. While it had been bombed numerous times before, it had escaped the 1,000 bomber raids and, as a strategic industrial and port city, Harris felt it was an essential target. He also announced the use of 'window' for the first time. Both the night fighters and the ground defences depended on radar for early target acquisition and to guide and control their night fighters and searchlights. By certain aircraft releasing thousands of black paper strips backed with aluminium foil the radars were confused as they received signals from both aircraft and the clouds of 'window'. This technology was ready to deploy as early as May 1942 but there was much squabbling about its use between the chiefs of staff and the scientists, Harris being initially against its use. One concern was that as the Germans almost certainly had the technology they would also use it. This became a diminishing concern as their bombing of Britain had almost entirely stopped. No. 76 Squadron, flying Halifaxes, was trained in its use and deployed it over Hamburg most effectively. The radar-tracked master searchlights scanned randomly and found few targets, with the result that the anti-aircraft guns fired haphazardly or not at all and the night fighter controllers could not find their pilots any targets. The box system was rendered ineffective overnight. In the first two raids using window the loss percentages were only 1.5 per cent and 2.2 per cent.

You may remember that window, or radar paper as they called it, was made by the John Dickinson paper milling and printing works at Frogmore Mill, part of the Apsley Mills complex near Brian's home town, Hemel Hempstead, and one of the many packing stations staffed mainly by volunteer women was an old garage in the nearby town of Berkhamsted.

181

The first raid of Operation Gomorrah was on 24 July and Brian and his crew were in their favourite ED984 with sixteen other 83 Squadron aircraft, the most they had put up since joining No. 8 Group. As Hamburg was beyond both Gee and Oboe range the Pathfinders relied on H2S and visuals; luckily the weather and visibility was good. At the briefing two things were different that signalled an important raid. Firstly, they were read a personal message from their commander-in-chief, Arthur Harris, and secondly – and to much excitement – they were told of the use of window. The squadron crews were allocated their roles – seven to back up, three of which would have to re-centre if required, one visual marker, two blind markers using H2S and six in the main force. They all took off between 2145 and 2230 hours into a clear sky.

Alec Shipway and Brian were the squadron's two blind markers and first in, due to drop at 0057 hours but Shipway was early. Most of his instruments became u/s on the way but instead of turning back he guessed both speed and altitude and, although helped by accurate route-marking flares, arrived a full six minutes early. It must have been eerie to circle the blacked out city, but not for long. While he and his navigator picked out landmarks on their H2S, Hamburg's air defences woke up and soon the air was full of searchlights and flak and he got a hole in his bomb bay doors for his trouble. This prompted him to tell his crew: 'It's about time someone started this party,' and smack on time he dropped his markers and bombs, as did two other Pathfinder aircraft with Brian a minute or so later; the raid was under way.

The Pathfinder pilots were getting used to complex marking plans and this was no exception. The twenty blind markers, using their 'special equipment', were to drop yellow markers and illuminating flares. Under that light, and precisely one minute later, the eight visual markers were to identify the aiming point and drop red markers for the main force four minutes later, with backers up ready to re-mark with reds. The main force of 667 aircraft bombed in 6 waves in less than 50 minutes.

The advantages of window were immediate. The scattering started mid-Channel and regularly on to the target, resulting in very few combats on their way out. When over the city it was clear that the usual coordination between searchlights and flak was absent, which many crews described. 'The searchlights hadn't got a clue,' presumably being bamboozled by the false radar signals 'and yet flak was being poured into the cones regardless of the absence of aircraft.' The overall loss of twelve aircraft was the lowest percentage for some time on a big raid.

Shipway and Brian reported later that they were happy with their work but at that early stage could see little evidence on the ground. Overall they felt content that the squadron and the Pathfinders put on a 'particularly fine show'. A number of squadron crews had problems with instruments, mainly u/s H2S.

Post-op analysis suggested that the marking was actually scattered but the main bombing stream dropped nearly 2,300 tons of bombs widely over the city. There was 'creep back' but much damage was done to the central and north-west of the city. A total of 1,500 people were killed in Hamburg but this was nothing to what happened on their next raid three days later.

One of the squadron crews at their post-op debrief mentioned that 'Boozer functioned', which was written up in the ORB. Boozer was a passive radar receiver that was designed to alert the operator when they were targeted by a German radar, both from the ground but typically from a night fighter. It was only introduced a few months earlier and the fact that only this aircraft mentions Boozer would suggest that few aircraft had them and they were still experimental.

That was the first of four Bomber Command raids and two USAAF daylight raids on Hamburg between 24 July and 2 August. I had always imagined it was after the event that it was named the Battle of Hamburg but apparently not. The ORB after that first raid reported: 'The Battle of Hamburg certainly started with a vengeance.'

With so many aircraft going through the target so quickly, they arrived home into crowded East Anglian skies from 0330 hours onward and, not untypically, there was a mist and visibility was down to 0.25 mile at times. It was an accident waiting to happen and sure enough Searby, who had been told to circle at 1,000ft and so could not see the flare-lit runway, was struck by another Lancaster from 156 Squadron, which was circling before landing at neighbouring Warboys. The collision took off his tail fin and rudder and smashed the upper turret, just as the lucky air gunner, Pilot Officer Coley, jumped out of his seat. Now damaged, Searby was given a priority landing slot. As he approached the runway, a 139 Squadron Mosquito appeared ahead of him from out of nowhere and landed, forcing Searby to land on the grass next to the runway, safely and with an uninjured but shaken crew. The other Lancaster, piloted by Squadron Leader Sammy Hall, also landed safely at Warboys but with his starboard outer engine ablaze and the propeller missing from another. Hall was a friend of Searby and admitted later to be very frightened by the incident. This type of situation was not uncommon, with tired crews and

183

damaged aircraft battling with poor early morning weather and a less than sophisticated air traffic control system. So, once again, it was calm heads and instinctive seat of the pants piloting that saved the day. A test that so many young inexperienced pilots failed.

According to his post-op debrief, Brian bombed precisely at 0059 hours, some fifty-nine minutes into his 19th birthday, even though his crew thought it was his 21st: what a way to spend your birthday.

It was not the only celebration that week as two days later Brian was promoted to flight lieutenant. They needed no excuse for a party and I hope they celebrated both these events. One of the reasons the Pathfinders of No. 8 Group was a popular posting was that crews received a promotion of one rank and the appropriate increase in pay. As a pilot officer Brian had been paid 14s 6d, about 74p in post-decimal currency. As a flight lieutenant his pay went up to £1 9s 9d, about £1.50p – so nearly doubled. I wonder how important that was to Brian? I suspect it was very important. There were, after all, mess bills to pay, pubs to visit and girls to take out.

For the first time the United States Eighth Air Force were invited to join the operation against Hamburg by carrying out two daylight raids immediately after the first Bomber Command raid. On 25 July, 100 B-17s bombed the shipyards and a day later seventy-one aircraft bombed the U-boat docks.

Although they intended to concentrate on these industrial targets, they were hampered by the smoke over the targets from the fires caused by the previous night's raids and so withdrew from Operation Gomorrah after those two daylight visits.

Although Brian was stood down, on the night of the 26th, 7 aircraft from 83 Squadron were employed on a raid to Essen with two backing up, the remaining 5 in the main stream, in a total force of 705 aircraft. Canadian Flight Lieutenant 'Rickie' Garvey had a passenger that night, Brigadier General Fred Anderson, the commander of USAAF 8 Bomber Command, who wanted to witness at first-hand what a night bombing operation was all about. Strange that they were back in the Ruhr so soon but it did achieve considerable damage to industrial and residential buildings as well as killing 500 people and injuring more than 1,200. One of the most important Essen targets, the Krupp factories, were hit and severely damaged on a very successful raid. Although window was deployed and the crews described the searchlights as 'being clueless', it was less effective as twenty-six aircraft, 3.7 per cent, were lost. General Anderson returned a day later for another trip, this time to Hamburg. Apparently he remarked after the raid that the fires were one of the most awe-inspiring sights he had ever seen and returned a few days later with gifts for Garvey and his crew. Garvey was briefly a reporter on the *Vancouver Province* newspaper, where his father, Art, was the sports editor. Garvey was 1 of a number of pilots to skipper Lancaster R5868, famous for completing 135 operations. He was one of the first to fly sixty operations without a break and completed his tour with a DFC but then cruelly was killed in a training accident flying an 'Ox Box' a few weeks later.

The second raid of the Hamburg offensive that General Anderson witnessed was a day later on 27 July and used 787 aircraft. At the squadron briefing Wing Commander Searby read out a personal message from Harris congratulating them on the first raid's success. The ORB sums up the atmosphere in that briefing room:

> We are all given to understand that our last few raids have done more to end this war and save thousands of 'Brown Types' [RAF slang for the British Army] than anything so far. The aircrew do feel that they are at last really achieving something vital towards ending this war and their spirit and press on attitude is at a peak.

Fourteen Lancasters from 83 Squadron were involved with Brian in 'A' for Apple. Initially Brian was briefed as the sole visual marker but they suspected that smoke could still be present from previous raids and he joined the four blind markers using H2S, all with yellow TIs. They were followed by another five aircraft backing up with greens and four in the main force. The five markers were reduced as Alec Shipway went back early with instrumentation problems but the remaining four were in first and were all done within three minutes. The backers up did their stuff and the main force bombed on greens, yellows and the increasing numbers of fires. The 700-plus aircraft went through their bombing run at the rate of about one every four seconds and dropped 2,326 tons of bombs. They all commented on the extent of the fires at the debrief. Warrant Officer Finding saw fires and smoke from 100 miles away. Flight Sergeant Turp reported a vast column of smoke up to 20,000ft and about 6 miles of fires. Pilot Officer Reid, who was backing up, said the crew could feel the heat of the fires in the aircraft – he bombed from 20,000ft. There is a difference of opinion as to how accurate the marking was but there is no doubt that the main force was remarkably accurate, putting a heavy concentration of bombs in a small area. It was later estimated that 550–600 bombs fell on an area 2 miles by 1 mile. The ORB reported the crews' high spirits on return and added:

> The pall of smoke over the target hung like a tremendous cumulus cloud complete with anvil where a light wind dispersed the top at 23,000ft. It was the most unholy sight lit up by the raging fires and visible for hundreds of miles.

The weather over the preceding days contributed to what transpired with hot, dry days and low humidity and an exceptional high evening temperature of 30°C. Most of the firefighters and their vehicles were on the other side of the city still damping down from the previous raids. The extreme concentration of bombing caused fires almost immediately, which were centred on the densely populated working-class areas of Hammerbrook, Hamm and Borgfelde and soon developed into a firestorm. The fires were so intense they sucked in air, creating winds that in turn generated incredibly high temperatures and thus spreading the firestorm widely. The asphalt roads burnt and the underground shelters were starved of oxygen. The fire burned for three hours, destroying about 16,000 apartment buildings and killing close to 40,000 people.

Whatever the airmen might have seen from the air, they could not have imagined the carnage on the ground and for one member of Brian's crew that would have been far from his mind. Following that operation Harold Allen, the mid-upper gunner, was off home to Birkenhead as on Saturday, 31 July, while the rest of his crew took ED984 for a test sortie, Harold was married to Dorothy 'Dolly' Farley in the Holy Trinity Church. He took a week's leave for his honeymoon.

Brian was stood down for the third raid on 29 July, which again, while not accurate, caused further damage. Fourteen squadron crews took part in a force of 777 aircraft. Much of the marking drifted 2 miles east and the main force crept back to mainly residential areas, creating more fires that the overstretched fire services could do little about. The city defences had improved and one crew had to fight off a night fighter, which damaged one wing, and Pilot Officer King's aircraft was hit by flak over the target, lost brake pressure and was instructed to land at Wittering. He mistook Sibson for Wittering and soon recognised his mistake as Sibson is grass and very short, so the landing was completed using the surrounding farmland. All were safe but the aircraft was wrecked. On the last day of the month, fourteen crews were prepped and briefed and in their aircraft ready for take-off before the op was scrubbed. As the ORB recorded: 'There was a rush for the bar, to drown those blues.'

Brian went back on the fourth and last raid of Operation Gomorrah on 2 August with fourteen 83 Squadron Lancasters as part of a total force of 740 aircraft. About thirty aircraft were lost to both Hamburg-based flak and night fighters, which as well as the normal *Himmelbett* system had an entire *Gruppe* – about thirty aircraft – acting freelance to attack the stream on the way in and back. This was the first time these novel tactics in such numbers had been used and would become the conventional night fighter *Zahme Sau* (Tame Boar) tactics of the next few months.

It was for most crews, particularly the less experienced, one of their more terrifying trips but not due to the actions of the Luftwaffe but at the hands of the other airmen's enemy, the weather.

As the first aircraft crossed the Dutch coast they flew straight into cloud, or *vis nil* as they put it, and within a few minutes were into thunderstorms, many trying and failing to weave their way through the vast towers of menacing cumulonimbus clouds. Every time they hit a storm they hit hail, started to ice up and the lightning blinded them for seconds at a time. The largest and fiercest of the storms hung over Hamburg, all crews experienced severe icing and the 10/10 cloud cover prevented any visual marking. As a consequence, the marking was scattered and the main force aircraft bombed poorly over a wide area, with many crews jettisoning their loads or, as Brian and three others did, bombing secondary, last-resort targets. As they turned for home, they passed over a port at the end of the Elbe estuary known to be a communications hub and Brian's log reported:

Electrical Storms – bombed Cuxhaven

A number of crews had eventful nights; one crew lost one engine and returned on three, while King lost his rear turret and his H2S just before the run and his Gee and bombsight just after. Wing Commander Shaw lost one engine and the other three surged dramatically, although he went on to bomb and skilfully nursed the aircraft home at 110 knots, while Maurice Chick went as low as 9,000ft to bomb. However, they all returned, a credit to their skill and training. Many experienced the natural phenomenon of St Elmo's Fire on their wings, which appeared to light up, and one aircraft was struck by lightning, adding to the bizarre nature of the night's work. Few crews returned without such experiences and it was fortunate that so very few succumbed to the appalling conditions. An operation to be forgotten.

Jack Currie, a Lancaster pilot, in his atmospheric and amusing book *Lancaster Target* describes his harrowing experiences of that raid vividly. After the war, and in the knowledge of the destruction of the first three raids, he wrote:

> Nature, more terrible and more effective than all man-made defences, had thrown her arms around the city and its ravaged streets and protected it from further horrors.

The use of window on these Hamburg raids had an immediate positive effect, much to the joy of the crews. However, these would be short-lived as the Luftwaffe would mitigate these advantages with the new *Wilde Sau* and *Zahme Sau* night fighter tactics, which were less dependent on ground radar. The early success of these tactics encouraged their widespread use and further developments would be introduced over the coming months with even more devastating effect.

Operation Gomorrah was over and it had demonstrated the appalling destruction these concentrated, large-scale area bombing raids could inflict. Later Alfred Speer (Hitler's architect and Reich Minister of Armaments and War Production) would write in his book published after the war, *The Secret Diaries*:

> It was quite a surprise to us when the first Hamburg raid took place because you used some new device which was preventing the anti-aircraft guns to find your bombers, so you had a great success and you repeated these attacks on Hamburg several times and each time the new success was greater and the depression was larger, and said, in those days, in a meeting of the Air Ministry, that if you would repeat this success on four or five other German towns, then we would collapse.

As far as Bomber Command was concerned, the four Hamburg raids employed 3,091 sorties and 87 aircraft were lost (a further nine were written off after take-off or landing crashes or from irreparable battle damage), most of which were heavies. About 552 aircrew were killed and a further 65 became PoWs. No. 83 Squadron sent fifty-seven sorties, of which fifty-six bombed their targets without losing a single aircraft, an outstanding record.

More than 8,000 tons of bombs were dropped over the four night raids and most reasonable estimates suggest that more than 42,000 people, possibly nearer 45,000, were killed. Eight square miles of the city were destroyed, including over 250,000 dwellings, resulting, incredibly, in about 1.2 million people, about two thirds of the city's population, displaced and leaving the city after the second raid's firestorms.

The statistics are appalling and it was, for the people of Hamburg, an utterly terrifying week.

Military historians, with the benefit of hindsight, search for wartime 'turning points' and the second raid on Hamburg appears regularly on these lists. As Speer pointed out, that operation clearly exposed Germany's vulnerability to area bombing and for Bomber Command it justified their strategy and persuaded the War Cabinet to let it continue. The second Hamburg raid added to the invasion of Sicily and the Soviet Army offensive at Kursk to make July 1943 a pivotal month in the war.

August 1943 was to be the busiest of the war to that point, with Bomber Command completing more than 7,800 sorties and for 83 Squadron it started on the 7th. Fourteen crews were briefed for another raid to Italy, for which Brian and his crew were stood down, but it was an interesting raid on a number of levels. It was the first of seven over a period of ten days from 7 to 16 August. The Italian bombing campaign was now politically motivated. Factory workers had been striking for some time as their workplaces were targeted and the continued bombing of the major cities in the north and the American campaign in the south did for once in the history of strategic bombing seriously affect the morale of the Italian people, putting Mussolini's regime under pressure. Allied forces invaded Sicily on 10 July and Rome was bombed for the first time on 19 July. That was enough and on 24 July command of the Italian armed forces was returned to the king and Mussolini was arrested the next day. Pietro Badaglio was appointed prime minister but did not surrender. This raid and more throughout August were intended to put further pressure on the Badaglio government to give up, which at last it did on 9 September, followed soon after by the invasion of mainland Italy at Salerno by British and American forces to remove the German occupying forces. It is widely believed that, for once, the psychological effects of the bombing campaign on the Italian people and subsequently on the Badaglio government far outweighed the physical damage.

The operation on 7 August was to Turin, Genoa and Milan, with the first two targets dealt with as one op and Milan separately. The plan was that twenty-four Pathfinder Lancasters would mark Turin for a main force of fifty from No. 1 and No. 5 groups. Twenty-two of the markers would then go on to mark Genoa for a further fifty aircraft from the same groups. It's a long journey and the Wyton crews took off in fading daylight, either side of 2130 hours, all loaded with flares and TIs. They marked Turin at around 0100 and Genoa at about 0130 hours. All returned safely between 0530 and 0615 hours. A long night's work with crews seeming happy with the Turin result but less so at Genoa, which was scattered. As far as the squadron was concerned, it was of particular interest in that it was controlled by a master bomber, who was their boss, John Searby. For him, this was a rehearsal for another master bomber-controlled operation that was to take place ten days later and was one of the most famous raids of the Bomber Command campaign.

The Italian job was Flight Lieutenant Tommy Wilmot's last with the squadron, having completed his tour. As was traditional, it gave all concerned another excuse for a party to send him on his way. The ORB noted: 'He was seen heading rapidly in a southerly direction towards Huntingdon Station with a bag and a "I've got 14 days leave" gleam in his eye.' What that report did not include was that Tommy went on leave with a broken arm received after a rather too vigorous mess game at his leaving bash. Mess games stimulated by an excess of alcohol were rarely violent but boisterous and often dangerous. It was decided that Tommy should leave Wyton with an impression of his backside on the ante-room ceiling. The de-bagged Tommy, with his rear end anointed with soot, fell from the pyramid of mess furniture stacked for his final ascent. It was his only injury in two tours.

The next day, ops were laid on but soon scrubbed and after a lecture from the commanding officer about his ferry pilot days, the rest of the evening was enjoyed at a squadron party. The ORB describes 'dancing and drinking (as far as 800 bottles will divide among 1,000 parched throats)'. It seems they ran out of booze and when the armourers turned up, having had to bomb up a visiting squadron, it was all gone. They were compensated by a special bus laid on for them into Cambridge a few days later.

On 10 August Brian, in ED984, and 652 other aircraft bombed the hub city of Nuremburg, the second largest city in Bavaria, with varied military production sites but, as the home of a number of pre-war Nazi Party rallies, a symbolic target. Fourteen crews from 83 Squadron were briefed for this operation, which was their first to this target. Brian, once again, was one of two visual markers. The targets were marked but cloud obscured their results, although and they all seemed unhappy with this rather scattered effort. Nonetheless, the main force did well and significant damage was done to the central and southern parts of the city. Sixteen aircraft were lost but all squadron aircraft returned, although a couple of them nearly didn't. The dangers of the proximity of other aircraft in the stream was brought home to Pilot Officer Allcroft when another aircraft, having been shot up, exploded, sending debris into his Lancaster and putting the front turret out of action and holing the fuselage. Brian's log had a curious comment, the truth of which the Squadron Operation Report Book revealed. The single comment he wrote was:

Shaky Do!!!

It seems that he had one engine fail before he reached the target but went on to bomb successfully on three. As soon as he finished his bomb run, a second engine 'went 3 parts u/s', which left him seriously underpowered. Having lost about 4 tons of bombs and half his fuel, he was just able to maintain a much lower altitude. He and Vernie would have had a lot of work to do. The fuel would have to be redistributed across the six wing fuel tanks to balance the aircraft and the two good engines monitored carefully to prevent overheating and to conserve fuel. The danger when two engines failed was that the remaining Merlins were overworked, overheated and drank too much. At the lower altitude, almost certainly below 10,000ft, he then had to get away from Nuremberg's defences, cross the French fighter belt on the German-France border and return over occupied France and the Channel. Not surprisingly, he was the last aircraft to land back at Wyton after a rather nervous seven-and-three-quarter-hour flight. The ORB noted that: 'F/Lt Slade put up a magnificent show ...'

The author of the ORB that night had some other pithy comments: 'The route as usual went through Mannheim, Karlsruhe, Stuttgart, Frankfurt area and it was of paramount importance that navigators kept the aircraft on the track otherwise veritable hornets nests would be stirred up and the hostility of the natives proved beyond doubt.' The raid was not a success as the marking was scattered and low cloud impaired everyone's view of the target. The ORB went on to note that: 'The fires seen through the cloud were not the funeral pyre of Nazism but the work of RAF Charcoal Production Unlimited setting the surrounding woods ablaze.'

Brian's Flight Commander Norman Hildyard was the one other visual marker that night. He had already collected a DFC when in 58 Squadron in June 1941 and collected a Bar to that over Nuremberg later in the month when, having escaped a coning on his bomb run, he went round again and bombed successfully.

Bomber Command now swung back to Italy to continue the pressure on Badaglio. On 12 August Brian was part of fourteen squadron aircraft in a 504 aircraft operation to Milan. All 83 Squadron aircraft were involved, with Wyton's station commander Group Captain Graham taking Sergeant Miller's aircraft and crew. All were happy with their marking and overall the operation was deemed successful. Only three aircraft were lost, none from 83 Squadron. The ORB remarked: 'Another pin was knocked from under the feet of tottering Italy.' Brian had an extra crew member that night, one Sergeant Ralph Henderson, but more of him later.

These visits to Italy were long tiring nights and on the 13th crews rested in the morning and there was no flying, giving ground crews some time to 'make and mend'.

The following night, however, 140 Lancasters took off once again on another raid to Milan with fourteen squadron aircraft for marking and backing up duties. It was deemed successful, with the newly promoted Group Captain Searby the senior pilot.

On 15 August there was another raid to Milan, with 199 Lancasters producing some very effective and concentrated bombing. Seven aircraft were lost and once again 83 Squadron suffered no casualties, which meant a clean sheet over the seven Italian raids. As most of these ops took over seven and a half hours and the journey back was normally in the company of pre-warned night fighters, it was an excellent record. The Badaglio government would last only another three weeks.

Chapter 19

Peenemünde

While there were a number of specific military industrial targets during the Ruhr and Hamburg campaigns, it was the area bombing of their surrounding built-up areas, whether deliberately or collaterally, that had the greatest effect. Not only through the destruction of buildings and the displacement of civilians but also in creating a significant distraction for Luftwaffe and civilian resources in their defence of the Reich.

Developing technology, however, and the ability to use it was improving accuracy. So, when a vitally important and relatively small target arose, Bomber Command was used. If it had been closer to mainland Britain a special forces raid such as that which brought back parts of the Würzburg radar from Bruneval in early 1942 would have been contemplated but this next target was too large, too complex and too far away in Pomerania, a place unheard of to most, on the Baltic coast of northern Germany.

The story of the creation of a centre for German rocket research and testing starts in the early 1930s. Although a scientist led project, the military soon hijacked the work as a clear route to the creation of new weapon systems and as such were in breach of the rearmament agreement imposed at Versailles. Consequently, the work of these military scientists was carried out under strict security. As early as 1931, the Wehrmacht built a research centre near Berlin but soon needed to expand to more remote and secure premises. They selected an isolated peninsula on the north German Baltic coast about 160 miles from Berlin. With water on three sides and no established transport links, it was easy to develop controlled security, and the small fishing village of Peenemünde on the mouth of the River Peene was its only close neighbour. Early occupants of the site loved its peace and tranquility, the pleasant summer climate, the beaches and its isolation.

By 1937 it was a fully established complex but continued to grow after the outbreak of war and by 1943 had extensive new accommodation, a power station, rail links, an airfield (controlled by the Luftwaffe) and vast areas of laboratory, testing and manufacturing infrastructure. It was highly technologically advanced. The power station, for instance, was the largest and most advanced in Germany. A coal-fed, steam turbine produced 20,000 kilowatts of power. The wind tunnel, or Aerodynamic Institute as it was known, was the most advanced in the world and capable of simulating conditions up to Mach 4.4. It alone employed 200 scientists and technicians. The whole site, about 12 square miles, was home to about 17,000 people, a mixture of military, scientists, an army of forced labourers and the families of many of the scientific and military personnel. Its location made it a popular posting.

The man in charge was a military scientist called Walter Dornberger. A number of the senior scientists were given military rank and, although there were tensions between the military and scientific 'wings' of Peenemünde, as far as the core work was concerned it was the scientists who prevailed, the most prominent of whom was Wernher von Braun. This brilliant young physicist quickly led a team of some of the best scientific and engineering talent in Germany, which in the 1930s was a powerhouse of scientific innovation. Von Braun was also an attractive, charismatic personality and an excellent administrator. At the outset of war it was clear that the entire establishment was working towards the creation of rocket-propelled projectiles and by the beginning of 1943 von Braun personally met and persuaded Hitler that he had weapon systems capable of delivering a potent payload of explosives up to 200 miles. Fully resourced, von Braun and his team were now close to mass production and widespread deployment. At a time when the war was looking increasingly unwinnable, these *Vergeltungswaffen* (retaliation weapons) or V-weapons provided Hitler with hope.

The visionary von Braun, although using Third Reich funding for his own research, was savvy enough to realise that in the event of Germany's defeat this unique knowledge would make him attractive to the Allies.

From as early as December 1942 and from various sources, the British intelligence community picked up information that Germany was developing rocket technology. However, not until April 1943 did the chiefs of staff recognise the possible significance of this scant information and appointed a man to coordinate the effort to establish what was happening at Peenemünde, and if necessary consider how to neutralise that threat. A young former MP with a background in rocketry was selected, and it did no harm that Duncan Sandys was also Churchill's son-in-law. His appointment ruffled feathers in the scientific intelligence community, within which varying views about the accuracy of the intelligence existed.

Over the next month or so the various strands of intelligence were collated and analysed, resulting in Sandys tasking the RAF to carry out photographic sorties. It was the Leuchars-based 540 (Photoreconnaissance) Squadron, which was familiar with the Baltic and the North German coast, that sent a single Mosquito on five sorties in May and June. Although there were flak boats close to Peenemünde, they were ordered not to fire so as not to alert the aircraft that there was anything worth protecting and these reconnaissance and photographic sorties progressed unopposed. The analysis of all this information and the work done by the photographic interpreters of RAF Medmenham convinced Sandys that Peenemünde had developed a rocket-propelled weapon that was very close to being deployed and the War Cabinet accepted his report. They were correct to do so as the weapons were already being manufactured.

There were two weapons being developed at Peenemünde. The V-2 was a liquid-fuelled rocket with a 2,200lb payload and a range of 200 miles. The production line for the manufacture of these weapons was ready just before the RAF arrived. The V-1, known in the UK as the 'doodlebug', was more of a flying bomb, manufactured away from Peenemünde but tested from its launch sites by the Luftwaffe. It was the same team that were working on the first rocket-propelled fighter, the Messerschmitt Me 163, and the first jet fighter, the Me 262. V-1s were already in production, and many of their factory sites were targeted by Bomber Command. The V-1 had a warhead of 1,870lb and a range of 160 miles. The intention was to launch the V-1 and V-2 towards London from sites in occupied France and Holland. The V-1 had no guidance but was simply pointed in the right direction and would drop onto the target when it ran out of fuel; an inaccurate but effective terror weapon.

As a small special forces raid was instantly dismissed knowing the size of the target, it fell to the chief of the air staff, Air Chief Marshal Charles Portal, to organise an operation to destroy Peenemünde. There was some dispute initially, with some senior officers wanting a smaller precision approach but Harris eventually went for a large-scale operation with both a large force bombing Pathfinder-marked targets and a smaller group bombing on 'time and distance' techniques, all controlled by a master bomber. By early August the plan was taking shape but at this stage no one was informed of the nature or location of the target outside High Wycombe. Security was tight and even John Searby, who had rehearsed his command and control skills on the first Turin raid on 7 August, was not told what that rehearsal was for. On 16 August he was invited up to Pathfinder HQ with his navigator and bomb aimer, where Don Bennett showed them a detailed model of a target they would be attacking. They were not told what or where this was but the three key parts of the target were pointed out.

Harris, at his regular meeting on the morning of 17 August, knew that the next few days provided the moonlight he required, and when told that the weather was good he decided that the operation was to happen that night. As usual, the news went down to the squadrons that an operation was on but not until 1000 hours and with no details of target or route. Normally, to enable them to fuel and bomb up the aircraft the 'erks' and the armourers would be told fuel and bomb load details early, but not today. Brian and his crew took ED984 for an hour's NFT in the morning and when they returned there were still no orders for the ground crews. The armourers did not get their orders until after lunch. The normal clues were absent, which will have puzzled both ground and aircrew alike.

As the ORB comments: 'A fine day with normal work up to about 1000 hours when a target came through that even the route and other details were withheld from all but the CO. Details were late through, the armourers had to wait until after lunch loads [sic] and suspense grew apace.'

Searby was called up to Group HQ for a meeting at 1130 hours, where he was informed of the location and more details on the nature of the target but not precisely what went on at Peenemünde.

Most of the Pathfinder aircraft, as usual, were loaded with flares, markers or a marker/HE mix but for the main force crews scattered around a number of East Anglian airfields, when they saw their loads early that afternoon they were HE bombs, not incendiaries. In fact, 75 per cent of aircraft had HE only. Whatever the target, it was one that needed to be blown to smithereens rather than incinerated. The fuel load, when it eventually came in, indicated Berlin, which was not met with delight as a clear, moonlit night over the city that had the most intense defences was not a great prospect. The crews' puzzlement carried on right up to their final briefing.

Although the Peenemünde peninsula was large (2 miles by 6 miles) and most of it was used by the research establishment or its support buildings, three specific targets were identified that would provide three separate aiming points. The first was the experimental works (A/P E), the second was the new V-2 production works (A/P B) and the third was the housing estate, which included the Wehrmacht barracks and some of the forced labourers' accommodation (A/P F). It was felt that as well as the specific building targets it was crucial to disrupt production by killing scientists and workers. It was a weekday night, so the houses and accommodation blocks should be full.

It was August, a relatively short night and a seven-hour round trip, so aircraft would be getting airborne in daylight. To make this work, crew briefings would normally have been early but for this operation they went into the briefings in late afternoon and they would have noticed that security was particularly tight, with a greater number than usual of military police on station. This would have added to the mystery of the fuel and bomb load. At that time squadron morale was high, they had experienced successes over the Ruhr and Hamburg and 83 Squadron specifically had refined many of the Pathfinder techniques that had contributed directly to these successes; the continuing use of window had also eased the threat of the night fighters.

The original operation order from High Wycombe was issued on 9 July, over a week before the raid, and was subject to various amendments but included the clearest indication of the importance of the target: 'If the attack fails to achieve the object it will have to be repeated the next night and on ensuing nights regardless … of casualties.'

No. 83 Squadron's commanding officer, Group Captain John Searby, was the night's nominated master bomber and led the briefing. There would have been a great buzz of excitement as the various maps and plans had their coverings removed and they were informed of the target, though few would have ever heard of it and none knew of its significance. Even after the raid security was maintained, and in his logbook Brian's description of the target was:

Peenemünde Radio – Location Factory

Firstly, the announcement that 596 aircraft were to be involved would have told them instantly that this was a big and important operation. The news that it was not Berlin and known not to have sophisticated ground-based air defences would have been met with relief, as would the route mainly over the sea and Denmark.

The atmosphere was heightened by the presence of Don Bennett and Duncan Sandys to hear Searby's briefing to his squadron. Searby rose to the occasion, and with the added responsibility of that night's role, he delivered what he later considered to be one of his best briefings.

Searby later recalled in his book *The Great Raids – Peenemünde*:

> From the low dais in front of the large map of Europe with its coloured tapes and pins, which marked the heavily defended areas of occupied territory, I watched the faces of my crews. They were impressed by the urgency but not worried, for the job would be done to the best of their ability. I caught the eye of Brian Slade, veteran Pathfinder captain at 21 years of age, and he grinned; he was all for it.
>
> Against the background of Essen, Berlin, Hamburg, Munich, Cologne and similar bloodbaths Peenemünde did not, at this stage, make much impression … No one had heard of this insignificant pimple sticking out of Pomerania and there was nothing humdrum about the operation; hence Brian's smile.

Brian's smile was as much due to the fact that Searby was to give him the opportunity to be the first aircraft over the target.

The secrecy continued, with the crews given not a hint of what happened at Peenemünde. Bomber Command was paranoid that any captured crew would potentially give away all their intelligence and worked on the basis that the less they knew the better. Although the crews were not told target details, some of the younger, inexperienced men responded to the general buzz: this was their Hamburg, their Dams raid. Nobody would have missed the importance of this raid, especially as Searby's parting shot was to pass on High Wycombe's order that they would do it again tomorrow if unsuccessful.

Soon after the briefings, the crews may have heard sixteen Merlin engines thundering down the Wyton runway but it was not four Lancasters, it was eight Mosquitos. These 139 Squadron aircraft were off to refuel closer to the coast before heading on a 'spoof' operation to Berlin.

It had been a hot August afternoon and was now a perfect summer's evening as 83 Squadron's fifteen Lancasters took off close to 2100 hours in daylight, passing through their assembly areas and heading north-east across the North Sea at the low altitude of 1,000ft. One crew returned quickly with engine trouble, but the rest pressed on with more than 580 heavies behind them. The North Sea is calm and after about an hour and thirty minutes, as they approached the Danish coast they dropped to 250ft. Their efforts to avoid detection worked but just after the Mosquitos started to mob up

Berlin, the Luftwaffe's early warning radar spotted the first wave of the main force on a different route and a higher altitude and circulated 'many hostile aircraft north of Ameland' (off the north Holland coast).

The decoy Mosquitos, after an uneventful flight, arrived over the German capital at about 2300 hours. They were briefed to fly at different headings and at different altitudes, and each dropped three 500lb bombs and some TIs. This had the desired effect as the sight of Mosquitos dropping TIs convinced the Berlin defences that the main force spotted over Ameland was on its way to them. Of the eight Mosquitos, one was lost but the rest reported hundreds of searchlights and that the flak was hot and heavy. The ground defences around Berlin and the radar stations controlling the night fighters were completely fooled by the main force's direction and the Mosquito attack. As far as they were concerned, this large force of bombers was clearly taking the northern route to Berlin. The night fighter controllers dispatched 158 twin-engine fighters to act with *Wilde Sau* tactics (many of which would have normally been tasked into the *Himmelbett* boxes) and fifty-five single-engine fighters and told them 'the hostile formation ... is close to Berlin'. The Berlin ground defences were thrown into confusion and a number of twin-engine night fighters were shot down by their own flak defences, having confused them with the decoy Mosquitos. The decoy raid was working perfectly, and it would save many aircrew's lives.

Earlier that day, the USAAF had carried out two large-scale daylight raids on the ball bearing factory at Schweinfurt and the Messerschmitt factory at Regensburg, which Bomber Command hoped would further stretch the day and night fighter squadrons of the Luftwaffe. Some 376 B-17 Flying Fortresses took off from their bases in England and, although the Regensburg bombing was a success, the losses were appalling; 60 aircraft did not return and 552 aircrew were initially reported missing. It was the Americans' worst loss percentage, nearly 16 per cent, of the war to date. Those raids fully occupied the Luftwaffe daylight fighters and a few twin-engine night fighters were also deployed, but they soon refuelled and rearmed. It did little to deter the night fighters from their coming night's work.

The Luftwaffe also had something new up its sleeve, which by coincidence was introduced that night. Night fighters had cannon and machine guns fixed in their wings or noses, which meant that an aircraft had to be pointing directly at its target when firing and the normal direction of approach was from behind, making them vulnerable to the rear gunner's attentions. Two enterprising Luftwaffe officers had put two 20mm cannon in a Messerschmitt pointing in an upward direction. This enabled the attacking fighter to approach unseen from underneath, where not only was he safer from the bomber's gunners but would be firing into the bomb bay and the wing fuel tanks. This weapon was nicknamed *Schräge Musik* (oblique music), and coupled with the new *Wilde Sau* tactics they hoped to further counter the use of the window. As the 596 aircraft crossed Denmark and the Baltic Sea, these night fighters were congregating around Berlin only 150 miles south of Peenemünde, looking forward to the arrival of such a large number of targets on a clear moonlit night.

The approach flight for the vast majority of the bombers, other than the release of bundles of window, was uneventful and as it was unusual to fly in such clear conditions many of the crews simply enjoyed the view as they crossed the North Sea, Denmark and the Baltic. Brian and the 83 Squadron aircraft were the first to cross the North Sea at a few hundred feet, rising to about 4,000ft to avoid the light flak deployed across Denmark and weaving continuously to give the air gunners the best change of spotting night fighters that infested the area of southern Denmark near Sylt. The Pathfinders' orders described the night's work as a 'Newhaven ground marking' job, but there was a complex plan of route marking, illuminating, blind and visual markers and the usual backers up that would mark three aiming points for three waves of main force bombers. Further Pathfinders would re-mark where possible, with the master bomber guiding the backing up and the main force of bombers by reference to the visible coloured markers. The seven blind markers from 83 Squadron (there were sixteen in all) were Brian, Pilot Officer Alec Shipway, Squadron Leader Guy Sells, Squadron Leader John Manton, Pilot Officer John Reid, Squadron Leader Ambrose Smith and Flying Officer Maurice Chick (his was the aircraft that turned back with engine trouble). Searby had chosen his most experienced crews for this initial marking role, one of the privileges of being the master bomber and the squadron commander.

They were all described in the No. 8 Group order as blind illuminator markers, which suggested their impending role. Their loads were appropriate, with each aircraft having four containers of flares, three red spot cookies as well as 7,000lb of HE. With a fuel load for a seven-hour trip, these aircraft were taking off with near maximum payload.

The overall marking plan and the timings were precise and complex. The blind markers were to approach from the north-west, locate the Árcona peninsula on the northern tip of the Island of Rügen and turn to the south-east some 45 miles north of the target. Then they would mark the route in by putting one of their 'red spot fires' on the small Ruden Island, continue on the same heading, drop their flares to illuminate the target area and another red spot to try and mark the aiming point, then circle for a second run and drop their high explosives. Immediately, the visual markers would re-mark the identified aiming point with yellows under the light of the flares. The blind markers would, of course, achieve all this using their H2S as the radar experts assured them that all the key landmarks would be visible on their screens, most crucially Ruden Island, which would then be continuously backed up, providing a datum that subsequent markers could use for a time and distance run. This was seen as a belt and braces approach using the new and the old navigating techniques.

That was just the start of it. The first aiming point would then be re-marked by the backers up with greens for the first wave of main force, and once they had finished the 'aiming point shifters' would then mark the second aiming point. That would be adjusted for the second wave and that repeated for the third and last aiming point. The whole operation was to be observed and controlled by the circling master bomber.

Martin Middlebrook, in his detailed book *The Peenemünde Raid*, noted:

> The first markers were released at 12.10am – one minute
> early – by the crew Flight Lieutenant Brian Slade, a senior
> Pathfinder captain at the age of only twenty-one!

As we know, he was in fact 19.

However, the raid did not get off to the best of starts. Although the weather was clear as they approached, on arrival Searby observed a thin layer of cloud between 2,000 and 3,000ft. It proved not to be an issue as he initially flew beneath it but the smoke generators, part of Peenemunde's ground defences, were a problem. Although they had started belching, the early arrivals could still see the target but by the time they had circled, even under the flares, the smoke generators were doing their job and the visual markers would struggle, particularly as they were operating from about 16,000ft. Worse was that Ruden was not visible on the blind markers' H2S screens, which led to the initial red spots landing either short or beyond the aiming point. In Brian's post-op debriefing he admits his marking fell in the sea well short of the aiming point. The timing of the blind markers was nearly perfect, with all marking within their allotted four minutes. The marking schedule was now into its fourth minute and between the reds short of and beyond the target a yellow marker appeared smack on aiming point 'F'. This was quickly marked by backers up with greens and that became the aiming point for the first wave, which arrived on time, a minute later. That yellow, dropped by a 156 Squadron Lancaster visual marker, saved the day or at least made Searby's job much easier.

A combination of further continuous accurate backing up controlled by Searby kept the markers in the right place despite the entire target area now being a mass of fires, explosions and smoke. In order to observe and correct the markers, his circuit was at a lower altitude to the main force, This proved an unnerving experience for his crew, who watched many main force 4,000lb cookies falling past them. The Darky frequency would have been fizzing as he directed the backers up and then the aiming point shifters and next two waves to bomb on the subsequent two aiming points. A constant problem that all crews had to deal with was not only the smoke generators, probably the most effective component of the site's defences, but also smoke from the early markers and fires that obscured the entire area for much of the duration of the operation in a gentle crosswind.

By now most the early Pathfinders were on their way home. Brian and most of the early markers knew H2S had let them down and their debriefs very accurately described those early marking errors, but equally as they left they will have seen the aiming point marked accurately and on return learned how successful the marking overall had been.

There was some light flak over the target from ground-based light machine guns, some heavier flak guns and from the flak ship moored off Peenemünde that bothered a few aircraft that strayed in their direction, including the master bomber, who was shot at on most of his circuits. The first two waves of main force aircraft were not troubled by night fighters but those spoofed into circling Berlin had already seen the early target markers and flares 150 miles to the north and raced towards them. Clarification of the target was not confirmed by the German defences until 0130 hours but most of those night fighters circling Berlin were already on their way to Peenemünde. They arrived as the third wave of 180 Halifaxes and Stirlings were bombing and making their exit from the target area.

In bright moonlight the night fighters first up from Berlin had an easy time finding targets. Unencumbered by their *Himmelbett* radar controllers, they enjoyed the freedom to pick off bombers on their bombing runs from above silhouetted against the ground fires and then from the bomber stream as they headed home. In total, forty aircraft were lost, with twenty-eight of those from the last wave. It is thought that six of those were the result of the new *Schräge Musik* tactics. There is no doubt that had not the diversionary tactics of the Mosquito raid on Berlin been so effective in keeping the Berlin defences on station they would have reached Peenemünde much earlier with even more devastating consequences. The night fighters followed the last bombers back and those who flew low to avoid them had to fly through the flak defences on the Danish Islands, which claimed some more.

No. 83 Squadron did not lose a single aircraft that night, although Searby, as one of the last to leave, was attacked by a night fighter on his last circuit but managed to fight it off. For once the first bombers over the target were not greeted by the heaviest flak or the fresh night fighter crews and all were well on their way home before the night fighters from Berlin created such havoc. Searby witnessed the carnage of many bombers brought down by night fighters.

Operation Hydra, as it was code-named, was deemed a success as V-2 production was halted for some months. In fact, the experimental works were hardly touched but the V-2 production works were damaged, although only hit by a few bombs. The greatest damage was done to the accommodation blocks and their inhabitants, although many of them reached their shelters before the bombs reached them, including most of the senior scientists. The labour camp was hard hit as the accommodation was wooden huts with no decent shelters. In the longer term, the V-1 and V-2 attacks on London that started in June and September 1944 were almost certainly delayed and limited in terms of the number of weapons that were deployed.

Group Captain Searby put much of the raid's success down to the selection of the most experienced crews to carry out the early marking and backing up but it was his control of the operation from his circling Lancaster that was seen as the single factor that prevented the raid from failing. His special report on the operation makes fascinating reading. He was constantly observing the target area and directing the main force on which colours to bomb. More than ninety Pathfinder aircraft were tasked, many of which would have been circling awaiting Searby's instructions. He made seven circuits of the target area under fire from that pesky flak boat every time. Duncan Sandys remained at Wyton for the duration of the raid and Searby was able to report personally of the success. The following day Searby was awarded the Distinguished Service Order. His deputy master bomber that night was Wing Commander Johnny Fauquier, who in a few days' time would be given the responsibility of his own master bomber operation, the first to 'the Big City'.

The Pathfinder post-op narrative pulls no punches and almost certainly came from the blunt pen of Don Bennett, No. 8 Group's commander.

The initial marking was praised but some of the time and distance visual markers were heavily criticised. That to Bennett was poor execution of a basic navigator's skill:

> The crews concerned are doubly blameworthy as the attack undoubtedly opened on the right spot and the aiming point accurately marked by the 1st visual marker. However this phase was short lived, thanks largely to the instructions of the Master of Ceremonies and to the subsequent markers having their fingers out.

In hindsight the Peenemünde raid remains an important and significant operation. Plenty went wrong: the bombing by recent standards was reasonably concentrated but not enough on such small targets and the damage was disappointingly temporary. The losses in the third wave were extremely high, with 6.7 per cent of aircraft lost. However, plenty went right. The threat of the work at Peenemünde was identified and action taken. The decoy raid was a great success and prevented the loss of many more bombers. The damage significantly stalled work on V-1 and V-2 development, production and deployment for two or three months at a critical period of the war. For the Pathfinders, a complex marking plan worked and the nascent master bomber concept was launched and would become a feature of many future raids, and often their reason for success. It is remarkable that after flying about 600 miles, the important players arrived to the minute at their allotted times.

Whether it was the USAAF at Schweinfurt and Regensburg or Bomber Command at Peenemünde, the previous twenty-four hours was the last straw for the man answerable to Göring for the defence of the Reich. The following day the chief of the general staff of the Luftwaffe, Hans Jeschonnek, committed suicide.

Von Braun was unscathed by the raid and, as he himself predicted, after the war was whisked away to the United States, received immunity from war crimes prosecution and became a key player at NASA. In July 1969, as a 15-year-boy, I watched Neil Armstrong take his famous giant leap. He was delivered to the Moon by the Saturn rocket, designed by von Braun. Little did I know that twenty-three years earlier my uncle and his chums had flown nearly 600 miles to try and kill him.

Don Bennett had a house at Wyton and invited Searby and some of his pilots to look at the post-op reconnaissance photos. Brian, 'Punch'

Thompson, Alec Shipway and a couple of others enjoyed a glass of sherry and looked at the photos with a small stereoscopic viewer to see the damage. The normally distant and difficult Bennett was clearly cheered by the success of the operation. Searby was happy that his boss was happy, so this group of senior pilots were very satisfied with their night's work and returned to the mess for further celebration.

An operation was planned for the following day but scrubbed at the briefing, where Searby paid a special tribute to the crews who took part in the Peenemünde raid. Life at Wyton soon returned to normal. Two days of stand down with various training carried out including clay pigeon shooting for the air gunners, a lecture on 'window' and some fighter affiliation. On 21 August they had a crew conference where new and old raid tactics were discussed, and then a general airing of everybody's grouses, 'including of course Sergeants' Messing'. The ORB comments: 'Everything went to show we are a happy squadron.' A number of buses to Cambridge only slightly lifted the monotony and frustration of more scrubbed operations, but on 23 August crews were excited to hear that day's target: Berlin.

Chapter 20

Berlin

The Big Mystery

Berlin had long been an ambition for Harris and although it had been attacked a number of times, it had not received the large-scale attention of his other city targets. Now, he had more heavies, more sophisticated radar systems and tactics that were improving navigation, accuracy and effectiveness, or so he hoped. The increased involvement of the USAAF also increased his irrepressible belief that the Allies' bombing strategy was working and if increased with more bombers and more high-profile city targets, Bomber Command could have a decisive role in ending the war. Germany's heavily defended capital city, which in 1943 had a population of 4.4 million, was that next prestigious target.

What became known as the 'Battle of Berlin' is often described as starting with an operation on 18 November 1943 and continuing until the end of March 1944. Over that period there were sixteen major raids on the city as well as large and small operations to other city targets. However, I believe that the Battle of Berlin started earlier than November with three significant operations in late August and early September, the first of which was on 23 August.

On that night 727 aircraft took part from Nos. 1, 4, 5 and 6 groups, with No. 8 Group's Pathfinder Lancasters and Halifaxes providing fifty-one H2S-equipped blind markers and re-centrers, thirty-seven backers up and thirty-four with the main force. Brian, in 'A' for 'Apple', was one of the blind markers and for the first time on a city target a master bomber was to be used. He was the Canadian Wing Commander J.E. Fauquier, the feisty commanding officer of 405 (Canadian) Squadron, who would go on to command 617 Squadron.

That morning two possible targets were given and the squadron prepped for both but as one was Berlin 'the other was given very little thought.

At briefing the crews showed great enthusiasm as this target had been expected daily and now was their chance to hit right at the nerve centre of Germany.' The ORB also comments that crews were unhappy with the overlong route. Other than a slight turn south to avoid some flak hot spots, it was fairly direct from the Dutch coast to their first turning point 30 miles south-east of Berlin. From there they would turn back sharply and head north-west, across the city, the Baltic and Denmark towards home. The planners hoped that this backdoor approach would enable them to avoid the flak defences that they believed were concentrated around the western perimeter of the city. To a degree they were correct but that night, flak was not to be the greatest threat.

For the last sixteen operations, in fact since 22 June, the squadron had not lost an aircraft on operations. That night sixteen squadron crews took off, three for the main force and five with green TIs. The rest with reds, including Brian, would go in first. As well as 4 × red TIs, they also carried 2 × 4,000lb cookies, (a high capacity and a red spot), 3 × 1,000 HE and a flare. That is a bomb bay with over 4 tons of high explosive and incendiaries. The first ten aircraft left Wyton every minute from 2015 hours with ED984, sixth away, leaving the ground on a cloudy evening just after sunset. Across the east of England's airfields there were the normal tragic take-off accidents and collisions, and of the 727 aircraft tasked, a relatively high number of seventy turned back listing various problems, mainly from the Halifax and Stirling squadrons. There was to be no diversionary raids as there had been the previous week. The sky over Germany was clear that night and the Berlin defences were notorious.

For someone with so many operations under his belt, it is notable that this was Brian's first raid on Berlin. It was also his fifty-ninth, so only this and one more to do.

The No. 8 Group aircraft crossed the Dutch coast over Texel with the main force crossing further south near Egmond aan Zee. The Luftwaffe's early warning radar picked up the approaching bombers early as they passed Amsterdam, with early *Himmelbett* sorties starting at 2133 hours and continuing all night, about seventy-nine in all. It is worth remembering that the use of window was severely decreasing the *Himmelbett* boxes' effectiveness and therefore many more night fighters were tasked on *Wilde Sau* sorties, several groups of which were scrambled at 2135 hours from the four main night fighter bases in the Low Countries, Germany and northern France. It was only the second major run out for this still experimental tactic and those freelancing night fighters were given a running commentary to help them track and follow the bomber stream as it crossed Holland, even though flying conditions that night were near perfect.

As the first Pathfinder Lancasters entered Germany, the weather was clear and, as one pilot commented, 'You could almost see Berlin'. They soon will have seen the first route markers about 30 miles over the border provided by eight Oboe Mosquitos that dropped TIs 20 miles apart, reds to their port side and greens to starboard to provide a visual 'gateway' across the North German Plain towards Berlin. At about the same time, a further tranche of Luftwaffe night fighters were scrambled from three further airfields across Germany. Now a total of between 120–150 freelancers were airborne.

At 2216 hours the commentary continued with 'Target still unknown', and a minute later 'Enemy aircraft flying towards Berlin'. Then, at 2238 hours, 'Berlin is probably the target', which was confirmed soon after at about 2300 hours, by which time all freelance twin and single-engine *Wilde Sau* night fighters were following their orders to get to Berlin. There seems not to have been a concerted effort to attack the bomber stream on their outward journey, although a few fell to flak. Most of the night fighters flew on to Berlin, where presumably they believed their targets would be more concentrated and the flak searchlights would help them out. Only a few of the lower-flying Stirlings and Halifaxes were picked off by the more experienced night fighter pilots, who in doing so were practising *Zahme Sau* or Tame Boar tactics rather than just following the stream and conducting Wild Boar tactics over the target.

At the same time as the night fighters were ordered to Berlin, the city's ground defences manned their radars, searchlights and anti-aircraft guns. Every man involved in the defence of Germany's capital was now poised to defend their city from what would be its largest attack to date.

After another hour or so Brian and the other blind markers would have seen the next route markers about 8 miles south of the town of Brandenburg on the River Havel. These were the large 4,000 cookie variants named 'red spot fires' dropped by a group of Pathfinder Lancasters and topped up every few minutes as the main force approached. As Brian passed over the burning red spots he was now only about 25 miles from the edge of 'the Big City'. The route was a continuation of the same heading, and they were to pass south of Berlin to their next turning point near the small village of Märkisch Bucholz, where they would turn sharply to port and head north-west towards the aiming point on the far side of Berlin.

The 83 Squadron aircraft, as part of the larger group of H2S Lancaster and Halifax markers, were the first aircraft over Berlin. The plan required the primary markers to drop their reds accurately on the aiming point and then the backers up and re-centrers would drop greens just beyond. The main force would then bomb on the greens with the intention that as they crept back they would shower the target and the centre of Berlin on a line to the south-east.

Brian wasn't through first but was only a few minutes behind the leading markers, who were yet to drop their first reds. The blind markers were all using H2S, the hope being that it would be able to detect the aiming point, which was a particular bulge of a built-up area on the north-west edge of the city. It seems that not only did many of the crews later report that their 'Y' equipment had failed but even those whose worked could not identify the aiming point. The ORB later confirmed: 'There was an unfortunate and unforeseen failure of our "Y" equipment.'

I suspect that Brian's H2S was one that failed and his instinct as an experienced visual marker took over. On a clear cloudless night, he had a better chance of finding the aiming point visually than using H2S. The Bomber Command Night Raid Report also suggested that many aircraft were late and if he was Brian knew that if he cut the corner and headed north he would be at the aiming point smack on time. With his H2S out of action his next move was an easy one.

It was also likely that as the first blind markers were ahead of him, by the time he got closer the first reds would be on the ground, making his visual approach easier. What happened over the next few minutes is unclear but what developed over the next hour was an intense aerial battle over the city.

'The first aircraft in were amazed to find that the flak was not forthcoming as expected,' the ORB reported.

Although this was the hoped for advantage of this route, to experienced crews this would indicate only one thing. 'The searchlights were numerous and Jerry's set up was as near daylight as he could make it. It soon became clear that the night fighters were up in great number and were predominant in the defence. Aircraft were being shot down on all sides as they became illuminated.'

They were right; the flak batteries were ordered to set their fuzes to 14,800ft between 2300 and 0047 hours. This was a well-co-ordinated defensive tactic that gave the *Wilde Sau* night fighters a safe altitude above which to operate. It was just after 2330 hours, Brian and his crew were now close to starting their bomb run and less than ten minutes from the target at 20,000ft. Bill Baker would now have retuned the radio to listen in to the master bomber's commentary and Brian would be listening in.

With no H2S, Cliff Robinson would have dropped out of his turret and be half crouching, half lying to peer through the bombsight. He would have rapidly checked all the settings for the TIs and the flares. Harold Allen, in the mid-upper, and Ronald Turner, in the rear turret, would have been scanning wildly for the last thirty minutes. Alexander Niven Macpherson would have been ready to give Brian the heading for their return.

The defence of Berlin was comprehensive and well co-ordinated, and the next forty minutes above Berlin were chaotic. The 600 or so bombers that had made it that far passed over the city and competed for space with the 150 night fighters. More than 370 searchlight beams were probing the clear night sky, coning aircraft for the 31 heavy flak batteries, that is more than 500 guns. It is recorded that more than eighty bombers were coned.

Of the thirty blind markers, only nineteen dropped their markers mainly due to H2S failures and those markers fell well away from the aiming point; five of them were shot down.

As the OBR put it … 'which led the attack to develop approx. 6 miles W of actual A/P. The success of the raid was not due to our accurate bombing but to the Germans for building so large a city.'

Over the next hour the main force streamed over the city dodging searchlights and night fighters, resulting in most of the bombs falling significantly south and west of the aiming point.

The confusion of that night over Berlin has been described by many but none more vividly than by a young Me 110 pilot, Leutnant Peter Spoden, who shot down a Stirling and a Halifax before being shot down himself:

> On the ground the big city was ablaze, first the detonations of the high explosive bombs and then the phosphorous incendiaries in amongst the lacerated houses. It was an unparalleled inferno. Hundreds of searchlights loomed towards us and moved across the sky like the fingers of corpses and ghostly hands, dazzling friend and foe alike. The flak fired a barrage up to 3000 meters as if in a frenzy, above that the night fighters flew as 'wild boars'. Many times I saw 30–40 aircraft all at once, cruising around. Everywhere were tracer, target indicators of all colours, night fighters recognition flares when the flak opened up on one of them. Vast clouds of smoke that rose into the sky, luridly lit from within. White vapour trails everywhere; and down below, the dreadful explosions.

A Lancaster tried to escape the searchlights by looping. I had the impression that everyone was shooting at everyone else. Me in the middle of it all – it was hell – Dante's Inferno … in my fear of death I thought of my mother and how many other young soldiers must have called out for theirs.

I have dreams that always return to me: for almost sixty years this night over Berlin is a nightmare that repeats itself every month and from which I can never escape.

Back in High Wycombe, the reviewed operation was deemed a success, despite it not developing as planned due to the scattered early marking. The initial red markers were 4 miles south-west of the aiming point and although this point was re-marked it did not attract the remainder of the main force and the centre of the attack crept back a further 2 miles. Central Berlin escaped serious damage but the Charlottenburg and Wilmersdorf areas suffered severely and the city authorities reported that it was the worst raid of the war to date with 2,611 buildings damaged and 854 people killed.

The operation was to that point in the bombing campaign the greatest loss suffered on a single night. In addition to the five aircraft that were victims of collisions or take-off and landing accidents, there were fifty-six lost, thirty-six over the target. That was 8.7 per cent of the bombers despatched. Bomber Command lost 276 aircrew and a further 110 became prisoners of war. The 335 Lancasters got off relatively lightly, with 5.1 per cent lost, the 251 Halifaxes lost 9.2 per cent but the 124 Stirlings lost 12.9 per cent.

Just north of the route in and about 20 miles south of Berlin centre, the residents of the village of Nunsdorf would have taken what shelter they could as the raid developed. A mile to their west the nearby searchlight units scanned for targets and the flak battery deployed in the next-door village of Trebbin took on the first few illuminated targets. What they heard though was not exploding bombs or flak guns firing but the impact of a Lancaster crashing on the outskirts of their village.

That Lancaster was ED984 'A' for Apple.

There is a great deal of evidence of what might have happened to Brian's aircraft.

There were at least 150 night fighters active in the bomber stream and over Berlin that night most of them were *Wilde Sau* sorties. One was a Messerschmitt Bf 110 G2 piloted by Oberleutnant Heinz Rökker of 1./NJG 2 based at Gilze-Rijen airfield in the North Brabant area of the Netherlands.

He took off at 2145 hours and, by radio, was guided towards the bomber stream to the edge of the city. Rökker joined the Luftwaffe on 1 October 1939, a month after the Wehrmacht's invasion of Poland and just a few weeks before his 19th birthday. Having qualified as a pilot, his first posting saw him join a night fighter unit in Sicily and then he was sent to Libya. By the time his unit was sent back to Europe in July 1943 he had flown well over fifty operations and claimed six 'kills' but was yet to prove himself in the defence of Germany. By 23 August, Rökker was 22 years old.

Another night fighter active was Bf 110 (2Z+LH) from 3.NJG 6 from Mainz-Finthen airfield, about 320 miles south-west of Berlin, which was scrambled at 2315 hours. Its pilot was Feldwebel Günther Bahr who, having served as a flying instructor, was posted to the Eastern Front, where he claimed his first kill. He then retrained as a night fighter pilot and was posted to 3.NJG 6 from 1 August 1943, he was also 22 years old.

Both Rökker and Bahr claimed to have shot down ED984 but neither claim was accepted by the *Abschusskommission*. They both made a second *Abschuss* claim that night, which were accepted. Rökker had a claim accepted against another 83 Squadron Lancaster and Bahr against a Stirling of 199 Squadron. Rökker's accepted claim was against the aircraft flown by former policeman Pilot Officer John Reid, who was on his tenth trip with the squadron. That night, night fighters claimed seventy-eight bombers but only fourteen were officially accepted. We now know that fifty-six bombers failed to return, of which thirty-one were shot down over Berlin.

Darkness and distance prevented night fighter crews ever being able to identify an individual bomber, so their claims were based on estimated position and altitude and timings, with as detailed a description of the attack as possible and, of course, the type of aircraft. This was then compared by the *Abschusskommission* to reports from crash sites, which where possible they formally inspected, other claims and reports from night fighter units, flak and searchlight units, radar reports and whatever intelligence they could pick from their scant knowledge of Allied losses. This was a typically thorough system but didn't prevent pilots making exaggerated claims, the acceptance of which brought prestige and recognition. It is possible that both Rökker and Bahr attacked ED984 but it was by no means conclusive that either shot it down.

Further claims on ED984 were also made by various ground defences. Two searchlight units (*2. & 4. Flakschweinwerfer Abteilung 808*) claimed to have coned ED984 and no fewer than four flak units covering the south-west of Berlin claimed to have shot it down. As the night fighter claims were rejected it is possible that one or more of the coning/flak claims was accepted, but no records of these remain and neither the acceptance or indeed the rejection of any claim was conclusive. None of these claims therefore are irrefutable.

There is, however, some more compelling evidence as there may have been eye witnesses. One of the crew, Flight Lieutenant Ron Turner, the tail gunner, survived the initial attack and was blown clear. His accounts add another dimension to the mystery.

Among of the myriad of RAF forms that were obsessively updated and cross-referenced during the war were the aircraft loss cards. On those cards every snippet of information was recorded from a variety of sources, leading, it was hoped, to a better understanding of the circumstances of each loss. The card for ED984 tells us a lot, albeit the handwritten entries are difficult to decipher and the contents contradictory. For instance, on the front of the card are two contradictory handwritten notes: 'N/fighter after being coned by S/lights' and 'shot down by flak'.

The edges of the card are printed with a variety of options – date, squadron etc. – that when marked by a hole punch confirm the option. For instance, there is a row of unlabelled options describing the fate of the crew. In the case of ED984, the 'some prisoners' and 'some known to be dead' are punched and both were true. There is then space for handwritten entries on both sides. I will look at the loss card in more detail in the next chapter but some entries extracted by censors from Ron Turner's letters home, written only weeks after the event, help us to understand what might have happened: 'Think the a/c exploded after we had been told to put on parachutes' and 'both wing and ?????? on fire & spread to fuselage while I (Turner) prepared to abandon. A/C must have exploded.'

Looking through some old letters between my mother and Brian's old friend 'Punch' Thompson, who was flying JA940 that night, we may have had another eyewitness, which he also mentions in his book. He had taken off later than Brian and was carrying green TIs, so was due over the target later than Brian, who you may remember was carrying reds. He recalls:

> It was probably Slade whom we saw hit as we entered Berlin because we saw an aircraft far to the north of us, coned in searchlights; it blew up in a shower of red Target Indicators.

Was there any other evidence that could help? What about witnesses on the ground? In 1947 news came back from local sources in Nunsdorf that

ED984 had crashed having 'been hit by anti-aircraft fire from the battery at Trebbin'. I will also explain the source of this in the next chapter.

So where does this leave us? Sadly not with a definitive answer. Let's look at the claims from the flak batteries, which may or may not have been officially supported. Certainly, evidence from the ground suggested a flak *Abschuss* and was recorded as such on the loss card. I believe this is kept as the official cause on RAF records stored by the Air Historical Branch. We know that ED984 was flying above the ordered fuze settings and, although it may have been coned, could not theoretically have been hit by flak exploding some 3,000ft below. If so, how did five German night fighters, also flying above that height, get hit by flak with two being shot down, Spoden being one of them? They knew they had to fly above the fuze setting altitude but could have strayed lower. More likely is that on that night (but also more generally), not all flak batteries followed their orders. On a clear night with so many searchlights and so many targets and where kills were so prestigious, who can blame the flak gunners for bending the rules?

Only two flak claims were officially accepted that night, so on probabilities alone it seems unlikely that ED984 fell to flak, but it is still possible. It is, though, quite possible that she was coned.

The night fighter evidence is more compelling but again flawed and contradictory. If all was going to plan, ED984 would have been on track and about 3 miles south of Nunsdorf as she headed for the turning point, but for some reason she was north of track. As I have said, I suspect their H2S was one of the many squadron radars that was not working and the night op report suggests a slighter stronger headwind than predicted. Maybe he was running late. Brian therefore decided to swing north and head direct to the aiming point (and a number of other aircraft did the same), which he could find visually and arrive on time at 2343 hours, two minutes before zero hour. If that is so he would have been passing over Nunsdorf somewhere between 2335 and 2340 hours. Rökker claimed his kill at 2335 hours and Bahr at 2340 hours. Rökker suggests 20km south-west of Berlin and Bahr 'near/over Berlin'. Rökker is more accurate as the crash site is about 20km from Berlin centre. Brian's early turn to the north would also explain why 'Punch' Thompson, who would have still been on track to the turning point, saw him 'far to the north of us'.

At this point it seems that Rökker's claim could have been valid but there are a number of inconsistencies in his story. He mentions neither that the aircraft exploded or the sight of a parachute, even though he says he watched the aircraft in flames all the way down to the crash site. There is no detailed record of Bahr's attack but Rökker did keep a diary. His books were written and published much later (1997 and 2006) and he gave various interviews to other authors but all were made some forty or fifty years later and, as with many veterans' accounts made so long after the event, are understandably inaccurate and short on detail. Both Rökker's accounts in other books, the detail of which were based on his diaries, while compelling are ambiguous. In one description he is unsure whether the aircraft was a Halifax or a Lancaster.

It was clear that there was only one person who could add first-hand evidence and possibly solve the mystery. Once again I was too late. Ron Turner died in 1991 but perhaps his family could help and, although it took me some years, eventually I met his widow and two of his three sons, both of whom, incidentally served in the RAF. Initially they were able to tell me very little that would help unlock the mystery as their father never spoke of his wartime life but I learned more about him and what happened to him after his escape from ED984, but more of that later.

The revelation came when they showed me his logbook. From the moment they took off to about 1946, Ron was separated from his logbook and therefore the Berlin trip would not have been written up immediately. Clearly though, when reunited with his logbook, he wanted to record the details of his last operational sortie and there, in his own hand, he wrote that on the night of 23 August 1943 their Lancaster, piloted by Brian, took off at 2030 hours and in the traditional red ink he recorded:

Operations – Berlin
SHOT DOWN BY NIGHT FIGHTER OVER TARGET

That part of the mystery seemed now to be solved and although I will never know for certain, it is most likely that Heinz Rökker was the night fighter's pilot.

Chapter 21

The Knock at the Door

Many hundreds of families were affected by the losses that night and over the course of the war tens of thousands would go through the trauma that the Slades were now to experience. I don't know who was at home in Chapel Street that day; whether it was Bernard or Emily who opened the door to receive the small buff envelope. A ghastly job to deliver but a shattering blow to receive. However much they lived with the possibility, the reality of that news must have been crushing. I have not seen that telegram but having read many similar, the wording would have been:

> We deeply regret to inform you that your son, 121451 Flight
> Lieutenant Ivor Charles Brian Slade DFC is missing as a result
> of air operations on the night of 23/24 August 1943. Letter
> follows. Please accept my profound sympathy. Any further
> information will be communicated to you immediately.

This would have been delivered sometime on 24 August, following which were a number of ways that further news about Brian could reach them.

In cases where death was determined quickly and definitively (often the case in UK training accidents) the next of kin would have been informed promptly of the certainty of death rather than the uncertainty of 'missing'. An aircraft missing did not mean that crews had perished, with many ending up in POW camps or evading capture and eventually returning home. That would have been Bernard and Emily's hope. Within a few days they would have received a letter from Brian's commanding officer, John Searby. It was customary for squadron commanders to write promptly and he was assiduous in contacting the families of all his lost crews, although at that stage Searby could have done no more than report what he knew, that ED984 had failed to return. I wish I could read that letter, which I'm sure would have reflected not only their friendship but also the high regard he had for one of his senior and most capable pilots. Searby, in his book *The Everlasting Arms*, described Brian as 'an outstanding officer'. In his book on Peenemünde he also wrote:

> [Brian was] a most courageous young Officer in all he undertook, only a few days earlier he had had occasion to 'feather' one engine soon after take-off for Germany but had continued to the target, marked it, and returned, on his remaining 3 engines.

It's quite likely that he would have shared his own glimmer of hope by suggesting that Brian could have survived, perhaps baled out or crash-landed. He often expressed this on the many letters he wrote to other lost crew's families. At that stage he knew nothing off their fate, particularly that Ron Turner was alive.

Throughout the war, medium wave broadcasts were made by the Reich Ministry of Public Enlightenment and Propaganda daily and by a number of different broadcasters, the most well known of which was William Joyce, aka Lord Haw-Haw. Although the content was highly exaggerated and sarcastic, it was listened to widely by families as the broadcasts would often mention downed, surviving aircrew by name and the POW camp where they would be interned. This almost certainly happened after the loss of ED984.

How do we know this? Back to the loss card. One of the hole punch groups is Sources of Information with Place of Burial, Special Message and Letter from PW. The hole for special message is punched. There was a radio broadcast, so could that have been the Special Message? There are also a number of written entries and the first suggests this and informs us that there was a German radio broadcast that stated Turner had been captured, was a POW and went on to comment: 'At the time of speaking he has probably left hospital and is quite well.' Why was Ron in hospital? Was he injured in the explosion or perhaps when he landed?

Ron's parents, who lived in the Royal Crescent in Bath, would have been living with the same uncertainty as the Slades, having received Searby's letter. They then received letters from friends who had also heard the radio broadcast. Did the Slades listen to this or did someone mention it to them? If that news did reach them it must have given them hope that, as well as

Ron, Brian was also alive. That false hope also reached Vernie's parents when Ron's parents wrote to them to tell them of Ron's survival.

The International Red Cross Committee (IRCC) were normally the first to be informed by the German authorities that a prisoner had been taken and they could have informed the RAF, but in any event, having arrived at a camp, prisoners were encouraged to write promptly, which, as all letters were censored at both ends, served to inform the German authorities, the RAF and in due course, the families. It was once again MI9 that monitored and analysed letters from POWs, which typically took four weeks to get home. Within five to five weeks the first letter from Ron Turner would have got back to his family, having first informed both the IRCC (via the German censor) and the RAF (via MI9), which now would know he'd survived.

And so it was that, having arrived at Stalag Luft III, Ron did write home and relevant extracts of that letter were noted by MI9 and sent to the RAF.

This first letter must have been a joyful moment for Ron's family but Brian's parents would have received little comfort had they read it. In what was probably his first letter, dated 5 October 1943, some six weeks after the Berlin operation, this paragraph was extracted by the RAF onto their loss card for ED984:

> Have no news of rest of crew, think the A/C exploded after we
> had been told to put on parachutes because the next I remember
> I was falling through the air and thinking it was about time
> I pulled the rip-cord. Was I relieved when I was pulled up with
> a jolt. I afterwards descended more peacefully.

For crashes in Germany, local and regional authorities, who typically kept efficient records, would inform the IRCC if bodies were recovered and identified but rarely the precise crash location. We know that local residents of Nunsdorf recovered the crew's remains, with some identifying items being handed to the local authorities and the German military. They were then buried in a single grave in Nunsdorf village cemetery.

To assist families in tracing their missing relatives, the Air Ministry established as part of its Casualty Branch a small Missing Research Section in 1942, which expanded in 1944 after D-Day as it was able to send teams into France behind the advancing Allies. This then became the Royal Air Force and Dominion Air Forces Missing Research and Enquiry Service (MRES), established with five officers in Paris in January 1945. Their painstaking work was mainly to research crash sites and initial burial sites but they were not allowed to exhume or move bodies, a role taken by the army and their grave concentration units (GCUs) under control of the Army Graves Service. Their laborious, detailed work focused on identification of crews and reburials. The work would eventually be taken over by the Commonwealth War Graves Commission. At the end of the war the RAF had 41,881 missing aircrew. It was these organisations that were able through their meticulous research to provide most families with precious news about their loved ones.

The vast majority of the MRES work was carried out post-war with small teams visiting every possible crash site and interviewing local people, particularly members of local government down to village level. As most of these kept detailed records, it would have been in Nunsdorf that the MRES team would have found the crew of ED984. Having located the crash site and initial burial site, the GCUs would then arrange for the exhumation, detailed identification and often reburial in larger cemeteries.

Back in Hertfordshire, fifty days after the Berlin raid, the Slades received another well-meaning but ghastly sheet of officialdom with the confirmation they were dreading:

> I am commanded by the Air Council to inform you that they have with great regret to confirm the telegram in which you were notified that, in view of information now received from the International Red Cross Committee, your son, Acting Flight Lieutenant Ivor Charles Brian Slade, DFC, Royal Air Force, is believed to have lost his life as the result of the air operation on the night of 23rd/24th August 1943.

How did the Air Ministry Casualty Branch know enough to inform them of this? The letter goes on:

> The Committee's telegram, quoting official German information, states that Acting Flight Lieutenant Turner, one of the occupants of the aircraft in which your son was flying on that night, was captured on the 24th August, and that the six other occupants were dead. It contains no information regarding the place of their burial nor any other details.

The 'official German information' was almost certainly obtained from Turner's interrogation. Parts of that would have been released to the IRCC.

However, further extracts from his intercepted letters home from Stalag Luft III entered on to the aircraft loss card were also received about the same time.

Another entry records:

> Turner POW, HE Allen and 5 unknown dead and buried at Nunsdorf and Zossen Kreis Teltow 5227N 0925E

The source of that is unknown but is almost certainly from the IRCC, which the Air Ministry clearly felt could not be passed on to the family at that time without confirmation.

The last entry of particularly poor handwriting and from a Turner letter was more intriguing:

> Attacked by army and wounded but did not realise it. Both wing and ???? on fire and spread to fuselage while I (Turner) prepared to abandon. Aircraft must have exploded, find I was temporarily stone deaf. Saw pay chit of Allen's and payment chit of Robinsons. Germans said bodies were badly mutilated so deaths must have been instantaneous.

The first sentence answers the question of Turner's wounds, which were mentioned in the radio broadcast and why he was hospitalised. They were not from baling out but from the treatment he received from the German soldiers who captured him. In fact, he was shot in the backside and initially treated by a Red Cross nurse. The Brandenburg area outside Berlin where Ron Turner landed was very pro-Nazi, so whether captured by soldiers or locals he would not have been well treated.

The next two sentences explain further the damage to the aircraft and the last two suggest that during his interrogation he was shown items recovered from the bodies soon after the crash that identified the crews. Aircrew were, of course, strictly forbidden from carrying anything of a personal nature but Allen's and Robinson's breach of these rules did enable a quicker identification. 'Pay chit' was the slang name for an airman's paybook, a throwback to when they were paid in cash and received a 'chit' with it. Although this detailed information was never passed to Bernard and Emily, it enabled the Air Ministry to write that more definitive letter of 13 October.

At Wyton, Brian's belongings would have been collected, listed and, along with his paperwork, sent to the RAF Central Depository. This department was responsible for passing on to next of kin any news from the MRES about their relatives and in due course returning their belongings. Neither the issuing of a death certificate nor the return of personal belongings could be carried out until that official presumption of death was made.

A further telegram from the IRCC in Geneva to the Air Ministry in January 1944 confirmed that the German Totenliste 181 (released by a department of the Wehrmacht) listed that Allen and five unknown were buried at Nunsdorf. This confirmation allowed the Air Ministry in February to declare officially that Brian and the other five members of his crew were 'missing presumed dead' and their personal effects could be released and their estate settled.

In May 1945, captured German documents further confirmed that a number of bodies had been buried at Nunsdorf following the crash on 23 August 1943.

Three years later, in January 1947, Brian's logbook was sent to the Slades, its last blunt entry, a red stamp declaring 'DEATH PRESUMED'. The arrival of this logbook so long after his death must have reopened the painful memories, three and a half years after ED984 went down and still no precise location or identification of Brian's remains. It took until May 1947 before a Missing Research Section made it to Berlin and eventually No. 4 MRES moved into the area of Nunsdorf, but as it was in the Soviet-controlled zone, the unit had to be accompanied by a Russian conducting officer. The MRES discovered the crash site on the south-east of the village and, following interviews with local people and officials, believed that the Lancaster had been hit by the anti-aircraft battery at nearby Trebbin. On exhumation of the communal grave it was impossible to identify individuals as a result of the explosion, crash and fire but once again the crew identity was confirmed by personal items of Allen's and a book, most likely the same items that Turner's interrogators showed him. The remains were then transferred and temporarily reburied in Berlin on 16 May on Heerstrasse, which became the Berlin 1939–1945 Cemetery. The Slades now knew beyond any doubt where Brian was buried and they received a note from the Air Ministry in October 1949 with a photograph of the first grave. That precise identification was important and ended their anxiety about his whereabouts. No mother wanted her missing son to be the next generation's 'unknown soldier'.

From the arrival of the first telegram, the effect on the family was shattering, the shock and fading optimism like a slow death over the fifty days it took to confirm. Emily had cause now to remember those family discussions back in 1940 when her reticence held no truck with her enthusiastic son and supportive husband. Her feeling of loss was now combined with the blame she put on Bernard for supporting Brian's under-age enlistment. She must have pondered what could have happened if his entry to the RAF had been delayed until he was 17 or 18? The effect on Bernard was more extreme, his feeling of guilt continually stabbing at his broken heart. He was never the same again.

At the time of Brian's death, his sister Norma was 14 years old. More than four years later my father met Norma (my mother) when they were both working at John Dickinson at Apsley Mills and he recalled on many occasions that when visiting the Slades' house to see her their sitting room was a shrine to their son. A sideboard was covered in his photographs, his medals, his side cap and a large oil painting of Brian hung on the wall. Norma said Bernard would spend all his time in that room. He didn't want to see or speak to anyone about Brian, not even Emily. Two days before Christmas in 1949, Bernard's injured leg gave way, he broke his femur and soon afterwards died of a pulmonary embolism only a few months before his daughter (my mother) married my father.

After her husband's death, Emily collected every reminder of her son and they went into the attic. She never mentioned him again. For my mother, those years as a teenager in a house full of pain and guilt strongly influenced how she dealt with Brian's death and it is hardly surprising that the atmosphere in her parents' house determined her fifty years of silence.

Brian's loss was a tragedy to his parents and sister but to me the greater tragedy was that they could not, even long after his death, be more openly proud of what he achieved. Their grief reflected the nation's attitude; it was time to move on. Brian wanted to fly, he wanted adventure and he wanted to fight, to do his bit as did countless others. However guilty Bernard may have been, his son was doing what he wanted to do and he did it professionally and gallantly, and he deserved to be remembered. Bernard's guilt and grief silenced him and dominated his last few years, and this was all the more acute as he had influenced and inspired his own son's demise. To a degree, and I suspect it was the same for thousands of fathers who served in the First World War, Bernard was living the Second World War vicariously through his son, whose death broke him.

After Bernard's death, Emily, as with so many families, tried to banish the tragedy, the horrors and the losses of the war. The generation of those who suffered those losses directly are themselves gone and we, thank goodness, can now recognise the qualities, commitment and sacrifice of those who died without the crippling, silencing grief my parents' generation suffered.

It wasn't until late 1952, after Bernard's death, that the final iconic CWGC headstone was erected. The inscription they wanted on his headstone was the entire third verse of the hymn *Lead, Kindly Light* but space allowed only the last two lines:

> *And with the morn*
> *those angel faces smile*
> *Which I have loved ...*
> *and lost awhile*

It was nearly fifteen years later that Emily felt ready to visit Brian's grave. In 1958, she wrote to a contact in Berlin to investigate how best she could get to Berlin, which at that time was in East Germany, but sadly a stroke prevented her from ever visiting her son's grave. Emily died in 1972.

In her later years my mother's attitude also altered and she wanted to know more about her brother. First was her curiosity about where Brian was buried. She knew it was in Germany but she had no details. As it happens, this was the easiest piece of information to research as the Commonwealth War Graves Commission has outstanding records, most of which are available through their website, and very soon I had the name of the cemetery on the outskirts of Berlin, the precise location of his grave and a photograph of his gravestone. To my surprise, she wanted to visit the grave and my sister and I took our parents to Berlin in 1998. She saw the end of her life approaching and wanted to say her goodbyes. It was a strange trip for them. My sister had been to Germany before and I had previously lived there but they treated it and reacted as if it was a trip into enemy territory. Our parents were tense and nervous, and they bristled at any contact with German people. It brought home to me that for many of their generation, the notion of forgiveness or reconciliation was impossible. Our trip to the cemetery exemplified this when our young taxi driver, in excellent English, explained that his grandfather had been a member of a Luftwaffe air defence battery on the outskirts of Berlin. It was a staggering irony that unsettled my mother. The cemetery was, of course, immaculate with an atmosphere of formality and peace unique to CWGC cemeteries. The Berlin cemetery contains 3,595 Commonwealth casualties from the Second World War, of which 397 remain unidentified.

It was a tearful occasion, but my mother left Berlin having said farewell to her beloved big brother. I have often wondered if she could only have embraced her brother's story and visited his grave earlier she may have had a very different view of the country where he died.

That visit prompted her to find out more and she obtained some of the books that mentioned Brian and tried to track down some of his old friends. She never grasped exactly what Brian did but she certainly knew in her later years that he was well respected and adored by many he served with. She also never knew exactly how he died and I would have liked her to have known that he and his five friends died together and instantly as their bomb load exploded in a vast red fireball.

Chapter 22

A Single Death is a Tragedy ...

... a million deaths is a statistic'

Wherever that quote came from, it almost certainly was not from Stalin, although he often receives the credit. It must, though, have been the sentiment of the families of aircrew casualties.

In the middle of 1943 the extent of casualty numbers on whichever side and whether military or civilian were reported inaccurately. RAF casualty lists were published internally within the Air Ministry and more widely through magazines and *The London Gazette* but were not studied closely as out of date and merely confirmation of bad news already received. As far as the general public were concerned, most were unaware of the extent of Bomber Command casualties.

Of the 384,000 British and Commonwealth military deaths in the war, about 70,000 came from the RAF (and RAFVR) and close to 57,000 were from Bomber Command, both operational and in training. Add to that about 8,000 injured and 9,800 that became POWs and you have total casualties close to 60 per cent of the total 125,000 Bomber Command aircrew who served.

Much has been written about the statistics of the war and particularly of Bomber Command, and I have scattered a few of those details throughout this story but see no reason to repeat endless lists of total sorties, operations, tonnages, dwellings destroyed, people displaced and the appalling casualties on all sides, however fascinating they are. Wars aren't won by politicians or generals alone, nor by industrial muscle or better technology, nor by better strategy or more ruthless tactics but by a complex blend of all those and other elements, including the actions of the 'boot wearers'. To end this story I want to dwell on the combatants, the combined efforts of millions of ordinary people doing remarkable things, so will I now look at what happened to the many crew members Brian flew with, and as you will see, they mirror those wider Bomber Command losses.

So what happened to them all?

Brian had his regular crew in 115 Squadron but he also flew with another seven airmen as temporary replacements or second pilots. Their stories are remarkably varied.

Their two-time front gunner, Hugh Dalton, who you may remember had travelled halfway around the world from New Zealand via Canada for training, completed two trips with Brian in December 1941. He had arrived at Marham on 8 December, the day after Japan attacked Pearl Harbor. The shock of that event reverberated around the world, not least in the Antipodes where the Japanese landings in Thailand and Malaya the following day further confirmed their vulnerability. Unsurprisingly, at 1100 hours that morning Hugh's homeland declared war on Japan. Many from New Zealand and Australia serving abroad now found themselves with split loyalties and Hugh quite clearly felt his place was back home. He volunteered to return home and within two months was once again at sea, arriving in New Zealand three months later. This part of Hugh's story illustrates the time and logistical effort it took to move colonial troops, particularly from New Zealand and Australia, to their training and theatre of operations. In the seventeen months between leaving and returning to New Zealand, Hugh spent more than twelve months in transit, most of that on troopships. After a further six months' training on home soil, he was posted to 6 (Flying Boat) Squadron flying Catalinas, spending time on Fiji, the New Hebrides (now Vanuatu) and the Solomon Islands between October 1943 and March 1944. He returned for a second tour from April 1944 to July 1945 with 5 Squadron, also as aircrew on Catalinas. They had a mixed role carrying out anti-submarine patrols, mining, reconnaissance and air-sea rescue, particularly of downed American airmen. Hugh flew on a number of successful 'Dumbo' operations, where a Catalinas would accompany the American-led island hopping operations specifically tasked with picking up US aircrew. Within a few days of returning home in July 1945, he was married and a month later the first atomic bomb was dropped on Hiroshima. He was finally discharged in October, two months after the Japanese surrender and the end of the Pacific War. In addition to his two trips with Brian, Hugh Dalton flew forty-one operations in the Pacific over his five years' service. He survived the war and died in April 1999.

The second front gunner was Sergeant Brown, who did three operations with Brian, the first of which was the Channel Dash trip. He also did five operations in the Sword crew and was with them on 6 May when, having been hit by flak and all baling out, Flight Lieutenant John Sword and his navigator Sergeant Batty were killed but the rest were taken prisoner. Brown saw out the war in Stalag Luft I, being liberated by the advancing Russians on 1 May 1945, the German guards having abandoned the camp the day before. Two weeks later, the British prisoners, including Brown, were flown home in B-17s.

As we know, when a new pilot arrived in the squadron he typically flew a few trips as a second pilot with an experienced skipper, just as Brian had done. One of those was Pilot Officer Lesley Bales, who flew with Brian on one operation to Cologne on 30 May 1942. He flew a further six operations with Sergeant McKee and four with Pilot Officer Croxton, who also flew in the dicky seat on one operation with Brian to Essen on 1 June. Bales was sitting in Croxton's dicky seat on 25 June when they ditched returning from Bremen. Despite searches, nothing was found and although one body was washed up on the German coast, there was no sign of the others. Croxton, Bales and the rest of the crew are commemorated at Runnymede.

On 1 and 3 June, Brian once again did some 'babysitting', this time with another new pilot to the squadron, Pilot Officer Malcolm Freegard. He attended Highgate School, which had been evacuated to North Devon, and as a 17-year-old cycled from there to Bristol with a friend in order to join up. Freegard also had two dicky seat trips with Sergeant Perry but his first as skipper was to Saint-Nazaire a few days later. And then on 22 June, on his way back from Emden, he had engine trouble and, as we know, Wellingtons weren't that easy to fly on one engine. Freegard ditched safely about 60 miles off the Norfolk coast and, whether via Morse or pigeon, the Air Sea Rescue (ASR) were alerted and soon on their way managing to land their Walrus and pick up the five crew members. The Walrus pilot, Pilot Officer Trevallian, was told he had endangered the aircraft by having too many people on board and simply replied: 'Which one should I have left behind.'

Freegard's luck was to change a month later when returning from Duisburg when he was attacked and shot down by a night fighter, crashing in Holland. Three of the crew were killed but Freegard and his front gunner, Sergeant Rogers, survived, the latter's injuries being patched up by local Dutch families. They both would see out the war in Stalag Luft III. After repatriation, Freegard went to Pembroke College Cambridge, where he read English and, following his marriage, lived in Norfolk and taught at Gresham's School. After four years teaching at St Luke's College, Exeter, he became a producer with the BBC and then established the Audio Visual

Centre at UEA. He had spent his childhood in Norfolk and retired there, not far from Marham, which he visited in 1999 to give a talk on his wartime experiences. Freegard had shown great fortitude, both in 115 Squadron and as a POW, and lived to enjoy a fulfilling and happy post-war life. His family told me, however, that as he aged he had bouts of guilt about those of his friends who died and also those German civilians who suffered on the ground. His son wrote:

> On a positive note, Malcolm's wartime encounters did bestow on him a perspective and healthy disregard – possibly, even, contempt – for many of the petty and comparatively insignificant trials and tribulations of daily life thereafter. He disdained the 'puffed-up' pomposity of bank managers, tax inspectors and other aficionados of officialdom! He was a man of much humour, humility and humanity.

He died in February 2004.

Another of Brian's novice second pilots also spent some time as a POW. Sergeant Baden Fereday did a number of trips as second pilot, the last a minelaying job with Brian on 7 June. He then had to wait a month before his first trip as skipper but on his sixth operation, when on his way back from Hamburg, he was hit by coastal flak. Two of his crew were injured and at one point, with the aircraft out of control, his wireless operator Sergeant Clerides, having lost his intercom, thought the crew had baled so he also jumped, ending up in a hospital in Bremen. Fereday, having regained control, headed out across the North Sea, losing altitude as both engines failed and eventually ditching about 50 miles off the Dutch coast. Their dinghy was holed and useless, so the four of them clung on to each other and a wooden box from their wrecked and sinking aircraft. By the time a Luftwaffe air-sea rescue seaplane found them six hours later, Sergeants Shoesmith and Skelley had died. The rescuers refused to pick up their bodies, which eventually came ashore, were recovered and buried in Denmark and Holland respectively. Fereday, Lindley and Clerides became POWs. After the war, Clerides became a barrister and in 1993 became President of Cyprus. Fereday and Lindley visited Cyprus and supported him during an earlier failed election campaign in 1988.

The fifth and last of the second pilots who flew with Brian was a 22-year-old Canadian, Flight Sergeant James Newman from Ontario, who was posted in from his conversion course on 12 June. His first operation with Brian on 25 June was the '1,000' raid to Bremen, when they had a complete hang-up and came home with a full bomb bay. He didn't fly on another operation until he piloted a minelaying job on 21 July and over the next month completed another ten trips. It was on his thirteenth that it all went wrong. Ten aircraft were part of a larger mining operation that was Bomber Command's only operation that night. One of the squadron aircraft was shot up but managed to get back to Exeter, however, Newman's Wellington failed to return. No trace of aircraft or crew was ever found. Their names appear on the Runnymede Memorial.

Most of Brian's operations were carried out with his regular team, which dispersed at the end of their tour. This must have been a bittersweet moment for Brian and his crew. A time for great celebration as they had now completed their tour of operations. I have photographs of Brian at this time and his DFC ribbon is fixed on his tunic as firmly as the grin on his face.

With their tour over, it could be the end of operational sorties for some months but whatever each of them intended to do next, it signalled the break-up of this very close-knit group of great friends who night after night had done their job, worked together in the harshest of conditions, looked out for each other and, with a fierce instinct for survival, had stayed alive. Whether or not it is better to be lucky than good, this crew had proven to be both. For these young men away from home, the crew that they flew with was their family, their brothers with a bond that even they found difficult to explain. After their last operation, and I've no doubt a few beers, Brian's Wellington crew slipped out of Marham in their different directions.

Sergeant Ken Swann was posted to 12 OTU at Chipping Warden, where Brian had done his Wellington training, as a gunnery instructor but he wanted to retrain as a pilot. After a year at Chipping Warden, he did his basic flying training and then in May 1944 went to America to No. 5 British Flying Training School in Florida. He didn't fly operationally again and on return in early 1945 he became a flying instructor at Worcester and Yatesbury, where he remained until the end of the war. He left the RAF in February 1946 and trained as a teacher, working in a number of Norfolk secondary schools where he taught science and PE. Later, after retirement, he worked with young offenders. Ken had been a devout Baptist all his life, having met his wife of fifty-seven years, Mollie, in the Silver Road Baptist Church in Norwich, where they were married in November 1943. He was active and independent to the end and died aged 92. Ken's daughter told me that he was not unduly affected by his experiences and, like most things in his life, took it in his stride. He was a 'glass half full' character and there is no doubt that his faith sustained him. He, like many Wellington crew, had great respect for the aircraft that kept them safe and often told of his great love and enthusiasm for the Wimpy.

You may remember that John Burbidge, having returned from his lengthy tryst on the French Riviera with his sweetheart, who incidentally not only shared John's love of classical music but became a professional cellist in London after the war, returned at the behest of his rowing chums keen that they all volunteer for the RAF. After he went through the gates of RAF Marham for the last time, he would not fly operationally again.

From 115 Squadron he went to 12 OTU as a signals leader instructor for a year, then to an Advanced Flying Unit as a signals instructor. In June 1944 he was posted to No. 14 Radio School, where after his promotion to squadron leader he was a senior instructor until July 1945. His last day was in February 1946 and he was able to retain the rank of wing commander into civilian life.

After the war John married Dorothy, who had worked as a nurse in Great Ormond Street Hospital during the blitz. Following a few years in Shrewsbury as the Chief Administrator in the County Education Department they had a son and when he was 3 they all moved to Hampshire ,where Dorothy became a headmistress.

During the period that John Burbidge and the rest of Brian's crew were at Marham, 115 Squadron had a torrid time. Although throughout the war they had a fine record of operational service, they paid a high price as the only squadron to lose more than 200 aircraft. During Brian's tour they lost thirty-three aircraft in eighty-six days, which resulted in 161 deaths and a further eighteen in POW camps. John would have known many of them, some of them were friends. All those losses bore heavily on John but there was worse as he also lost some closer friends. Before he left Marham, all seven of John's rowing crew were dead. It is clearly his son's view that it was these personal losses that had a long-term effect on his mental health.

Having spoken and corresponded with him at length, it is clear he believes their wartime experiences traumatised both his parents. He suffered a terrible relationship with his father, whose short temper and intolerance frequently resulted in violence towards him. He told me that his father understood that all his rowing chums were killed in training accidents due in part to their laissez-faire attitude to training. Whenever John heard that his son was not concentrating at school, a beating would result. He was terrified of his father, grew to hate him and left home as soon as he could, having little contact with him until Dorothy died when John was 83. John lived alone and was visited once a year at Christmas by his son until his death in 2006 at the age of 95. A tragic tale where not only a participant of war suffered from post-traumatic stress but it severely impacted the next generation.

Sergeant Sam Lowry, the popular young Royal Australian Air Force air gunner who manned the rear turret, would spend the next twelve months at 27 OTU based at RAF Lichfield teaching mainly RAAF crew how to operate Wellingtons.

In 1941, just before he was posted to Marham, he'd met Aileen Pattison, an Australian girl living in London, who had moved there from Sydney with her mother and younger sister Angela in 1938. At the outbreak of war, both girls joined the Air Transport Auxiliary in London. During and after his time at Marham, Sam would spend as much of his leave as he could with Aileen and they were married on 27 April 1943 at Caxton Hall in London. The best man was another Australian pilot, Colin Chapman, and Aileen was attended by her sister. A few days after his wedding, he was commissioned and was now Pilot Officer Lowry, so plenty to celebrate. I'd like to think some of Sam's old crew from Marham went to the wedding but I doubt Brian was there as he'd been busy the night before bombing Duisburg.

A couple of months after his wedding Sam was posted to 1661 Heavy Conversion Unit to convert to Lancasters. In late August 1943 he would have been close to finishing his course and on 3 September he was in Lancaster R5492 with his new crew on a training flight near Exeter. There was some mystery about this flight as one of the other crew member's family was told unofficially that the aircraft had been shot down by friendly anti-aircraft fire, part of the defences of Exeter. There is no evidence to suggest the family's suspicions were correct but some believed that the exercise involved flying around Exeter to enable its searchlight defences to practise tracking aircraft. On this part of the incident they were correct as they were the Bullseyes exercises. The official record states that the Lancaster crashed due 'a structural failure of the tailplane'. While manoeuvring to evade the searchlights, it plunged, tracked by the lights for several thousand feet before crashing. The orders for Bullseye sorties encouraged 'gentle evasive action', so perhaps that sudden plunge was caused either by the tailplane failure or excessive corkscrewing. Either way, it's not difficult to see where the misunderstanding came from. That Lancaster was an old one, being one of the first to be built in March 1942 and having served with 44 and 106 squadrons before going as a conversion trainer. None were able to bale out and the aircraft crashed less than a mile west of the airfield. The crew, three from the RAAF and five from the RAF, all died. Sam is buried in Exeter High Cemetery, 2 miles west of the crash site, and left his young widow, Aileen. They were married for less than five months.

Ken Dodwell's skills as Brian's navigator were not to be wasted and he became a navigation instructor at a conversion unit for seven months, and then on promotion to squadron leader went to join the staff at No. 3 Group Headquarters. Although under no obligation, experienced crew in staff or training roles did occasional operations when one of the crew was sick or they were required to observe at first-hand what effect their tactical changes were having, and Ken completed a further seven operations. In December 1945 he married his WAAF girlfriend, Jean, who he had met at Marham four years earlier, and after a number of other staff jobs, he left the RAF in 1946. Many years later it was one of his grandchildren asking about his time in the war that prompted Ken to write his memoirs, which I was delighted to discover and quote from extensively here. On 28 June 2012 Ken attended the unveiling of the Royal Air Force Bomber Command Memorial by Queen Elizabeth II at Hyde Park Corner in London. Ken died on 20 December 2014 aged 94, leaving Jean, his wife, a son and three daughters. While I did not have the opportunity of meeting Ken, I did meet with Jean and their children and heard many great stories of their time at Marham.

When I went to the International Bomber Command Centre at Lincoln to research and to look at Brian's name on the rusting memorial walls, I returned to the low, modern building down the wide paved path flanked by remembrance stones, each one dedicated by a veteran or his family. Ken's family told me that they wanted one for their father and, when I found it, there was another name engraved. It was Brian's. On their father's stone they had engraved the name of his closest friend.

Ken's family told me he was often troubled by his wartime experiences and he found his survival and the loss of his friends hard to accept even decades after the war. Although he had heard of Brian's death, he lost track of his other good friend, Sam Lowry. He believed Sam had survived the war and returned home. In 1995 Ken wrote to the Royal Australian Air Force to try and find him, only to hear that Sam had been killed in 1943. He wrote again asking them to check and expressing his guilt of not knowing Sam's fate. That guilt never left him, and in his memoirs he wrote: 'I would have loved to have had these young men as my lifelong friends. They were the best … I cannot believe that they were lost forever.' Ken's family are close and supportive and he, after the RAF, had a successful business and family life. They did, though, know of his occasional periods of introspection and his youngest daughter wrote a most moving poem, *Wheels Up*, of which this a short extract:

> *He went his way, proliferated, wife and children surrounded ...*
> *how strange it is life's amnesia ... the mask the worlds*
> *demands – convenience of politics.*
>
> *Cracks and blemishes appear as life continues on, deep*
> *crevices and canyons hiding behind polite facade, lies*
> *everyday occurrences.*
>
> *Tiny little traumas dissolve and reverberate deep into*
> *the caverns of unresolved pain, lying dormant all the years,*
> *emerging in jets and flashes of disturbance.*
>
> *Wheels Up ... the droning goes on ... it won't die ... why did*
> *they die, why did I live? Loss of friendships deep.*

No. 83 Squadron, as part of No. 8 Group, were typically populated by more experienced crews, often on their second tours, but as with Brian, there was a few who came in from conversion units having not flown in heavies before. They would have a number of training flights, both as crew and skipper, but then would fly as an eighth crew member on an operation with a more experienced skipper. The first of two 'guests' who flew with Brian was the Canadian Ernest Stiles from Apohaqui, New Brunswick. He joined the squadron from 1661 HCU in July 1943 and had three guest trips with Squadron Leader Sells, Brian and Flight Sergeant Britton, all very experienced pilots. Stiles then had to wait ten days before he had his maiden trip as a skipper, which was to Berlin on 23 August. That, of course, was Brian's last. Stiles went through much of the winter and made many trips to Berlin but on 2 January 1944 his aircraft was shot down as it approached Berlin and crashed near Timmenrode in the Hertz Mountains. The crew are buried in the Berlin 1939–1945 Cemetery.

You may remember that back on 9 June the officers' mess was excited to greet Flight Lieutenant 'Joe' Ogilvie back after his epic evasion from France to Gibraltar. He wasn't the only member of the Mackie crew to complete that journey. One of the others was the 33-year-old Northumbrian Sergeant Ralph Henderson, who flew with Brian on 12 August to Milan, now on his second episode at 83 Squadron. He was first posted in from 1661 HCU in early March 1943 as a flight engineer and his first operation was with Squadron Leader Hurry (who would soon have Vernie Lewis as his engineer) and his second was with Flight Lieutenant Mackie, who was on his second tour with 83 Squadron. On 11 March, returning from Stuttgart, they were attacked by a Bf 110, their aircraft crash landing about 100 miles east of Paris. Two of the crew were killed, two became POWs and Mackie, Ogilvie and Ralph Henderson evaded capture. With help from locals, Mackie and Henderson met up within twenty-four hours, were fed, given French clothes, slept for twenty-four hours and introduced to the resistance. After several days' travel, mainly by train, via Paris and through Vichy France, they arrived in Toulouse. After eleven days they were moved on with false papers and just avoided a sweep by the Gestapo, who arrested several of those who had helped them. By train, bus and foot, helped by their guide, they crossed the Pyrenees and into Spain, where they were arrested until the British Consulate had them released. Joe spent another week in Spain but Ralph, now in the care of MI9, was taken straight to Gibraltar and flown back, arriving in the UK in mid-May. It was a 1,300-mile, two-month evasion for which both were decorated, Ralph receiving the DFM. He then decided to retrain as a pilot and also get married, which he did to Muriel on 14 August. A few days later he was back at Wyton with his wings on his chest. Like Stiles, Henderson's first operation as a skipper was to Berlin on 23 August, having only had one trip previously with Brian as an inductee pilot. He went on to complete a further sixteen operations, including two as flight engineer in the Davies crew. October was a good month as he was promoted to pilot officer and his DFM came through. He was now a senior blind marker, but the Battle of Berlin gathered pace and on a cloudy night over the big city, his aircraft was shot down, most likely by predicted flak, and crashed in Schiller Park. He and his crew were killed and are also buried in the Berlin 1939–1945 Cemetery.

Before Vernie Lewis joined the crew, Brian's flight engineer was Sergeant E. Maxwell, who did six operations with Brian during April and early May 1943. Prior to that he completed thirteen trips with Pilot Officer Oakes. His last job was on 23 May, after which he was posted out to the PFF Navigational Training Unit at its new station, RAF Upwood. As far as I can find out, he survived the war.

A second crew member who flew once with Brian as a stand-in mid-upper gunner was Warrant Officer J.N. Papworth, who took Harold Allen's place for one trip to Hamburg on 2 August while Harold was on leave getting married. By that time he had completed thirteen trips with his regular skipper, Flight Lieutenant H.P. Mason DFC, and a further seven afterwards. He was then posted out to the PFF Navigation School in

September and after his 'rest' tour at Upwood was posted as a mid-upper gunner to another Pathfinder unit, 582 Squadron at RAF Little Staughton, which had been formed in April 1944 as the plans for an Allied invasion of Europe were being finalised. D-Day, on 6 June 1944, was supported by Bomber Command with 1,211 sorties, the most in one single night and an extensive and complex fire plan was devised, jointly with a naval bombardment, to bomb the coastal batteries overnight on 5–6 June in order to support directly the early morning landings. It involved 1,012 aircraft, of which 946 actually bombed. Most of the targets were covered in cloud and Oboe was used extensively on a night when 5,000 tons of bombs were dropped. Although the cloud hampered the accuracy of the bombing, it combined with an unprepared and depleted German air defence to produce an incredibly low number of losses; only three aircraft. The only Lancaster lost was from 582 Squadron and its target was the battery at Longues, three quarters of a mile south of the west end of Gold Beach. It was skippered by Squadron Leader Raybould, with Papworth as his mid-upper gunner. The Lancaster disappeared without trace. Jonathan Papworth and the rest of the crew are remembered on the Runnymede Memorial.

The six crew mates in ED984 who perished over Berlin are buried side by side in the Berlin 1939–1945 Cemetery and the effect on their families was no less than that on the Slades.

Harold Allen, having had his week off to get married, rejoined Brian and took part in the Nuremburg raid, the two trips to Milan, Peenemünde and, of course, their fateful operation to Berlin. The 21-year-old was married to his 20-year-old bride Dolly for less than one month. His parents listed the announcement of his death in the local newspaper, which they ended with 'his brokenhearted Mum and Dad'. 'Greater love hath no man than he who lays down his life for his friends' appears on his headstone.

Another young bride prematurely widowed was Bill Baker's wife, Betty. They had been married just under a year. You may remember that Bill had six siblings, the youngest twin boys, Ken and Les. Ken was 84 when I spoke to him. He told me his earliest memories as a 5-year-old was the adventure of the family piling into their Anderson shelter in their back garden and the searchlights over Birmingham. He also remembered Bill coming home on leave and putting his cap on his head. 'I can still smell the Brylcreem,' Ken told me. On another occasion, Bill brought Ron Turner home to Birmingham for the weekend. The other enduring memory he has, although at that time he didn't fully understand it, was the moment his father told his mother 'Bill's missing'. A tragedy for the family but Bill's father, quite rightly, was incredibly proud of his eldest son, showing off his DFM at any opportunity. Ken and his twin brother Les, when they learned more about Bill's life, became very proud of their big brother, as Ken told me 'a pride that has never diminished'.

The inscription on his headstone reads: 'His Spirit Happy in the Knowledge of the Cause for Which he Died'.

In the first three days after the Berlin raid, Cliff Robinson's father received notification from the RCAF that Cliff was missing. He also had letters from John Searby and the station commander at RAF Wyton. They all held out hope for the crew's survival but on 16 October a letter from the RCAF confirmed that Cliff was 'missing believed killed'. Six months later his death was presumed but, as with the others, it was 1949 before his grave in Berlin was confirmed. The inscription on his headstone reads: 'Thy word is true, thy will is just; To thee we leave him Lord, in Trust'.

Towards the end of August 1943, Vernie Lewis, Brian's flight engineer, was nominated for a Distinguished Flying Medal, his citation reads:

> F/Sgt Lewis has completed 42 operations with the Pathfinder Force. He is a keen and efficient Flight Engineer and on many long distance trips, his knowledge and skill have been given full scope. On the ground, he is a tireless worker and enjoys the complete confidence of his Captain and crew. F/Sgt Lewis has always displayed great keenness to operate and he is commended for the award of DFM.

Clearly, he was awarded his DFM posthumously and his VC-winning father, Stokey Lewis, received it personally from King George VI in May 1946. That medal was not Vernie's only legacy for Stokey and Edith. Vernie had recently become engaged to his girlfriend at Wyton, Ann Elizabeth 'Betty' Dawson, a WAAF telephonist. When Vernie took off on 23 August, he was only three weeks away from their planned wedding and he had just arranged for his father to be his best man. What he may not have known, however ,was that Betty was about six weeks pregnant. Could he have flown to Berlin on his last operation not knowing he was to become a father? Betty remained on station for about three months, then in accordance with WAAF regulations was discharged 'on compassionate grounds'. Devastated by Vernie's death, she spent some time with the Lewis family in South Wales and just over seven months after Vernie's death, Betty gave birth to their son back at her family home in Irlam near Manchester.

Of course, it was not unknown for WAAFs to become pregnant, the predictable result of young men and women living and working in close proximity at an RAF station amidst the stresses and strains of wartime operations. Romance was inevitable and accidents happened. The consequences for these young women, assuming they did not pursue dangerous illegal abortions, was a swift discharge from the RAF and humiliation, the degree of which depended on their social and family background. For some the honourable conclusion was marriage, for others isolation then adoption were preferable.

Stokey Lewis's courage and compassion wasn't limited to his actions in 1916 but extended to his son's illegitimate child. He and Edith, both in their late 40s, adopted the boy soon after his birth. Christened Vernon Charles after his father and known to all as 'Young Vernie', he was brought up as their own son.

I can only speculate how the adoption came about but some station medical officers were sympathetic to these realities of station life and did their best to help resolve them. One such was 'Doc' Macgown, who as well as his empathy for stressed aircrew, also helped WAAFs who became pregnant. With great discretion and sympathy, he developed a scheme to help them, in contravention of the prevailing RAF policies. I just wonder if he didn't have a hand in helping the Dawsons and Vernie's parents with the adoption of their grandson.

Betty's daughter was able to tell me more. Having taken what must have been an incredibly difficult decision, Betty continued to keep in touch with the Lewises and regularly sent Young Vernie birthday and Christmas presents labelled 'from Auntie Betty'. In early 1946 she re-enlisted and after some training was posted to RAF St Eval in Cornwall, where she met and married Harold Townend, a Coastal Command navigator. Soon after their marriage, Harold was posted to South Africa and Betty was once again discharged from the RAF and went out to join him. They returned to Manchester in late summer 1947 to raise their two daughters. When he was old enough, Young Vernie was told that Betty was his birth mother and the Dawsons were delighted to hear that he was engaged. He had always intended to travel to Manchester to meet his mother and his two half-sisters.

Tragically for both families, that meeting never took place as Young Vernie was killed in a traffic accident aged 27 in 1971. Betty and Harold attended the funeral and Young Vernie is buried with his grandparents in Milford Haven Cemetery. The gravestone falsely but understandably describes Young Vernie as their son. Young Vernie may not have met his parents but his altruistic and loving grandparents were wonderful substitutes.

Vernie's headstone in Berlin reads: 'At the going down of the sun and in the morning we will remember him'.

I had assumed that the family of Brian's navigator, having a name like Alexander Niven Macpherson, would be easy to trace but I had underestimated the number of people with Scottish roots that shared it. The only distant family connection I contacted knew very little, but it was a pleasure to tell them of their forebear's early career, his bravery in winning a DFM and his time supporting Brian and becoming part of a very good and experienced Pathfinder crew. His headstone inscription reads: 'At the going down of the sun and in the morning we still remember'.

As you've read, the only survivor from Brian's Lancaster crew was the rear gunner, Ron Turner, who after the Lancaster exploded, and having been thrown clear of the spiralling blazing aircraft, found himself parachuting, but not to safety. He was shot, captured and after a spell in a German hospital and the mandatory questioning by the Gestapo, arrived at Stalag Luft III in Sagan on 11 September. While there he kept a brief diary, which is fascinating. It describes how he shared a room with five others, got drunk on 'Kriege Brew' at Christmas and the night of the Great Escape, where he was a lookout, which he describes as 'Bags of Panic', and then the news a few weeks later that fifty of the escapees had been shot by the Gestapo. The opening page of this unique and precious diary is a memorial to his Lancaster crew and also includes a pencil sketch of ED984 and a vivid poem describing an operation.

As the Soviet Army approached in January 1945, he and his fellow prisoners were marched in freezing temperatures and snow the 50 miles to another camp at Spremburg, and then trained to another camp near Nuremburg. There they remained until the US Army approached in April and once again they were moved, to Stalag VII-A, where 130,000 PoWs now congregated from a variety of camps until they were liberated on 29 April 1945. When it was safe to fly, most of these prisoners were flown by Bomber Command back to the UK and Ron Turner returned to his family on 9 June. He was awarded the DFC, which was gazetted in September 1943, but Ron was always very unhappy that his award was sent to him by post rather than being presented personally. One of the jobs he had soon after the war was to interview and debrief returning Japanese prisoners, to whose traumatic experiences he could relate. He stayed in the RAF and was promoted steadily to become a wing commander in 1968. He retired to Dorset in 1975 and became a school bursar. He frequently walked his favourite coastal path, where a memorial bench remains. He died on 28 September 1991, aged 71.

Having met his family, it is clear that he almost never shared his wartime experiences and enjoyed a successful and happy post-war life. His eldest son described him as the life and soul of any party. His logbook and diary gave me invaluable information and I am extremely grateful to his wife and sons for sharing those with me.

I hesitate to reduce these remarkable personal stories to mere statistics but they clearly illustrate the casualty rate among bomber crews. Of those I have tracked, and there is only one I cannot, there were twenty-three members, both regular and occasional, of Brian's two crews, including himself. Of those, twelve were killed in action and two in training, that total of fourteen representing 61 per cent of the total. Prisoners of War represent a further 17 per cent of the whole, which means only 22 per cent avoided the casualty lists.

These are only slightly worse than the overall Bomber Command statistics.

I am in no doubt that these young men became hardened to the continual losses of other crews and of those members of their respective messes that joined and soon were lost. But they never got over the loss of close friends with whom they flew and fought, celebrated, sang, drank and partied. Such shared times create great bonds and Brian had many. Part of the process of writing this story was to build an image of the person I never met and to get to know him better both as a pilot and as a man. It is easy now having researched and written this story to recognise the good pilot, a very good bomber pilot and latterly a highly respected and experienced Pathfinder. The combination of his professionalism and his character made him a good skipper, but also a great friend and enjoyable company for many. He was devoted to the task and, like many thousands of others, prepared to risk all to fight against something he believed threatened his way of life and his future. Of course, I wish I had met him. I know I would have liked him. It was one of his old friends and fellow pilots that described him so well.

Walter 'Punch' Thompson, after his time with 83 Squadron, returned to Canada and in 1944 he became what he described as 'an Air Force dummy', selling war bonds in the industrial plants of British Columbia. He became a skilled public speaker, told his audiences of Brian's story and they cried and bought bonds. While the war continued, he was restless and returned to Britain but too late to serve in the RAF again. He had often flown over

Oxford and fulfilled a long-held ambition by joining Lincoln College to read philosophy, politics and economics. He was there when the European war ended in May 1945 and soon after returned to Canada. In 2005 my mother tracked him down and they corresponded. He wrote:

> I was stunned and deeply moved by your letter and the picture of yourself and Brian. There was a camaraderie between pilots which was sometimes not shared with other crew members and the association between myself and Maurice Chick and Brian was quite close. I never met in all my long life a more fun loving, witty and effervescent man than Brian. It was a sheer delight to be in his company. He loved to sing, tell stories and frequent the company of WAAFs, as indeed Chick and I did also. I must confess that when I received your letter and picture I wept uncontrollably, I could not stop. Forgive the infirmity of character of an old man.

I do so wish I could have met Walter Thompson and all those who Brian flew with but yet again I was too late. I have great respect for all those who served and fought but Bomber Command aircrew in the Second World War were, I believe, an extraordinary and unique group of young men. They were intelligent, they were all volunteers, from many nations and with varied backgrounds and motivations. They were courageous, highly professional, determined and loyal. They fought a very different brand of war and in the main gelled into fiercely effective teams, at their best generating a group fighting spirit only seen in the very best of fighting men.

Over the years of my research I've become very close to Brian and it is a very strange emotion now, having told his tale, to miss a person you have never met, but I do.

Acknowledgements

Personal curiosity and the desire to inform my family started this process but there have been many people over the last decade that have encouraged, supported and helped. A key moment that inspired me to finish the book came on an idyllic summer day beside the River Test in Hampshire when Max Hastings, while cautioning me from any hope of publication, insisted that I should finish what for others would be both an informative and historical record in the future. I'm grateful for that push to the finish line.

The story would be nothing without knowing more about the aircrew who flew with Brian. I am eternally thankful to those families for their contributions. Key to me tracking down many of them was the skill and determination of Brenda Kelly, who has helped countless Bomber Command families discover the contributions of their forebears. Brenda, thank you so much.

Some of the families we traced deserve particular mention. Firstly, the Dodwell family, who provided Ken Dodwell's memoir and on meeting recounted so many more anecdotes of Brian's and Ken's time flying together. The Turner family gave me access to Ron's logbook and POW diary and I so enjoyed meeting them. Ken Swann's daughter provided his wartime memoirs and Ken Baker described his memories and some wonderful photographs of his big brother, Bill. Thank you all. For those unmentioned, thank you for your help and I hope you find this a useful and accurate record of your relations' wartime activities.

Primary sources were the essential starting point for so much. RAF Disclosures provided endless service records and I'm very grateful that some were provided promptly. The staff at the National Archives, who provided squadron ORBs, are an invaluable start for any Bomber Command researcher and I am grateful for all their help and patience. My principal secondary sources are listed in the bibliography and were all both helpful and enjoyable to read, but *The Bomber Command War Diaries*, by Martin Middlebrook and Chris Everitt, and Bill Chorley's *RAF Bomber Command Losses* are required reading and provided me with much detail.

'The Hemel at War' project between Hemel Hempstead School and Goldsmiths was very helpful in describing Brian's school days, as was the school website. The volunteer amateur websites of which there are too many to list provided me with so much useful additional detail. I would like to thank particularly Mark Evans of the Midland Aircraft Recovery Group and Dom Howard's Bomber Command History Forum and their comprehensive websites. The Friends of 115 Squadron website provided much useful information and The Royal Lancers and Nottinghamshire Yeomanry Museum shed additional light on Bernard Slade's service.

There are many excellent museums and aviation centres often linked to former wartime airfields and in finding out about RAF Marham I met Mark Avery and Ken Delves of the RAF Marham Aviation Heritage Centre. They were endlessly helpful and encouraging and were able to put me in touch with the Swann family. Thank you also to Caro Clark in New Zealand, the staff of The National Archives of Australia and Karl Kjarsgaard of the Bomber Command Museum of Canada for providing details of their aircrew who flew with Brian. To Uwe Benkel for establishing the true crash site of ED984 and Theo Boiten for information that helped me understand the confusion of the Berlin raid. To Corinne Mitchell, whose father flew with Brian over the same period with 83 Squadron and who now runs the 83 and 44 squadrons Facebook group and allowed me to use the photograph of R5626.

As an amateur I have to apologise for any errors and omissions. I have where possible checked the accuracy of everything but I've no doubt not all.

Closer to home, a thank you to my family for their encouragement, to my niece, Phillippa, who skilfully tweaked my publisher's submission, and to my wife, Julia. Her acceptance of my 'do not disturb' face and yet another obsession is a credit to her patience. Her proofreading and checking of these pages was at least on occasions marginally more interesting than endless articles on fly fishing.

Bibliography

Barker, R., *The Thousand Plan*, Pan Books Ltd, 1965

Barnes, M., *Despite The Elements: A History of 115 Squadron 1917–1982*, The Nettlebed Press, 1983

Bennett, D.C.T., *Pathfinder*, Crecy Publishing, 1983

Bendimer, E., *The Fall of Fortresses*, Pan, 1981

Bishop, P., *Bomber Boys*, Harper Collins, 2007

Boiten, T., *Nachtjagd Combat Archive Pt 2*, Red Kite, 2018

Bowman, Martin W., *Voices In Flight: The Path Finder Force*, Pen & Sword Books, 2016

Brenan J. and Frost R., *Fighter! Fighter!*, Redbek, 2008

Burtt-Smith, J. and French, F., *A Drop in the Ocean*, Pen & Sword Books, 1996

Bury, G., *Wellingtons of 115 Squadron over Europe*, Newton Books, 1994

Bushby, J., *Gunners Moon*, Ian Allan, 1972

Charlwood, D., *No Moon Tonight*, Goodall Publications, 2000

Chorley W.R., *Royal Air Force Bomber Command Losses Volumes 1–9*, Midland Publishing

Currie. J., *Lancaster Target*, Goodall Publications, 2020

Delve, K., *RAF Marham. Operational History: 1916 to 2019*, RAF Marham Aviation Heritage Centre, 2009

Frankland, N., *The Bombing Offensive Against Germany*, Faber and Faber, 1965

Hastings, M., *Bomber Command*, Michael Joseph Ltd, 1979

Hastings, M., *Chastise: The Dambusters*, Harper Collins, 2020

Holland, J., *Big Week*, Penguin, 2018

Iredale, W., *The Pathfinders*, Penguin, 2021

Ireland, W., *The Story of Stokey Lewis VC*, Zulu Books, 2021

Low, R. and Harper, F.E., *83 Squadron 1917–1969*, Compaid Graphics, 1997

Lumsden, A., *Wellington Special*, Ian Allan, 1974

McKinstry, Leo, *Lancaster: The Second World War's Greatest Bomber*, John Murray, 2009

Middlebrook, M., *The Peenemünde Raid: The Night of 17–18 August 1943*, Phoenix, 2000

Middlebrook, Martin and Everitt, Chris, *The Bomber Command War Diaries: An Operational Reference Book 1939–1945*, Pen & Sword Books, 2014

Middlebrook, Martin, *The Berlin Raids*, Pen & Sword Books, 2010

Middlebrook Martin, *The Battle of Hamburg*, Cassell, 2000

Moore, C., *Lancaster Valour: The Valour and the Truth*, Compaid Graphics, 1995

Overy R., *The Bombing War. Europe 1939–1945*, Allen Lane, 2013

Overy, R., *Bomber Command 1935–45*, Harper Collins, 1997

Overy, R., *The Birth of the RAF*, Penguin, 2018

Price, Alfred, *The Hardest Day: 18 August 1940*, New York: Charles Scribner's Sons, 1980

Richards, D., *RAF Bomber Command in the Second World War*, Penguin Books, 2001

Searby, John, *Everlasting Arms: A War Memoir*, William Kimber & Co Ltd, 1988

Searby, John, *The Bomber Battle for Berlin*, Airlife Publishing, 1991

Searby, John, *The Great Raids, Peenemunde*, Nutshell Press, 1978

Spoden, P., *Enemy in the Dark*, Cerberus, 2003

Swift, D., *Bomber County*, Penguin, 2010

Tavender, I.T., *The Distinguished Flying Medal Register for the Second World War*, Savannah, 2000

Thompson, W.R., *Lancaster to Berlin*, Goodall Publications, 1985

Ward, C., *83 Squadron*, Mention the War Ltd, 2016

Ward, C., *115 Squadron*, Mention the War Ltd, 2019

Webster and Frankland, *The Strategic Air Offensive Against Germany Vol. 1*, The Naval & Military Press, 1961

Whipple, T., *The Battle of the Beams*, Bantam, 2023

White, R., *Vulcan 607*, Corgi, 2007

Winchester, J., *Aircraft of World War II: The Aviation Factfile*, Grange Books plc, 2004

Yates, H., *Luck and a Lancaster*, Airlife Publishing, 2005

Index